Hands-On Artificial Inte for IoT

Expert machine learning and deep learning techniques for developing smarter IoT systems

Amita Kapoor

BIRMINGHAM - MUMBAI

Hands-On Artificial Intelligence for IoT

Commissioning Editor: Amey Varangaonkar
Acquisition Editor: Nelson Morris
Content Development Editor: Karan Thakkar
Technical Editor: Adya Anand
Copy Editor: Safis Editing
Project Coordinator: Hardik Bhinde
Proofreader: Safis Editing
Indexer: Tejal Daruwale Soni
Graphics: Jisha Chirayil
Production Coordinator: Arvindkumar Gupta

First published: January 2019

Production reference: 1310119

Published by Packt Publishing Ltd.
Livery Place
35 Livery Street
Birmingham
B3 2PB, UK.

ISBN 978-1-78883-606-7

www.packtpub.com

To my friend and mentor Narotam Singh for being my gradient ascent in the dataset called life.
A part of my royalties will go to smilefoundation.org, a non-profit organization based in India
working on welfare projects on education, healthcare, livelihood, and the
empowerment of women in remote villages and slums across the different states of India.

– Amita Kapoor

`mapt.io`

Mapt is an online digital library that gives you full access to over 5,000 books and videos, as well as industry leading tools to help you plan your personal development and advance your career. For more information, please visit our website.

Why subscribe?

- Spend less time learning and more time coding with practical eBooks and Videos from over 4,000 industry professionals

- Improve your learning with Skill Plans built especially for you

- Get a free eBook or video every month

- Mapt is fully searchable

- Copy and paste, print, and bookmark content

Packt.com

Did you know that Packt offers eBook versions of every book published, with PDF and ePub files available? You can upgrade to the eBook version at `www.packt.com` and as a print book customer, you are entitled to a discount on the eBook copy. Get in touch with us at `customercare@packtpub.com` for more details.

At `www.packt.com`, you can also read a collection of free technical articles, sign up for a range of free newsletters, and receive exclusive discounts and offers on Packt books and eBooks.

Contributors

About the author

Amita Kapoor is an associate professor in the Department of Electronics, SRCASW, University of Delhi, and has been actively teaching neural networks and artificial intelligence for the last 20 years. She completed her master's in electronics in 1996 and her PhD in 2011. During her PhD she was awarded the prestigious DAAD fellowship to pursue part of her research at the Karlsruhe Institute of Technology, Karlsruhe, Germany. She was awarded the Best Presentation Award at the Photonics 2008 international conference. She is an active member of ACM, AAAI, IEEE, and INNS. She has co-authored two books. She has more than 40 publications in international journals and conferences. Her present research areas include machine learning, artificial intelligence, deep reinforcement learning, and robotics.

I would like to thank Prof Ajit Jaokar, University of Oxford; his IoT course was the inspiration behind this book. Special thanks to Erin LeDell, Chief Machine Learning Scientist at H2O.ai for her thoughtful suggestions. I would also like to thank Armando Fandango, Narotam Singh, Ruben Olivas, and Hector Velarde for their input.
I am grateful for the support of my colleagues and students. Last but not least, I would like to thank the entire Packt team, with a special mention to Tushar Gupta, Karan Thakkar, and Adya Anand for their continuous motivation.

About the reviewers

Hector Duran Lopez Velarde received a B.Che.E. from UPAEP and an MSc in automation and artificial intelligence from Tecnologico de Monterrey ITESM, Mexico, in 2000. He has worked as a controls and automation engineer for companies such as Honeywell and General Electric, among others. He also has participated in several research projects as a technical lead. His experience in software development, process simulation, artificial intelligence, and industrial automation has led him to the current development of complete IoT solutions in the automotive, textile, and pharmaceutical industries. He is currently working on a research center of IoT.

Huge thanks to my wife, Yaz, and to my children, Ivana and Hector, for all their support and love.

Ruben Oliva Ramos is a computer engineer from Tecnologico of León Institute, with a master's degree in computer and electronics systems engineering with a networking specialization from the University of Salle Bajio. He has more than 5 years' experience of developing web apps to control and monitor devices connected to Arduino and Raspberry Pi, using web frameworks and cloud services to build IoT applications. He has authored *Raspberry Pi 3 Home Automation Projects*, *Internet of Things Programming with JavaScript*, *Advanced Analytics with R and Tableau*, and *SciPy Recipes* for Packt.

I would like to thank my savior and lord, Jesus Christ for giving me strength and courage to pursue this project, to my dearest wife, Mayte, our two lovely sons, Ruben and Dario, to my dear father (Ruben), my dearest mom (Rosalia), my brother (Juan Tomas), and my sister (Rosalia), whom I love. I'm very grateful to Packt Publishing for giving me the opportunity to collaborate as an author and reviewer, to belong to this honest and professional team.

Packt is searching for authors like you

If you're interested in becoming an author for Packt, please visit `authors.packtpub.com` and apply today. We have worked with thousands of developers and tech professionals, just like you, to help them share their insight with the global tech community. You can make a general application, apply for a specific hot topic that we are recruiting an author for, or submit your own idea.

Table of Contents

Preface

The mission of this book is to enable the reader to build AI-enabled IoT applications. With the surge in popularity of IoT devices, there are many applications that use data science and analytics to utilize the terabyte of data generated. However, these applications do not address the challenge of continually discovering patterns in IoT data. In this book, we cover the various aspects of AI theory and implementation that the reader can utilize to make their IoT solutions smarter by implementing AI techniques.

The reader starts by learning the basics of AI and IoT devices and how to read IoT data from various sources and streams. Then we introduce various ways to implement AI with examples in TensorFlow, scikit learn, and Keras. The topics covered include machine learning, deep learning, genetic algorithms, reinforcement learning, and generative adversarial networks. We also show the reader how to implement AI using distributed technologies and on the cloud. Once the reader is familiar with AI techniques, then we introduce various techniques for different kinds of data generated and consumed by IoT devices, such as time series, images, audio, video, text, and speech.

After explaining various AI techniques on various kinds of IoT data, finally, we share some case studies with the reader from the four major categories of IoT solutions: personal IoT, home IoT, industrial IoT, and smart city IoT.

Who this book is for

The audience for this book is anyone who has a basic knowledge of developing IoT applications and Python and wants to make their IoT applications smarter by applying AI techniques. This audience may include the following people:

- IoT practitioners who already know how to build IoT systems, but now they want to implement AI to make their IoT solution smart.
- Data science practitioners who have been building analytics with IoT platforms, but now they want to transition from IoT analytics to IoT AI, thus making their IoT solutions smarter.
- Software engineers who want to develop AI-based solutions for smart IoT devices.
- Embedded system engineers looking to bring smartness and intelligence to their products.

What this book covers

Chapter 1, *Principles and Foundations of IoT and AI*, introduces the basic concepts IoT, AI, and data science. We end the chapter with an introduction to the tools and datasets we will be using in the book.

Chapter 2, *Data Access and Distributed Processing for IoT*, covers various methods of accessing data from various data sources, such as files, databases, distributed data stores, and streaming data.

Chapter 3, *Machine Learning for IoT*, covers the various aspects of machine learning, such as supervised, unsupervised, and reinforcement learning for IoT. The chapter ends with tips and tricks to improve your models' performance.

Chapter 4, *Deep Learning for IoT*, explores the various aspects of deep learning, such as MLP, CNN, RNN, and autoencoders for IoT. It also introduces various frameworks for deep learning.

Chapter 5, *Genetic Algorithms for IoT*, discusses optimization and different evolutionary techniques employed for optimization with an emphasis on genetic algorithms.

Chapter 6, *Reinforcement Learning for IoT*, introduces the concepts of reinforcement learning, such as policy gradients and Q-networks. We cover how to implement deep Q networks using TensorFlow and learn some cool real-world problems where reinforcement learning can be applied.

Chapter 7, *Generative Models for IoT*, introduces the concepts of adversarial and generative learning. We cover how to implement GAN, DCGAN, and CycleGAN using TensorFlow, and also look at their real-life applications.

Chapter 8, *Distributed AI for IoT*, covers how to leverage machine learning in distributed mode for IoT applications.

Chapter 9, *Personal and Home and IoT*, goes over some exciting personal and home applications of IoT.

Chapter 10, *AI for Industrial IoT*, explains how to apply the concepts learned in this book to two case studies with industrial IoT data.

Chapter 11, *AI for Smart Cities IoT*, explains how to apply the concepts learned in this book to IoT data generated from smart cities.

Chapter 12, *Combining It All Together*, covers how to pre-process textual, image, video, and audio data before feeding it to models. It also introduces time series data.

To get the most out of this book

To get the most out of this book, download the examples code from the GitHub repository and practice with the Jupyter Notebooks provided.

Download the example code files

You can download the example code files for this book from your account at `www.packtpub.com`. If you purchased this book elsewhere, you can visit `www.packtpub.com/support` and register to have the files emailed directly to you.

You can download the code files by following these steps:

1. Log in or register at `www.packtpub.com`.
2. Select the **SUPPORT** tab.
3. Click on **Code Downloads & Errata**.
4. Enter the name of the book in the **Search** box and follow the onscreen instructions.

Once the file is downloaded, please make sure that you unzip or extract the folder using the latest version of:

- WinRAR/7-Zip for Windows
- Zipeg/iZip/UnRarX for Mac
- 7-Zip/PeaZip for Linux

The code bundle for the book is also hosted on GitHub at `https://github.com/PacktPublishing/Hands-On-Artificial-Intelligence-for-IoT`. We also have other code bundles from our rich catalog of books and videos available at `https://github.com/PacktPublishing/`. Check them out!

Download the color images

We also provide a PDF file that has color images of the screenshots/diagrams used in this book. You can download it here: `http://www.packtpub.com/sites/default/files/downloads/9781788836067_ColorImages.pdf`.

Conventions used

There are a number of text conventions used throughout this book.

`CodeInText`: Indicates code words in text, database table names, folder names, filenames, file extensions, pathnames, dummy URLs, user input, and Twitter handles. Here is an example: "This declares two placeholders with the names A and B; the arguments to the `tf.placeholder` method specify that the placeholders are of the `float32` datatype."

A block of code is set as follows:

```
# Declare placeholders for the two matrices
A = tf.placeholder(tf.float32, None, name='A')
B = tf.placeholder(tf.float32, None, name='B')
```

Bold: Indicates a new term, an important word, or words that you see onscreen. For example, words in menus or dialog boxes appear in the text like this. Here is an example: "At the bottom of the stack, we have the device layer, also called the **perception layer**."

Warnings or important notes appear like this.

Tips and tricks appear like this.

Get in touch

Feedback from our readers is always welcome.

General feedback: Email `feedback@packtpub.com` and mention the book title in the subject of your message. If you have questions about any aspect of this book, please email us at `questions@packtpub.com`.

Errata: Although we have taken every care to ensure the accuracy of our content, mistakes do happen. If you have found a mistake in this book, we would be grateful if you would report this to us. Please visit `www.packtpub.com/submit-errata`, selecting your book, clicking on the Errata Submission Form link, and entering the details.

Piracy: If you come across any illegal copies of our works in any form on the Internet, we would be grateful if you would provide us with the location address or website name. Please contact us at copyright@packtpub.com with a link to the material.

If you are interested in becoming an author: If there is a topic that you have expertise in and you are interested in either writing or contributing to a book, please visit authors.packtpub.com.

Reviews

Please leave a review. Once you have read and used this book, why not leave a review on the site that you purchased it from? Potential readers can then see and use your unbiased opinion to make purchase decisions, we at Packt can understand what you think about our products, and our authors can see your feedback on their book. Thank you!

For more information about Packt, please visit packtpub.com.

Principles and Foundations of IoT and AI

Congratulations on purchasing this book; it suggests that you're keenly interested in keeping yourself updated with the recent advancements in technology. This book deals with the three big trends in the current business scenario, **Internet of Things (IoT)**, big data, and **Artificial Intelligence (AI)**. The exponential growth of the number of devices connected to the internet, and the exponential volume of data created by them, necessitate the use of the analytical and predictive techniques of AI and **deep learning (DL)**. This book specifically targets the third component, the various analytical and predictive methods or models available in the field of AI for the big data generated by IoT.

This chapter will briefly introduce you to these three trends and will expand on how they're interdependent. The data generated by IoT devices is uploaded to the cloud, hence you'll also be introduced to the various IoT cloud platforms and the data services they offer.

This chapter will cover the following points:

- Knowing what's a *thing* is in IoT, what devices constitute things, what the different IoT platforms are, and what an IoT vertical is
- Knowing what big data is and understanding how the amount of data generated by IoT lies in the range of big data
- Understanding how and why AI can be useful for making sense of the voluminous data generated by IoT
- With the help of an illustration, understanding how IoT, big data, and AI together can help us shape a better world
- Learning about some of the tools needed to perform analysis

What is IoT 101?

The term IoT was coined by Kevin Ashton in 1999. At that time, most of the data fed to computers was generated by humans; he proposed that the best way would be for computers to take data directly, without any intervention from humans. And so he proposed things such as RFID and sensors, which gather data, should be connected to the network, and feed directly to the computer.

 You can read the complete article where Ashton talks about what he means by IoT here: `http://www.itrco.jp/libraries/RFIDjournal-That%20Internet%20of%20Things%20Thing.pdf`.

Today IoT (also called the **internet of everything** and sometimes, the fog network) refers to a wide range of things such as sensors, actuators, and smartphones connected to the internet. These things can be anything: a person with a wearable device (or even mobile phone), an RFID-tagged animal, or even our day-to-day devices such as a refrigerator, washing machine, or even a coffee machine. These things can be physical things—that is, things that exist in the physical world and can be sensed, actuated, and connected—or of the information world (a virtual thing)—that is, things that aren't tangibly present but exist as information (data) and can be stored, processed, and accessed. These things necessarily have the ability to communicate directly with the internet; optionally, they might have the potentiality of sensing, actuation, data capture, data storage, and data processing.

The **International Telecommunication Unit (ITU)**, a United Nations agency, defines IoT as:

> *"a global infrastructure for the information society, enabling advanced services by interconnecting (physical and virtual) things based on existing and evolving interoperable information and communication technologies."*

You can learn more at `https://www.itu.int/en/ITU-T/gsi/iot/Pages/default.aspx`.

The wide expanse of ICT already provided us with communication at any time or any place; the IoT added the new dimension of **ANY THING communication**:

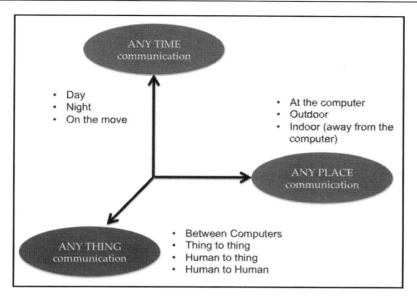

New dimension introduced in IoT (adapted from b-ITU-T Y.2060 report)

It's predicted that IoT as a technology will have a far-reaching impact on people and the society we live in. To give you a glimpse of its far-reaching effects, consider the following scenarios:

- You, like me, live in a high rise building and are very fond of plants. With lots of effort and care, you've made a small indoor garden of your own using potted plants. Your boss asks you to go for a week-long trip, and you're worried your plants won't survive for a week without water. The IoT solution is to add soil moisture sensors to your plants, connect them to the internet, and add actuators to remotely switch on or off the water supply and artificial sunlight. Now, you can be anywhere in the world, but your plants won't die, and you can check the individual plant's soil moisture condition and water it as needed.

- You had a very tiring day at the office; you just want to go home and have someone make you coffee, prepare your bed, and heat up water for a bath, but sadly you're home alone. Not anymore; IoT can help. Your IoT-enabled home assistant can prepare the right flavor coffee from the coffee machine, order your smart water heater to switch on and maintain the water temperature exactly the way you want, and ask your smart air conditioner to switch on and cool the room.

The choices are limited only by your imagination. The two preceding scenarios correspond to consumer IoT—the IoT with a focus on consumer-oriented applications. There also exists a large scope of **Industry IoT (IIoT)** where manufacturers and industries optimize processes and implement remote monitoring capabilities to increase productivity and efficiency. In this book, you'll find the hands-on experience with both IoT applications.

IoT reference model

Just like the OSI reference model for the internet, IoT architecture is defined through six layers: four horizontal layers and two vertical layers. The two vertical layers are **Management** and **Security** and they're spread over all four horizontal layers, as seen in the following diagram:

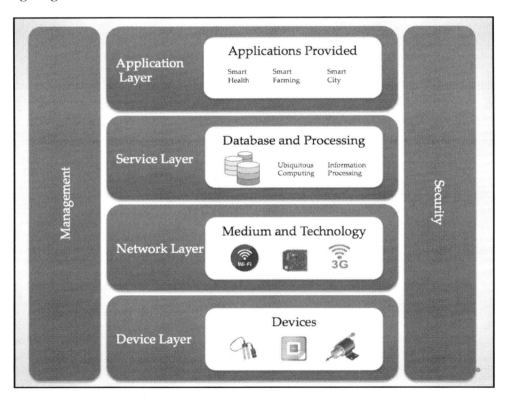

IoT layers

The **Device Layer**: At the bottom of the stack, we have the device layer, also called the **perception layer**. This layer contains the physical things needed to sense or control the physical world and acquire data (that is, by perceiving the physical world). Existing hardware, such as sensors, RFID, and actuators, constitutes the perception layer.

The **Network Layer**: This layer provides the networking support and transfer of data over either wired or wireless network. The layer securely transmits the information from the devices in the device layer to the information processing system. Both transmission **Medium and Technology** are part of the networking layer. Examples include 3G, UMTS, ZigBee, Bluetooth, Wi-Fi, and so on.

The **Service Layer**: This layer is responsible for service management. It receives information from the network layer, stores it into the database, processes that information, and can make an automatic decision based on the results.

The **Application Layer**: This layer manages the applications dependent upon the information processed in the service layer. There's a wide range of applications that can be implemented by IoT: smart cities, smart farming, and smart homes, to name a few.

IoT platforms

Information from the network layer is often managed with the help of IoT platforms. Many companies today provide IoT platform services, where they help not only with data but also enable seamless integration with different hardware. Since they function as a mediator between the hardware and application layer, IoT platforms are also referred to as IoT middleware and are part of the service layer in the IoT reference stack. IoT platforms provide the ability to connect and communicate with things from anywhere in the world. In this book, we'll briefly cover some popular IoT platforms such as the Google Cloud Platform, Azure IoT, Amazon AWS IoT, Predix, and H2O.

You can select which IoT platform is best for you based on the following criteria:

- **Scalability**: Addition and deletion of new devices to the existing IoT network should be possible
- **Ease of use**: The system should be perfectly working and delivering all its specifications with minimum intervention
- **Third party integration**: Heterogeneous devices and protocols should be able to inter-network with each other
- **Deployment options**: It should be workable on a broad variety of hardware devices and software platforms
- **Data security**: The security of data and devices is ensured

IoT verticals

A vertical market is a market in which vendors offer goods and services specific to an industry, trade, profession, or other groups of customers with specialized needs. IoT enables the possibility of many such verticals, and some of the top IoT verticals are as follows:

- **Smart building**: Buildings with IoT technologies can help in not only reducing the consumption of resources but also improving the satisfaction of the humans living or working in them. The buildings have smart sensors that not only monitor resource consumption but can also proactively detect residents' needs. Data is collected via these smart devices and sensors to remotely monitor a building, energy, security, landscaping, HVAC, lighting, and so on. The data is then used to predict actions, which can be automated according to events and hence efficiency can be optimized, saving time, resources, and cost.
- **Smart agriculture**: IoT can enable local and commercial farming to be more environmentally friendly, cost-effective, and production efficient. Sensors placed through the farm can help in automating the process of irrigation. It's predicted that smart agricultural practices will enable a manifold increase in productivity, and hence food resources.

- **Smart city**: A smart city can be a city with smart parking, a smart mass transit system, and so on. A smart city has the capability to address traffic, public safety, energy management, and more for both its government and citizens. By using advanced IoT technologies, it can optimize the usage of the city infrastructure and quality of life for its citizens.
- **Connected healthcare**: IoT enables critical business and patient monitoring decisions to be made remotely and in real time. Individuals carry medical sensors to monitor body parameters such as heartbeat, body temperature, glucose level, and so on. The wearable sensors, such as accelerometers and gyroscopes, can be used to monitor a person's daily activity.

We'll be covering some of them as a case study in this book. The content of this book is focused on information processing and the applications being implemented on IoT and so we'll not be going into details of the devices, architecture, and protocols involved in IoT reference stacks any further.

The interested reader can refer to the following references to know more about the IoT architecture and different protocols:

- Da Xu, Li, Wu He, and Shancang Li. *Internet of things in industries: A survey.* IEEE Transactions on industrial informatics 10.4 (2014): 2233-2243.
- Khan, Rafiullah, et al. *Future internet: The internet of things architecture, Possible Applications and Key Challenges.* **Frontiers of Information Technology (FIT)**, 2012 10th International Conference on. IEEE, 2012.
- This website provides an overview of the protocols involved in IoT:

  ```
  https://www.postscapes.com/internet-of-things-
  protocols/.
  ```

Big data and IoT

IoT has connected things never previously connected to the internet, such as car engines, resulting in the generation of a large amount of continuous data streams. The following screenshot shows explorative data by IHS of the number of connected devices in billions in future years. Their estimate shows that the number of IoT devices will reach **75.44** billion by **2025**:

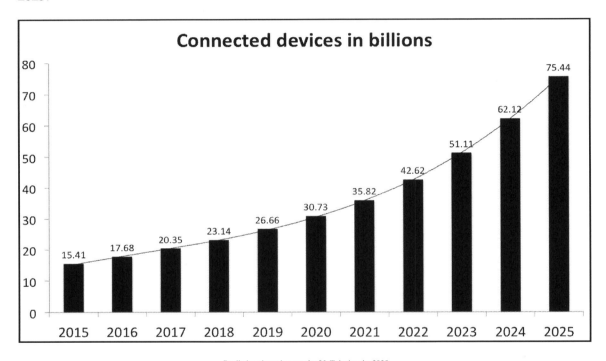

Prediction about the growth of IoT devices by 2025

The full whitepaper, *IoT platforms: enabling the Internet of Things*, by IHS is available as PDF at: https://cdn.ihs.com/www/pdf/enabling-IOT.pdf.

The reduction in sensor cost, efficient power consumption techniques, a large range of connectivity (infrared, NFC, Bluetooth, Wi-Fi, and so on), and the availability of cloud platforms that support IoT deployment and development are the major reasons for this pervasion of IoT in our homes, personal lives, and industry. This has also motivated companies to think about providing new services and developing new business models. Some examples include the following:

- **Airbnb**: It connects people so that they can rent out spare rooms and cottages to one another, and it earns the commission.
- **Uber**: It connects cab drivers with travelers. The location of the traveler is used to assign them to the nearest driver.

The amount of data generated in the process is both voluminous and complex, necessitating a big data. Big data approach and IoT are almost made for each other; the two work in conjunction.

Things are continuously generating an enormous amount of data streams that provide their statuses such as temperature, pollution level, geolocation, and proximity. The data generated is in time series format and is autocorrelated. The task becomes challenging because the data is dynamic in nature. Also, the data generated can be analyzed at the edge (sensor or gateway) or cloud. Before sending the data to the cloud, some form of IoT data transformation is performed. This may involve the following:

- Temporal or spatial analysis
- Summarizing the data at the edge
- Aggregation of data
- Correlating data in multiple IoT streams
- Cleaning data
- Filling in the missing values
- Normalizing the data
- Transforming it into different formats acceptable to the cloud

At the edge, **complex event processing (CEP)** is used to combine data from multiple sources and infer events or patterns.

The data is analyzed using stream analytics, for example, applying analytical tools to the stream of data, but developing the insights and rules used externally in an offline mode. The model is built offline and then applied to the stream of data generated. The data may be handled in different manners:

- **Atomic**: Single data at a time is used
- **Micro batching**: Group of data per batch
- **Windowing**: Data within a timeframe per batch

The stream analytics can be combined with the CEP to combine events over a time frame and correlate patterns to detect special patterns (for example, anomaly or failure).

Infusion of AI – data science in IoT

A very popular phrase among data scientists and machine learning engineers is *"AI is the new electricity"* said by Prof Andrew Ng in NIPS 2017, we can expand it as follows: *If AI is the new electricity, data is the new coal, and IoT the new coal-mine.*

IoT generates an enormous amount of data; presently, 90% of the data generated isn't even captured, and out of the 10% that is captured, most is time-dependent and loses its value within milliseconds. Manually monitoring this data continuously is both cumbersome and expensive. This necessitates a way to intelligently analyze and gain insight from this data; the tools and models of AI provide us with a way to do exactly this with minimum human intervention. The major focus of this book will be on understanding the various AI models and techniques that can be applied to IoT data. We'll be using both **machine learning** (**ML**) and DL algorithms. The following screenshot explains the relationship between **Artificial Intelligence**, **Machine Learning**, and **Deep Learning**:

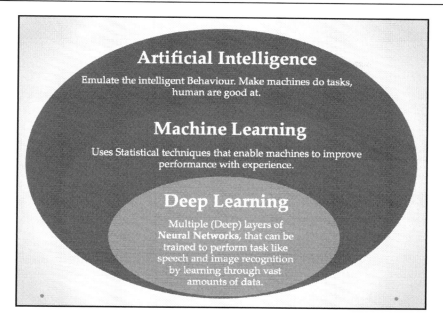

AI, ML, and DL

By observing the behavior of multiple things, IoT (with the help of big data and AI) aims to gain insight into the data and optimize underlying processes. This involves multiple challenges:

- Storing real-time generated events
- Running analytical queries over stored events
- Performing analytics using AI/ML/DL techniques over the data to gain insights and make predictions

Cross-industry standard process for data mining

For IoT problems, the most used **data management** (**DM**) methodology is **cross-industry standard process for data mining** (**CRISP-DM**) proposed by Chapman et al. It's a process model that states the tasks that need to be carried out for successfully completing DM. It's a vendor-independent methodology divided into these six different phases:

1. **Business understanding**
2. **Data understanding**
3. **Data preparation**
4. **Modelling**
5. **Evaluation**
6. **Deployment**

Following diagram shows the different stages:

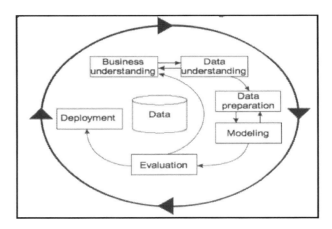

Different stages in CRISP-DM

As we can see, it's a continuous process model with data science and AI playing important roles in steps 2–5.

The details about CRISP-DM and all its phases can be read in the following:

Marbán, Óscar, Gonzalo Mariscal, and Javier Segovia. *A data mining & knowledge discovery process model. Data Mining and Knowledge Discovery in Real Life Applications.* InTech, 2009.

AI platforms and IoT platforms

A large number of cloud platforms with both AI and IoT capabilities are available today. These platforms provide the capability to integrate the sensors and devices and perform analytics on the cloud. There exist more than 30 cloud platforms in the global market, each targeting different IoT verticals and services. The following screenshot lists the various services that AI/IoT platforms support:

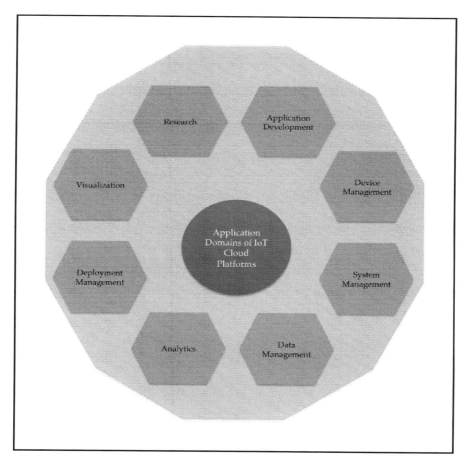

Services that different AI/IoT platforms support

Let's briefly find out about some popular cloud platforms. In `Chapter 12`, *Combining it all together*, we'll learn how to use the most popular ones. The following is a list of some of the popular Cloud platforms:

- **IBM Watson IoT Platform**: Hosted by IBM, the platform provides device management; it uses the MQTT protocol to connect with IoT devices and applications. It provides real-time scalable connectivity. The data can be stored for a period and accessed in real time. IBM Watson also provides Bluemix **Platform-as-a-Service (PaaS)** for analytics and visualizations. We can write code to build and manage applications that interact with the data and connected devices. It supports Python along with C#, Java, and Node.js.
- **Microsoft IoT-Azure IoT suite**: It provides a collection of preconfigured solutions built on Azure PaaS. It enables a reliable and secure bidirectional communication between IoT devices and cloud. The preconfigured solutions include data visualization, remote monitoring, and configuring rules and alarms over live IoT telemetry. It also provides Azure Stream Analytics to process the data in real time. The Azure Stream Analytics allows us to use Visual Studio. It supports Python, Node.js, C, and Arduino, depending upon the IoT devices.
- **Google Cloud IoT**: The Google Cloud IoT provides a fully managed service for securely connecting and managing IoT devices. It supports both MQTT and HTTP protocols. It also provides bidirectional communication between IoT devices and the cloud. It provides support for Go, PHP, Ruby, JS, .NET, Java, Objective-C, and Python. It also has BigQuery, which allows users to perform data analytics and visualization.
- **Amazon AWS IoT**: The Amazon AWS IoT allows IoT devices to communicate via MQTT, HTTP, and WebSockets. It provides secure, bi-directional communication between IoT devices and the cloud. It also has a rules engine that can be used to integrate data with other AWS services and transform the data. Rules can be defined that trigger the execution of user code in Java, Python, or Node.js. AWS Lambda allows us to use our own custom trained models.

Tools used in this book

For the implementation of IoT-based services, we need to follow a bottom-up approach. For each IoT vertical, we need to find the analytics and the data and, finally, implement it in code.

Due to its availability in almost all AI and IoT platforms, Python will be used for coding in this book. Along with Python, some helping libraries such as NumPy, pandas, SciPy, Keras, and TensorFlow will be used to perform AI/ML analytics on the data. For visualization, we will be using Matplotlib and Seaborn.

TensorFlow

TensorFlow is an open source software library developed by the Google Brain team; it has functions and APIs for implementing deep neural networks. It works with Python, C++, Java, R, and Go. It can be used to work on multiple platforms, CPU, GPU, mobile, and even distributed. TensorFlow allows for model deployment and ease of use in production. The optimizer in TensorFlow makes the task of training deep neural networks easier by automatically calculating gradients and applying them to update weights and biases.

In TensorFlow, a program has two distinct components:

- **Computation graph** is a network of nodes and edges. Here all of the data, variables, placeholders, and the computations to be performed are defined. TensorFlow supports three types of data objects: constants, variables, and placeholders.
- **Execution graph** actually computes the network using a `Session` object. Actual calculations and transfer of information from one layer to another takes place in the `Session` object.

Let's see the code to perform matrix multiplication in TensorFlow. The whole code can be accessed from the GitHub repository (`https://github.com/PacktPublishing/Hands-On-Artificial-Intelligence-for-IoT`) filename, `matrix_multiplication.ipynb`:

```
import tensorflow as tf
import numpy as np
```

This part imports the TensorFlow module. Next, we define the computation graph. `mat1` and `mat2` are two matrices we need to multiply:

```
# A random matrix of size [3,5]
mat1 = np.random.rand(3,5)
# A random matrix of size [5,2]
mat2 = np.random.rand(5,2)
```

We declare two placeholders, A and B, so that we can pass their values at runtime. In the computation graph, we declare all of the data and computation objects:

```
# Declare placeholders for the two matrices
A = tf.placeholder(tf.float32, None, name='A')
B = tf.placeholder(tf.float32, None, name='B')
```

This declares two placeholders with the names A and B; the arguments to the `tf.placeholder` method specify that the placeholders are of the `float32` datatype. Since the shape specified is `None`, we can feed it a tensor of any shape and an optional name for the operation. Next, we define the operation to be performed using the matrix multiplication method, `tf.matmul`:

```
C = tf.matmul(A,B)
```

The execution graph is declared as a `Session` object, which is fed the two matrices, `mat1` and `mat2`, for the placeholders, A and B, respectively:

```
with tf.Session() as sess:
    result = sess.run(C, feed_dict={A: mat1, B:mat2})
    print(result)
```

Keras

Keras is a high-level API that runs on top of TensorFlow. It allows for fast and easy prototyping. It supports both convolutional and recurrent neural networks, and even a combination of the two. It can run on both CPUs and GPUs. The following code performs matrix multiplication using Keras:

```
# Import the libraries
import keras.backend as K
import numpy as np

# Declare the data
A = np.random.rand(20,500)
B = np.random.rand(500,3000)
```

```
#Create Variable
x = K.variable(value=A)
y = K.variable(value=B)
z = K.dot(x,y)
print(K.eval(z))
```

Datasets

In the coming chapters, we'll be learning different DL models and ML methods. They all work on data; while a large number of datasets are available to demonstrate how these models work, in this book, we'll use datasets available freely through wireless sensors and other IoT devices. The following are some of the datasets used in this book and their sources.

The combined cycle power plant dataset

This dataset contains 9,568 data points collected from a **combined cycle power plant** (**CCPP**) in a course of six years (2006-2011). CCPP uses two turbines to generate power, the gas turbine and the steam turbine. There're three main components of the CCPP plant: gas turbine, heat recovery system, and steam turbine. The dataset, available at UCI ML (`http:/ /archive.ics.uci.edu/ml/datasets/combined+cycle+power+plant`), was collected by Pinar Tufekci from Namik Kemal University and Heysem Kaya from Bogazici University. The data consists of four features determining the average ambient variables. The averages are taken from various sensors located around the plant that record ambient variables per second. The aim is to predict the net hourly electrical energy output. The data is available in both `xls` and `ods` formats.

The features in the dataset are as follows:

- The **Ambient Temperature** (**AT**) is in the range 1.81°C and 37.11°C
- The **Ambient Pressure** (**AP**) is in the range 992.89—1033.30 millibar
- **Relative Humidity** (**RH**) is in the range 25.56% to 100.16%
- Exhaust **Vacuum** (**V**) is in the range 25.36 to 81.56 cm Hg
- Net hourly electrical energy output (PE) is in the range 420.26 to 495.76 MW

Further details about the data and the problem can be read from the following:

- Pınar Tüfekci, *Prediction of full load electrical power output of a baseload operated combined cycle power plant using machine learning methods*, International Journal of Electrical Power & Energy Systems, Volume 60, September 2014, Pages 126-140, ISSN 0142-0615.
- Heysem Kaya, Pınar Tüfekci, Sadık Fikret Gürgen: *Local and GlobalLearning Methods for Predicting Power of a Combined Gas & Steam Turbine*, Proceedings of the International Conference on Emerging Trends in Computer and Electronics Engineering ICETCEE 2012, pp. 13-18 (Mar. 2012, Dubai).

Wine quality dataset

Wineries around the world have to undergo wine certifications and quality assessments to safeguard human health. The wine certification is performed with the help of physicochemical analysis and sensory tests. With the advancement of technology, the physicochemical analysis can be performed routinely via in-vitro equipment.

We use this dataset for classification examples in this book. The dataset can be downloaded from the UCI-ML repository (`https://archive.ics.uci.edu/ml/datasets/Wine+Quality`). The wine quality dataset contains results of physicochemical tests on different samples of red and white wine. Each sample was further rated by an expert wine taster for quality on a scale of 0—10.

The dataset contains in total 4,898 instances; it has a total of 12 attributes. The 12 attributes are as follows:

- Fixed acidity
- Volatile acidity
- Citric acid
- Residual sugar
- Chlorides
- Free sulfur dioxide
- Total sulfur dioxide

- Density
- pH
- Sulfates
- Alcohol
- Quality

The dataset is available in the CSV format.

 Details about the dataset can be read from this paper: Cortez, Paulo, et al. *Modeling wine preferences by data mining from physicochemical properties.* Decision Support Systems 47.4 (2009): 547-553 (https://repositorium.sdum.uminho.pt/bitstream/1822/10029/1/wine5.pdf).

Air quality data

Air pollution poses a major environmental risk to human health. It's found that there exists a correlation between improved air quality and amelioration of different health problems such as respiratory infections, cardiovascular diseases, and lung cancer. The extensive sensor networks throughout the world by Meteorological Organizations of the respective country provide us with real-time air quality data. This data can be accessed through the respective web APIs of these organizations.

In this book, we'll use the historical air quality data to train our network and predict the mortality rate. The historical data for England is available freely at Kaggle (https://www.kaggle.com/c/predict-impact-of-air-quality-on-death-rates), and the air quality data consists of daily means of **ozone (O3)**, **Nitrogen dioxide (NO2)**, particulate matter with a diameter less than or equal to 10 micrometers (PM10) and PM25 (2.5 micrometers or less), and temperature. The mortality rate (number of deaths per 100,000 people) for England region is obtained by the data provided by the UK Office for National Statistics.

Summary

In this chapter, we learned about IoT, big data, and AI. This chapter introduced the common terminologies used in IoT. We learned about the IoT architecture for data management and data analysis. The enormous data generated by IoT devices necessitates special ways to handle it.

We learned about how data science and AI can help in both analytics and prediction generated by the many IoT devices. Various IoT platforms were briefly described in this chapter, as were some popular IoT verticals. We also learned about special DL libraries: TensorFlow and Keras. Finally, some of the datasets we'll be using throughout the book were introduced.

The next chapter will cover how to access the datasets available in varied formats.

Data Access and Distributed Processing for IoT

2

Data is everywhere: images, speech, text, weather information, the speed of your car, your last EMI, changing stock prices. With the integration of **Internet of Things (IoT)** systems, the amount of data produced has increased many-fold; an example is sensor readings, which could be taken for room temperature, soil alkalinity, and more. This data is stored and made available in various formats. In this chapter, we will learn how to read, save, and process data in some popular formats. Specifically, you will do the following:

- Access data in TXT format
- Read and write csv-formatted data via the CSV, pandas, and NumPy modules
- Access JSON data using JSON and pandas
- Learn to work with the HDF5 format using PyTables, pandas, and h5py
- Handle SQL databases using SQLite and MySQL
- Handle NoSQL using MongoDB
- Work with Hadoop's Distributed File System

TXT format

One of the simplest and common formats for storing data is the TXT format; many IoT sensors log sensor readings with different timestamps in the simple `.txt` file format. Python provides built-in functions for creating, reading, and writing into TXT files.

We can access TXT files in Python itself without using any module; the data, in this case, is of the string type, and you will need to transform it to other types to use it. Alternatively, we can use NumPy or pandas.

Using TXT files in Python

Python has built-in functions that read and write into TXT files. The complete functionality is provided using four sets of functions: `open()`, `read()`, `write()`, and `close()`. As the names suggest, they are used to open a file, read from a file, write into a file, and finally close it. If you are dealing with string data (text), this is the best choice. In this section, we will use `Shakespeare` plays in TXT form; the file can be downloaded from the MIT site: `https://ocw.mit.edu/ans7870/6/6.006/s08/lecturenotes/files/t8.shakespeare.txt`.

We define the following variables to access the data:

```
data_folder = '../../data/Shakespeare'
data_file = 'alllines.txt'
```

The first step here is to open the file:

```
f = open(data_file)
```

Next, we read the whole file; we can use the `read` function, which will read the whole file as one single string:

```
contents = f.read()
```

This reads the whole file (consisting of 4,583,798 characters) into the `contents` variable. Let's explore the contents of the `contents` variable; the following command will print the first `1000` characters:

```
print(contents[:1000])
```

The preceding code will print the output as follows:

```
"ACT I"
"SCENE I. London. The palace."
"Enter KING HENRY, LORD JOHN OF LANCASTER, the EARL of WESTMORELAND, SIR
WALTER BLUNT, and others"
"So shaken as we are, so wan with care,"
"Find we a time for frighted peace to pant,"
"And breathe short-winded accents of new broils"
"To be commenced in strands afar remote."
"No more the thirsty entrance of this soil"
"will daub her lips with her own children's blood,"
"Nor more will trenching war channel her fields,"
"Nor bruise her flowerets with the armed hoofs"
"Of hostile paces: those opposed eyes,"
"Which, like the meteors of a troubled heaven,"
```

```
"All of one nature, of one substance bred,"
"Did lately meet in the intestine shock"
"And furious close of civil butchery"
"will now, in mutual well-beseeming ranks,"
"March all one way and be no more opposed"
"Against acquaintance, kindred and allies:"
"The edge of war, like an ill-sheathed knife,"
"No more will cut his master. Therefore, friends,"
"As far as to the sepulchre of Christ,"
"Whose
```

If the TXT files contain numeric data, it is better to use NumPy; if data is mixed, pandas is the best choice.

CSV format

Comma-separated value (CSV) files are the most popular formats for storing tabular data generated by IoT systems. In a `.csv` file, the values of the records are stored in plain-text rows, with each row containing the values of the fields separated by a separator. The separator is a comma by default but can be configured to be any other character. In this section, we will learn how to use data from CSV files with Python's `csv`, `numpy`, and `pandas` modules. We will use the `household_power_consumption` data file. The file can be downloaded from the following GitHub link: `https://github.com/ahanse/machlearning/blob/master/household_power_consumption.csv`. To access the data files, we define the following variables:

```
data_folder = '../../data/household_power_consumption'
data_file = 'household_power_consumption.csv'
```

Generally, to quickly read the data from CSV files, use the Python `csv` module; however, if the data needs to be interpreted as a mix of date, and numeric data fields, it's better to use the pandas package. If the data is only numeric, NumPy is the most appropriate package.

Working with CSV files with the csv module

In Python, the `csv` module provides classes and methods for reading and writing CSV files. The `csv.reader` method creates a reader object from which rows can be read iteratively. Each time a row is read from the file, the reader object returns a list of fields. For example, the following code demonstrates reading the data file and printing rows:

```
import csv
import os
```

```
with open(os.path.join(data_folder,data_file),newline='') as csvfile:
    csvreader = csv.reader(csvfile)
    for row in csvreader:
        print(row)
```

The rows are printed as a list of field values:

```
['date', 'time', 'global_active_power', 'global_reactive_power', 'voltage',
'global_intensity', 'sub_metering_1', 'sub_metering_2', 'sub_metering_3']
['0007-01-01', '00:00:00', '2.58', '0.136', '241.97', '10.6', '0', '0',
'0'] ['0007-01-01', '00:01:00', '2.552', '0.1', '241.75', '10.4', '0', '0',
'0'] ['0007-01-01', '00:02:00', '2.55', '0.1', '241.64', '10.4', '0', '0',
'0']
```

The csv.writer method returns an object that can be used to write rows to a file. As an example, the following code writes the first 10 rows of the file to a temporary file and then prints it:

```
# read the file and write first ten rows
with open(os.path.join(data_folder, data_file), newline='') as csvfile, \
        open(os.path.join(data_folder, 'temp.csv'), 'w', newline='') as
tempfile:
    csvreader = csv.reader(csvfile)
    csvwriter = csv.writer(tempfile)
    for row, i in zip(csvreader, range(10)):
        csvwriter.writerow(row)
# read and print the newly written file
with open(os.path.join(data_folder, 'temp.csv'), newline='') as tempfile:
    csvreader = csv.reader(tempfile)
    for row in csvreader:
        print(row)
```

The delimiter field and the quoting field characters are important attributes that you can set while creating reader and writer objects.

By default, the delimiter field is , and the other delimiters are specified with the delimiter argument to the reader or writer functions. For example, the following code saves the file with | as delimiter:

```
# read the file and write first ten rows with '|' delimiter
with open(os.path.join(data_folder, data_file), newline='') as csvfile, \
        open(os.path.join(data_folder, 'temp.csv'), 'w', newline='') as
tempfile:
    csvreader = csv.reader(csvfile)
    csvwriter = csv.writer(tempfile, delimiter='|')
    for row, i in zip(csvreader, range(10)):
        csvwriter.writerow(row)
```

```
# read and print the newly written file
with open(os.path.join(data_folder, 'temp.csv'), newline='') as tempfile:
    csvreader = csv.reader(tempfile, delimiter='|')
    for row in csvreader:
        print(row)
```

If you do not specify a `delimiter` character when the file is read, the rows will be read as one field and printed as follows:

```
['0007-01-01|00:00:00|2.58|0.136|241.97|10.6|0|0|0']
```

`quotechar` specifies a character with which to surround fields. The `quoting` argument specifies what kind of fields can be surrounded with `quotechar`. The `quoting` argument can have one of the following values:

- `csv.QUOTE_ALL`: All the fields are quoted
- `csv.QUOTE_MINIMAL`: Only fields containing special characters are quoted
- `csv.QUOTE_NONNUMERIC`: All non-numeric fields are quoted
- `csv.QUOTE_NONE`: None of the fields are quoted

As an example, let's print the temp file first:

```
0007-01-01|00:00:00|2.58|0.136|241.97|10.6|0|0|0
0007-01-01|00:01:00|2.552|0.1|241.75|10.4|0|0|0
0007-01-01|00:02:00|2.55|0.1|241.64|10.4|0|0|0
0007-01-01|00:03:00|2.55|0.1|241.71|10.4|0|0|0
0007-01-01|00:04:00|2.554|0.1|241.98|10.4|0|0|0
0007-01-01|00:05:00|2.55|0.1|241.83|10.4|0|0|0
0007-01-01|00:06:00|2.534|0.096|241.07|10.4|0|0|0
0007-01-01|00:07:00|2.484|0|241.29|10.2|0|0|0
0007-01-01|00:08:00|2.468|0|241.23|10.2|0|0|0
```

Now let's save it with all fields quoted:

```
# read the file and write first ten rows with '|' delimiter, all quoting
and * as a quote charachetr.
with open(os.path.join(data_folder, data_file), newline='') as csvfile, \
        open('temp.csv', 'w', newline='') as tempfile:
    csvreader = csv.reader(csvfile)
    csvwriter = csv.writer(tempfile, delimiter='|',
quotechar='*',quoting=csv.QUOTE_ALL)
    for row, i in zip(csvreader, range(10)):
        csvwriter.writerow(row)
```

The file gets saved with the specified quote character:

```
*0007-01-01*|*00:00:00*|*2.58*|*0.136*|*241.97*|*10.6*|*0*|*0*|*0*
*0007-01-01*|*00:01:00*|*2.552*|*0.1*|*241.75*|*10.4*|*0*|*0*|*0*
*0007-01-01*|*00:02:00*|*2.55*|*0.1*|*241.64*|*10.4*|*0*|*0*|*0*
*0007-01-01*|*00:03:00*|*2.55*|*0.1*|*241.71*|*10.4*|*0*|*0*|*0*
*0007-01-01*|*00:04:00*|*2.554*|*0.1*|*241.98*|*10.4*|*0*|*0*|*0*
*0007-01-01*|*00:05:00*|*2.55*|*0.1*|*241.83*|*10.4*|*0*|*0*|*0*
*0007-01-01*|*00:06:00*|*2.534*|*0.096*|*241.07*|*10.4*|*0*|*0*|*0*
*0007-01-01*|*00:07:00*|*2.484*|*0*|*241.29*|*10.2*|*0*|*0*|*0*
*0007-01-01*|*00:08:00*|*2.468*|*0*|*241.23*|*10.2*|*0*|*0*|*0*
```

Remember to read the file with the same arguments; otherwise, the * quote character will be treated as part of the field values and printed as follows:

```
['*0007-01-01*', '*00:00:00*', '*2.58*', '*0.136*', '*241.97*', '*10.6*',
'*0*', '*0*', '*0*']
```

Using the correct arguments with the `reader` object prints the following:

```
['0007-01-01', '00:00:00', '2.58', '0.136', '241.97', '10.6', '0', '0',
'0']
```

Now let's see how we can read CSV files with pandas, another popular Python library.

Working with CSV files with the pandas module

In pandas, the `read_csv()` function returns a DataFrame after reading the CSV file:

```
df = pd.read_csv('temp.csv')
print(df)
```

The DataFrame is printed as follows:

```
          date      time  global_active_power  global_reactive_power
voltage   \
0   0007-01-01  00:00:00                 2.580                  0.136
241.97
1   0007-01-01  00:01:00                 2.552                  0.100
241.75
2   0007-01-01  00:02:00                 2.550                  0.100
241.64
3   0007-01-01  00:03:00                 2.550                  0.100
241.71
4   0007-01-01  00:04:00                 2.554                  0.100
241.98
5   0007-01-01  00:05:00                 2.550                  0.100
```

```
241.83
6  0007-01-01  00:06:00                    2.534                    0.096
241.07
7  0007-01-01  00:07:00                    2.484                    0.000
241.29
8  0007-01-01  00:08:00                    2.468                    0.000
241.23

   global_intensity  sub_metering_1  sub_metering_2  sub_metering_3
0            10.6               0               0               0
1            10.4               0               0               0
2            10.4               0               0               0
3            10.4               0               0               0
4            10.4               0               0               0
5            10.4               0               0               0
6            10.4               0               0               0
7            10.2               0               0               0
8            10.2               0               0               0
```

We see in the preceding output that pandas automatically interpreted the date and time columns as their respective data types. The pandas DataFrame can be saved to a CSV file with the to_csv() function:

```
df.to_csv('temp1.cvs')
```

pandas, when it comes to reading and writing CSV files, offers plenty of arguments. Some of these are as follows, complete with how they're used:

- header: Defines the row number to be used as a header, or none if the file does not contain any headers.
- sep: Defines the character that separates fields in rows. By default, the value of sep is set to , .
- names: Defines column names for each column in the file.
- usecols: Defines columns that need to be extracted from the CSV file. Columns that are not mentioned in this argument are not read.
- dtype: Defines the data types for columns in the DataFrame.

Many other available options are documented at the following links: https://pandas.pydata.org/pandas-docs/stable/generated/pandas.read_csv.html and https://pandas.pydata.org/pandas-docs/stable/generated/pandas.DataFrame.to_csv.html.

Now let's see how to read data from CSV files with the NumPy module.

Working with CSV files with the NumPy module

The NumPy module provides two functions for reading values from CSV files: `np.loadtxt()` and `np.genfromtxt()`.

An example of `np.loadtxt` is as follows:

```
arr = np.loadtxt('temp.csv', skiprows=1, usecols=(2,3), delimiter=',')
arr
```

The preceding code reads columns 3 and 4 from the file that we created earlier, and saves them in a 9 × 2 array as follows:

```
array([[2.58 , 0.136],
       [2.552, 0.1  ],
       [2.55 , 0.1  ],
       [2.55 , 0.1  ],
       [2.554, 0.1  ],
       [2.55 , 0.1  ],
       [2.534, 0.096],
       [2.484, 0.   ],
       [2.468, 0.   ]])
```

The `np.loadtxt()` function cannot handle CSV files with missing data. For instances where data is missing, `np.genfromtxt()` can be used. Both of these functions offer many more arguments; details can be found in the NumPy documentation. The preceding code can be written using `np.genfromtxt()` as follows:

```
arr = np.genfromtxt('temp.csv', skip_header=1, usecols=(2,3),
delimiter=',')
```

NumPy arrays produced as a result of applying AI to IoT data can be saved with `np.savetxt()`. For example, the array we loaded previously can be saved as follows:

```
np.savetxt('temp.csv', arr, delimiter=',')
```

The `np.savetxt()` function also accepts various other useful arguments, such as the format for saved fields and headers. Check the NumPy documentation for more details on this function.

CSV is the most popular data format on IoT platforms and devices. In this section, we learned how to read CSV data using three different packages in Python. Let's learn about XLSX, another popular format, in the next section.

XLSX format

Excel, a component of the Microsoft Office pack, is one of the popular formats in which data is stored and visualized. Since 2010, Office has supported the `.xlsx` format. We can read XLSX files using the OpenPyXl and pandas functions.

Using OpenPyXl for XLSX files

OpenPyXl is a Python library for reading and writing Excel files. It is an open source project. A new `workbook` is created using the following command:

```
wb = Workbook()
```

We can access the currently `active` sheet by using the following command:

```
ws = wb.active()
```

To change the sheet name, use the `title` command:

```
ws.title = "Demo Name"
```

A single row can be added to the sheet using the `append` method:

```
ws.append()
```

A new sheet can be created using the `create_sheet()` method. An individual cell in the active sheet can be created using the `column` and `row` values:

```
# Assigns the cell corresponding to
# column A and row 10 a value of 5
ws.['A10'] = 5
#or
ws.cell(column=1, row=10, value=5)
```

A workbook can be saved using the `save` method. To load an existing workbook, we can use the `load_workbook` method. The names of the different sheets in an Excel workbook can be accessed using `get_sheet_names()`.

The following code creates an Excel workbook with three sheets and saves it; later, it loads the sheet and accesses a cell. The code can be accessed from GitHub at `OpenPyXl_example.ipynb`:

```
# Creating and writing into xlsx file
from openpyxl import Workbook
from openpyxl.compat import range
from openpyxl.utils import get_column_letter
wb = Workbook()
dest_filename = 'empty_book.xlsx'
ws1 = wb.active
ws1.title = "range names"
for row in range(1, 40):
 ws1.append(range(0,100,5))
ws2 = wb.create_sheet(title="Pi")
ws2['F5'] = 2 * 3.14
ws2.cell(column=1, row=5, value= 3.14)
ws3 = wb.create_sheet(title="Data")
for row in range(1, 20):
  for col in range(1, 15):
  _ = ws3.cell(column=col, row=row, value="\
 {0}".format(get_column_letter(col)))
print(ws3['A10'].value)
wb.save(filename = dest_filename)

# Reading from xlsx file
from openpyxl import load_workbook
wb = load_workbook(filename = 'empty_book.xlsx')
sheet_ranges = wb['range names']
print(wb.get_sheet_names())
print(sheet_ranges['D18'].value)
```

 You can learn more about OpenPyXL from its documentation, available at `https://openpyxl.readthedocs.io/en/stable/`.

Using pandas with XLSX files

We can load existing `.xlsx` files with the help of pandas. The `read_excel` method is used to read Excel files as a DataFrame. This method uses an argument, `sheet_name`, which is used to specify the sheet we want to load. The sheet name can be specified either as a string or number starting from 0. The `to_excel` method can be used to write into an Excel file.

The following code reads an Excel file, manipulates it, and saves it. The code can be accessed from GitHub at `Pandas_xlsx_example.ipynb`:

```
import pandas as pd
df = pd.read_excel("empty_book.xlsx", sheet_name=0)
df.describe()
result = df * 2
result.describe()
result.to_excel("empty_book_modified.xlsx")
```

Working with the JSON format

JavaScript Object Notation (JSON) is another popular data format in IoT systems. In this section, we will learn how to read JSON data with Python's JSON, NumPy, and pandas packages.

For this section, we will use the `zips.json` file, which contains US ZIP codes with city codes, geolocation details, and state codes. The file has JSON objects recorded in the following format:

```
{ "_id" : "01001", "city" : "AGAWAM", "loc" : [ -72.622739, 42.070206 ],
"pop" : 15338, "state" : "MA" }
```

Using JSON files with the JSON module

To load and decode JSON data, use the `json.load()` or `json.loads()` functions. As an example, the following code reads the first 10 lines from the `zips.json` file and prints them nicely:

```
import os
import json
from pprint import pprint

with open(os.path.join(data_folder,data_file)) as json_file:
    for line,i in zip(json_file,range(10)):
        json_data = json.loads(line)
        pprint(json_data)
```

The objects are printed as follows:

```
{'_id': '01001',
 'city': 'AGAWAM',
 'loc': [-72.622739, 42.070206],
 'pop': 15338,
 'state': 'MA'}
```

The `json.loads()` function takes string objects as input while the `json.load()` function takes file objects as input. Both functions decode the JSON object and load it in the `json_data` file as a Python dictionary object.

The `json.dumps()` function takes an object and produces a JSON string, and the `json.dump()` function takes an object and writes the JSON string to the file. Thus, both these function do the opposite of the `json.loads()` and `json.load()` functions.

JSON files with the pandas module

JSON strings or files can be read with the `pandas.read_json()` function, which returns a DataFrame or series object. For example, the following code reads the `zips.json` file:

```
df = pd.read_json(os.path.join(data_folder,data_file), lines=True)
print(df)
```

We set `lines=True` because each line contains a separate object in JSON format. Without this argument being set to `True`, pandas will raise `ValueError`. The DataFrame is printed as follows:

```
          _id          city                        loc     pop
state
0         1001       AGAWAM      [-72.622739, 42.070206]   15338
MA
1         1002      CUSHMAN       [-72.51565, 42.377017]   36963
MA
...       ...          ...                         ...     ...
...
29351    99929     WRANGELL     [-132.352918, 56.433524]    2573
AK
29352    99950     KETCHIKAN      [-133.18479, 55.942471]     422
AK

[29353 rows x 5 columns]
```

To save the pandas DataFrame or series object to a JSON file or string, use the `Dataframe.to_json()` function.

> More information for both of these functions can be found at these links: `https://pandas.pydata.org/pandas-docs/stable/generated/pandas.read_json.html` and `https://pandas.pydata.org/pandas-docs/stable/generated/pandas.DataFrame.to_json.html`.

While CSV and JSON remain the most popular data formats for IoT data, due to its large size, it is often necessary to distribute data. There are two popular distributed mechanisms for data storage and access: HDF5 and HDFS. Let's first learn about the HDF5 format.

HDF5 format

Hierarchical Data Format (HDF) is a specification put together by the HDF Group, a consortium of academic and industry organizations (`https://support.hdfgroup.org/HDF5/`). In HDF5 files, data is organized into groups and datasets. A group is a collection of **groups** or **datasets**. A dataset is a multidimensional homogeneous array.

In Python, PyTables and h5py are two major libraries for handling HDF5 files. Both these libraries require HDF5 to be installed. For the parallel version of HDF5, a version of MPI is also required to be installed. Installation of HDF5 and MPI is beyond the scope of this book. Installation instructions for parallel HDF5 can be found at the following link: `https://support.hdfgroup.org/ftp/HDF5/current/src/unpacked/release_docs/INSTALL_parallel`.

Using HDF5 with PyTables

Let's first create an HDF5 file from the numeric data we have in the `temp.csv` file with the following steps:

1. Get the numeric data:

```
import numpy as np
arr = np.loadtxt('temp.csv', skiprows=1, usecols=(2,3),
delimiter=',')
```

2. Open the HDF5 file:

```
import tables
h5filename = 'pytable_demo.hdf5'
with tables.open_file(h5filename,mode='w') as h5file:
```

3. Get the `root` node:

```
root = h5file.root
```

4. Create a group with `create_group()` or a dataset with `create_array()`, and repeat this until all the data is stored:

```
h5file.create_array(root,'global_power',arr)
```

5. Close the file:

```
h5file.close()
```

Let's read the file and print the dataset to make sure it is properly written:

```
with tables.open_file(h5filename,mode='r') as h5file:
    root = h5file.root
    for node in h5file.root:
        ds = node.read()
        print(type(ds),ds.shape)
        print(ds)
```

We get the NumPy array back.

Using HDF5 with pandas

We can also read and write HDF5 files with pandas. To read HDF5 files with pandas, they must first be created with it. For example, let's use pandas to create a HDF5 file containing global power values:

```
import pandas as pd
import numpy as np
arr = np.loadtxt('temp.csv', skiprows=1, usecols=(2,3), delimiter=',')
import pandas as pd
store=pd.HDFStore('hdfstore_demo.hdf5')
print(store)
store['global_power']=pd.DataFrame(arr)
store.close()
```

Now let's read the HDF5 file that we created and print the array back:

```
import pandas as pd
store=pd.HDFStore('hdfstore_demo.hdf5')
print(store)
print(store['global_power'])
store.close()
```

The values of the DataFrame can be read in three different ways:

- `store['global_power']`
- `store.get('global_power')`
- `store.global_power`

pandas also provides the high-level `read_hdf()` function and the `to_hdf()` DataFrame method for reading and writing HDF5 files.

More documentation on HDF5 in pandas is available at the following link: `http://pandas.pydata.org/pandas-docs/stable/io.html#io-hdf5`.

Using HDF5 with h5py

The `h5py` module is the most popular way to handle HDF5 files in Python. A new or existing HDF5 file can be opened with the `h5py.File()` function. After the file is open, its groups can simply be accessed by subscripting the file object as if it was a dictionary object. For example, the following code opens an HDF5 file with `h5py` and then prints the array stored in the `/global_power` group:

```
import h5py
hdf5file = h5py.File('pytable_demo.hdf5')
ds=hdf5file['/global_power']
print(ds)
for i in range(len(ds)):
    print(arr[i])
hdf5file.close()
```

The `arr` variable prints an `HDF5 dataset` type:

```
<HDF5 dataset "global_power": shape (9, 2), type "<f8">
[2.58  0.136]
[2.552 0.1  ]
[2.55 0.1 ]
[2.55 0.1 ]
[2.554 0.1  ]
[2.55 0.1 ]
[2.534 0.096]
[2.484 0.   ]
[2.468 0.   ]
```

For a new `hdf5file`, datasets and groups can be created by using
the `hdf5file.create_dataset()` function, returning the dataset object, and the
`hdf5file.create_group()` function, returning the folder object. The `hdf5file` file
object is also a folder object representing /, the root folder. Dataset objects support array
style slicing and dicing to set or read values from them. For example, the following code
creates an HDF5 file and stores one dataset:

```
import numpy as np
arr = np.loadtxt('temp.csv', skiprows=1, usecols=(2,3), delimiter=',')

import h5py
hdf5file = h5py.File('h5py_demo.hdf5')
dataset1 = hdf5file.create_dataset('global_power',data=arr)
hdf5file.close()
```

`h5py` provides an `attrs` proxy object with a dictionary-like interface to store and retrieve
metadata about the file, folders, and datasets. For example, the following code sets and then
prints the dataset and file attribute:

```
dataset1.attrs['owner']='City Corp.'
print(dataset1.attrs['owner'])

hdf5file.attrs['security_level']='public'
print(hdf5file.attrs['security_level'])
```

For more information about the `h5py` library, refer to the documentation at the following
link: `http://docs.h5py.org/en/latest/index.html`.

So far, we have learned about different data formats. Often, large data is stored
commercially in databases, therefore we will explore how to access both SQL and NoSQL
databases next.

SQL data

Most databases are organized using relational models. A relational database consists of one or more related tables of information, and the relationship between information in different tables is described using keys. Conventionally, these databases are managed using the **Database Management System** (**DBMS**), software which interacts with end users, different applications, and the database itself to capture and analyze data. Commercially available DBMSes use **Structured Query Language** (**SQL**) to access and manipulate databases. We can also use Python to access relational databases. In this section, we will explore SQLite and MySQL, two very popular database engines that work with Python.

The SQLite database engine

According to the SQLite home page (`https://sqlite.org/index.html`), *SQLite is a self-contained, high-reliability, embedded, full-featured, public-domain SQL database engine.*

SQLite is optimized for use in embedded applications. It is simple to use and quite fast. We need to use the `sqlite3` Python module to integrate SQLite with Python. The `sqlite3` module is bundled with Python 3, so there is no need to install it.

We will use the data from the European Soccer Database (`https://github.com/hugomathien/football-data-collection`) for demonstrative purposes. We assume that you already have a SQL server installed and started:

1. The first step after importing `sqlite3` is to create a connection to the database using the `connect` method:

```
import sqlite3
import pandas as pd
connection = sqlite3.connect('database.sqlite')
print("Database opened successfully")
```

2. The European Soccer Database consists of eight tables. We can use `read_sql` to read the database table or SQL query into the DataFrame. This prints a list of all the tables in the database:

```
tables = pd.read_sql("SELECT * FROM sqlite_master WHERE
        type='table';", connection)
print(tables)
```

```
       type              name          tbl_name  rootpage  \
0     table    sqlite_sequence   sqlite_sequence         4
1     table  Player_Attributes  Player_Attributes        11
2     table             Player            Player        14
3     table              Match             Match        18
4     table             League            League        24
5     table            Country           Country        26
6     table               Team              Team        29
7     table    Team_Attributes   Team_Attributes         2

                                                    sql
0            CREATE TABLE sqlite_sequence(name,seq)
1     CREATE TABLE "Player_Attributes" (\n\t`id`\tIN...
2     CREATE TABLE `Player` (\n\t`id`\tINTEGER PRIMA...
3     CREATE TABLE `Match` (\n\t`id`\tINTEGER PRIMAR...
4     CREATE TABLE `League` (\n\t`id`\tINTEGER PRIMA...
5     CREATE TABLE `Country` (\n\t`id`\tINTEGER PRIM...
6     CREATE TABLE "Team" (\n\t`id`\tINTEGER PRIMARY...
7     CREATE TABLE `Team_Attributes` (\n\t`id`\tINTE...
```

3. Let's read data from the `Country` table:

```
countries = pd.read_sql("SELECT * FROM Country;", connection)
countries.head()
```

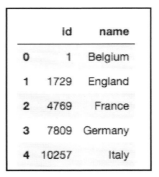

	id	name
0	1	Belgium
1	1729	England
2	4769	France
3	7809	Germany
4	10257	Italy

4. We can use SQL queries on tables. In the following example, we select players whose height is greater than or equal to 180 and whose weight is greater than or equal to 170:

```
selected_players = pd.read_sql_query("SELECT * FROM Player WHERE
        height >= 180 AND weight >= 170 ", connection)
print(selected_players)
```

	id	player_api_id	player_name	player_fifa_api_id \
0	1	505942	Aaron Appindangoye	218353
1	4	30572	Aaron Galindo	140161
2	9	528212	Aaron Lennox	206592
3	11	23889	Aaron Mokoena	47189
4	17	161644	Aaron Taylor-Sinclair	213569
5	20	46447	Abasse Ba	156626
6	24	42664	Abdelkader Ghezzal	178063
7	29	306735	Abdelouahed Chakhsi	210504
8	31	31684	Abdeslam Ouaddou	33022
9	32	32637	Abdessalam Benjelloun	177295
10	34	41093	Abdou Traore	187048

5. Finally, do not forget to close the connection using the `close` method:

```
connection.close()
```

If you made any changes in the database, you will need to use the `commit()` method.

The MySQL database engine

Though we can use SQLite for large databases, MySQL is generally preferred. In addition to being scalable for large databases, MySQL is also useful where data security is paramount. Before using MySQL, you will need to install the Python MySQL connector. There are many possible Python MySQL connectors such as, MySQLdb, PyMySQL, and MySQL; we will use `mysql-connector-python`.

In all three, after making a connection using the `connect` method, we define the `cursor` element and use the `execute` method to run different SQL queries. To install MySQL, we use the following:

```
pip install mysql-connector-python
```

1. Now that the Python MySQL connector is installed, we can start a connection with the SQL server. Replace the `host`, `user`, and `password` configurations with your SQL server configuration:

```
import mysql.connector
connection = mysql.connector.connect(host="127.0.0.1", # your host
        user="root", # username
        password="**********" ) # password
```

2. Let's check existing databases in the server and list them. To do this, we use the `cursor` method:

```
mycursor = connection.cursor()
mycursor.execute("SHOW DATABASES")
for x in mycursor:
    print(x)
```

```
('information_schema',)
('mysql',)
('performance_schema',)
('sys',)
```

3. We can access one of the existing databases. Let's list the tables in one of the databases:

```
connection = mysql.connector.connect(host="127.0.0.1", # your host
user="root", # username
password="**********" ,    #replace with your password
database = 'mysql')
mycursor = connection.cursor()
mycursor.execute("SHOW TABLES")
for x in mycursor:
    print(x)
```

NoSQL data

The **Not Only Structured Query Language (NoSQL)** database is not a relational database; instead, data can be stored in key-value, JSON, document, columnar, or graph formats. They are frequently used in big data and real-time applications. We will learn here how to access NoSQL data using MongoDB, and we assume you have the MongoDB server configured properly and on:

1. We will need to establish a connection with the Mongo daemon using the `MongoClient` object. The following code establishes the connection to the default host, `localhost` , and port (`27017`). And it gives us access to the database:

```
from pymongo import MongoClient
client = MongoClient()
db = client.test
```

2. In this example, we try to load the `cancer` dataset available in scikit-learn to the Mongo database. So, we first get the breast cancer dataset and convert it to a pandas DataFrame:

```
from sklearn.datasets import load_breast_cancer
import pandas as pd

cancer = load_breast_cancer()
data = pd.DataFrame(cancer.data, columns=[cancer.feature_names])

data.head()
```

3. Next, we convert this into the JSON format, use the `json.loads()` function to decode it, and insert the decoded data into the open database:

```
import json
data_in_json = data.to_json(orient='split')
rows = json.loads(data_in_json)
db.cancer_data.insert(rows)
```

4. This will create a collection named `cancer_data` that contains the data. We can query the document we just created, using the `cursor` object:

```
cursor = db['cancer_data'].find({})
df = pd.DataFrame(list(cursor))
print(df)
```

```
                              _id  \
0   5ba272f0d82f8a68a1fa33ab


                                          columns  \
0   [[mean radius], [mean texture], [mean perimete...


                                             data  \
0   [[17.99, 10.38, 122.8, 1001.0, 0.1184, 0.2776,...


                                            index
0   [0, 1, 2, 3, 4, 5, 6, 7, 8, 9, 10, 11, 12, 13,...
```

When it comes to distributed data on the IoT, **Hadoop Distributed File System (HDFS)** is another popular method for providing distributed data storage and access in IoT systems. In the next section, we study how to access and store data in HDFS.

HDFS

HDFS is a popular storage and access method for storing and retrieving data files for IoT solutions. The HDFS format can hold large amounts of data in a reliable and scalable manner. Its design is based on the **Google File System** (https://ai.google/research/pubs/pub51). HDFS splits individual files into fixed-size blocks that are stored on machines across the cluster. To ensure reliability, it replicates the file blocks and distributes them across the cluster; by default, the replication factor is 3. HDFS has two main architecture components:

- The first, **NodeName**, stores the metadata for the entire filesystem, such as filenames, their permissions, and the location of each block of each file.
- The second, **DataNode** (one or more), is where file blocks are stored. It performs **Remote Procedure Calls (RPCs)** using protobufs.

RPC is a protocol that one program can use to request a service from a program located on another computer on a network without having to know the network's details. A procedure call is also sometimes known as a **function call** or a **subroutine call**.

There are many options for programmatically accessing HDFS in Python, such as snakebite, pyarrow, hdfs3, pywebhdfs, hdfscli, and so on. In this section, we will focus mainly on libraries that provide native RPC client interfaces and work with Python 3.

Snakebite is a pure Python module and CLI that allows you to access HDFS from Python programs. At present, it only works with Python 2; Python 3 is not supported. Moreover, it does not yet support write operations, and so we are not including it in the book. However, if you are interested in knowing more about this, you can refer to Spotify's GitHub: https://github.com/spotify/snakebite.

Using hdfs3 with HDFS

hdfs3 is a lightweight Python wrapper around the C/C++ libhdfs3 library. It allows us to use HDFS natively from Python. To start, we first need to connect with the HDFS NameNode; this is done using the HDFileSystem class:

```
from hdfs3 import HDFileSystem
hdfs = HDFileSystem(host = 'localhost', port=8020)
```

This automatically establishes a connection with the NameNode. Now, we can access a directory listing using the following:

```
print(hdfs.ls('/tmp'))
```

This will list all the files and directories in the tmp folder. You can use functions such as mkdir to make a directory and cp to copy a file from one location to another. To write into a file, we open it first using the open method and use write:

```
with hdfs.open('/tmp/file1.txt','wb') as f:
    f.write(b'You are Awesome!')
```

Data can be read from the file:

```
with hdfs.open('/tmp/file1.txt') as f:
    print(f.read())
```

You can learn more about `hdfs3` from its documentation: `https://media.readthedocs.org/pdf/hdfs3/latest/hdfs3.pdf`.

Using PyArrow's filesystem interface for HDFS

PyArrow has a C++-based interface for HDFS. By default, it uses `libhdfs`, a JNI-based interface, for the Java Hadoop client. Alternatively, we can also use `libhdfs3`, a C++ library for HDFS. We connect to the NameNode using `hdfs.connect`:

```
import pyarrow as pa
hdfs = pa.hdfs.connect(host='hostname', port=8020, driver='libhdfs')
```

If we change the driver to `libhdfs3`, we will be using the C++ library for HDFS from Pivotal Labs. Once the connection to the NameNode is made, the filesystem is accessed using the same methods as for hdfs3.

HDFS is preferred when the data is extremely large. It allows us to read and write data in chunks; this is helpful for accessing and processing streaming data. A nice comparison of the three native RPC client interfaces is presented in the following blog post: `http://wesmckinney.com/blog/python-hdfs-interfaces/`.

Summary

This chapter dealt with many different data formats, and, in the process, many different datasets. We started with the simplest TXT data and accessed the `Shakespeare` play data. We learned how to read data from CSV files using the `csv`, `numpy`, and `pandas` modules. We moved on to the JSON format; we used Python's JSON and pandas modules to access JSON data. From data formats, we progressed to accessing databases and covered both SQL and NoSQL databases. Next, we learned how to work with the Hadoop File System in Python.

Accessing data is the first step. In the next chapter, we will learn about machine learning tools that will help us to design, model, and make informed predictions on data.

Machine Learning for IoT

3

The term **machine learning** (**ML**) refers to computer programs that can automatically detect meaningful patterns in data and improve with experience. Though it isn't a new field, it's presently at the peak of its hype cycle. This chapter introduces the reader to standard ML algorithms and their applications in the field of IoT.

After reading this chapter, you will know about the following:

- What ML is and the role it plays in the IoT pipeline
- Supervised and unsupervised learning paradigms
- Regression and how to perform linear regression using TensorFlow and Keras
- Popular ML classifiers and implementing them in TensorFlow and Keras
- Decision trees, random forests, and techniques to perform boosting and how to write code for them
- Tips and tricks to improve the system performance and model limitations

ML and IoT

ML, a subset of artificial intelligence, aims to build computer programs with an ability to automatically learn and improve from experience without being explicitly programmed. In this age of big data, with data being generated at break-neck speed, it isn't humanly possible to go through all of the data and understand it manually. According to an estimate by Cisco, a leading company in the field of IT and networking, IoT will generate 400 zettabytes of data a year by 2018. This suggests that we need to look into automatic means of understanding this enormous data, and this is where ML comes in.

The complete Cisco report, released on February 1, 2018, can be accessed at https://www.cisco.com/c/en/us/solutions/collateral/service-provider/global-cloud-index-gci/white-paper-c11-738085.html. It forecasts data traffic and cloud service trends in light of the amalgamation of IoT, robotics, AI, and telecommunication.

Every year, Gartner, a research and advisory firm, releases a graphical representation providing a visual and conceptual presentation of the maturity of emerging technologies through five phases.

You can find the image of *Gartner Hype Cycle for Emerging Technologies* in the year 2018 at `https://www.gartner.com/smarterwithgartner/5-trends-emerge-in-gartner-hype-cycle-for-emerging-technologies-2018/`.

We can see that both IoT platforms and ML are at the Peak of Inflated Expectations. What does it mean? The Peak of Inflated Expectations is the stage in the lifetime of technology when there's over enthusiasm about the technology. A large number of vendors and startups invest in the technology present at the peak crest. A growing number of business establishments explore how the new technology may fit within their business strategies. In short, it's the time to jump in to the technology. You can hear investors joking at venture fund events that *if you just include machine learning in your pitch, you can add a zero on to the end of your valuation.*

So, fasten your seat belts and let's dive deeper into ML technology.

Learning paradigms

ML algorithms can be classified based on the method they use as follows:

- Probabilistic versus non-probabilistic
- Modeling versus optimization
- Supervised versus unsupervised

In this book, we classify our ML algorithms as supervised versus unsupervised. The distinction between these two depends on how the model learns and the type of data that's provided to the model to learn:

- **Supervised learning**: Let's say I give you a series and ask you to predict the next element:

  (1, 4, 9, 16, 25,...)

  You guessed right: the next number will be 36, followed by 49 and so on. This is supervised learning, also called **learning by example**; you weren't told that the series represents the square of positive integers—you were able to guess it from the five examples provided.

In a similar manner, in supervised learning, the machine learns from example. It's provided with a training data consisting of a set of pairs (X, Y) where X is the input (it can be a single number or an input value with a large number of features) and Y is the expected output for the given input. Once trained on the example data, the model should be able to reach an accurate conclusion when presented with a new data.

The supervised learning is used to predict, given set of inputs, either a real-valued output (regression) or a discrete label (classification). We'll explore both regression and classification algorithms in the coming sections.

- **Unsupervised learning**: Let's say you're given with eight circular blocks of different radii and colors, and you are asked to arrange or group them in an order. What will you do?

Some may arrange them in increasing or decreasing order of radii, some may group them according to color. There are so many ways, and for each one of us, it will be dependent on what internal representation of the data we had while grouping. This is unsupervised learning, and a majority of human learning lies in this category.

In unsupervised learning, the model is just given the data (X) but isn't told anything about it; the model learns by itself the underlying patterns and relationships in the data. Unsupervised learning is normally used for clustering and dimensionality reduction.

Though we use TensorFlow for most of the algorithms in this book, in this chapter, due to the efficiently built scikit library for ML algorithms, we'll use the functions and methods provided by scikit wherever they provide more flexibility and features. The aim is to provide you, the reader, with to use AI/ML techniques on the data generated by IoT, not to reinvent the wheel.

Prediction using linear regression

Aaron, a friend of mine, is a little sloppy with money and is never able to estimate how much his monthly credit card bill will be. Can we do something to help him? Well, yes, linear regression can help us to predict a monthly credit card bill if we have sufficient data. Thanks to the digital economy, all of his monetary transactions for the last five years are available online. We extracted his monthly expenditure on groceries, stationery, and travel and his monthly income. Linear regression helped not only in predicting his monthly credit card bill, it also gave an insight into which factor was most responsible for his spending.

This was just one example; linear regression can be used in many similar tasks. In this section, we'll learn how we can perform linear regression on our data.

Linear regression is a supervised learning task. It's one of the most basic, simple, and extensively used ML techniques for prediction. The goal of regression is to find a function $F(x, W)$, for a given input-output pair (x, y), so that $y = F(x, W)$. In the (x, y) pair, x is the independent variable and y the dependent variable, and both of them are continuous variables. It helps us to find the relationship between the dependent variable y and the independent variable(s) x.

The input x can be a single input variable or many input variables. When $F(x, W)$ maps a single input variable x, it's called **simple linear regression**; for multiple input variables, it's called **multiple linear regression**.

The function $F(x, W)$ is approximated using the following expression:

$$y_i \approx F(x_i, W) = W_0 + \sum_{j=1}^{d} x_{ij} W_j$$

In this expression, d is the dimensions of x (number of independent variables), and W is the weight associated with each component of x. To find the function $F(x, W)$, we need to determine the weights. The natural choice is to find the weights that reduce the squared error, hence our objective function is as follows:

$$\mathcal{L} = \sum_{i=1}^{N} (y_i - F(x_i, W))^2$$

In the preceding function, N is the total number of the input-output pair presented. To find the weights, we differentiate the objective function with respect to weight and equate it to 0. In matrix notation, we can write the solution for the column vector $W = (W_0, W_1, W_2, ..., W_d)^T$ as follows:

$$\nabla_W \mathcal{L} = 0$$

On differentiating and simplifying, we get the following:

$$W = (X^T X)^{-1} X^T Y$$

X is the input vector of size $[N, d]$ and Y the output vector of size $[N, 1]$. The weights can be found if $(X^T X)^{-1}$ exists, that's if all of the rows and columns of X are linearly independent. To ensure this, the number of input-output samples (N) should be much greater than the number of input features (d).

 An important thing to remember is that Y, the dependent variable, isn't linear with respect to the dependent variable X; instead, it's linear with respect to the model parameter W, the weights. And so we can model relationships such as exponential or even sinusoidal (between Y and X) using linear regression. In this case, we generalize the problem to finding weights W, so that $y = F(g(x), W)$, where $g(x)$ is a non-linear function of X.

Electrical power output prediction using regression

Now that you've understood the basics of linear regression, let's use it to predict the electrical power output of a combined cycle power plant. We described this dataset in Chapter 1, *Principles and Foundations of AI and IoT*; here, we'll use TensorFlow and its automatic gradient to find the solution. The dataset can be downloaded from the UCI ML archive (http://archive.ics.uci.edu/ml/datasets/combined+cycle+power+plant). The complete code is available on GitHub (https://github.com/PacktPublishing/Hands-On-Artificial-Intelligence-for-IoT) under the filename ElectricalPowerOutputPredictionUsingRegression.ipynb.

Let's understand the execution of code in the following steps:

1. We import `tensorflow`, `numpy`, `pandas`, `matplotlib`, and some useful functions of scikit-learn:

```
# Import the modules
import tensorflow as tf
import numpy as np
import pandas as pd
import matplotlib.pyplot as plt
from sklearn.preprocessing import MinMaxScaler
from sklearn.metrics import mean_squared_error, r2_score
from sklearn.model_selection import train_test_split
%matplotlib inline # The data file is loaded and analyzed
```

2. The data file is loaded and analyzed:

```
filename = 'Folds5x2_pp.xlsx' # download the data file from UCI ML
repository
df = pd.read_excel(filename, sheet_name='Sheet1')
df.describe()
```

3. Since the data isn't normalized, before using it, we need to normalize it using the `MinMaxScaler` of `sklearn`:

```
X, Y = df[['AT', 'V','AP','RH']], df['PE']
scaler = MinMaxScaler()
X_new = scaler.fit_transform(X)
target_scaler = MinMaxScaler()
Y_new = target_scaler.fit_transform(Y.values.reshape(-1,1))
X_train, X_test, Y_train, y_test = \
  train_test_split(X_new, Y_new, test_size=0.4, random_state=333)
```

4. Now, we define a class, `LinearRegressor`; this is the class where all of the real work happens. The class initialization defines the computational graph and initializes all of the `Variables` (weights and bias). The class has the `function` method, which models the function $y = F(X,W)$; the `fit` method performs the auto gradient and updates the weights and bias, the `predict` method is used to get the output y for a given input X, and the `get_weights` method returns the learned weights and bias:

```
class LinearRegressor:
 def __init__(self,d, lr=0.001 ):
 # Placeholders for input-output training data
 self.X = tf.placeholder(tf.float32,\
 shape=[None,d], name='input')
 self.Y = tf.placeholder(tf.float32,\
```

```
name='output')
# Variables for weight and bias
self.b = tf.Variable(0.0, dtype=tf.float32)
self.W = tf.Variable(tf.random_normal([d,1]),\
dtype=tf.float32)

# The Linear Regression Model
self.F = self.function(self.X)

# Loss function
self.loss = tf.reduce_mean(tf.square(self.Y \
- self.F, name='LSE'))
# Gradient Descent with learning
# rate of 0.05 to minimize loss
optimizer = tf.train.GradientDescentOptimizer(lr)
self.optimize = optimizer.minimize(self.loss)

# Initializing Variables
init_op = tf.global_variables_initializer()
self.sess = tf.Session()
self.sess.run(init_op)

def function(self, X):
return tf.matmul(X, self.W) + self.b

def fit(self, X, Y,epochs=500):
total = []
for i in range(epochs):
_, l = self.sess.run([self.optimize,self.loss],\
feed_dict={self.X: X, self.Y: Y})
total.append(l)
if i%100==0:
print('Epoch {0}/{1}: Loss {2}'.format(i,epochs,l))
return total

def predict(self, X):
return self.sess.run(self.function(X), feed_dict={self.X:X})

def get_weights(self):
return self.sess.run([self.W, self.b])
```

5. We use the previous class to create our linear regression model and train it:

```
N, d = X_train.shape
model = LinearRegressor(d)
loss = model.fit(X_train, Y_train, 20000) #Epochs = 20000
```

Let's see the performance of our trained linear regressor. A plot of mean square error with **Epochs** shows that the network tried to reach a minimum value of mean square error:

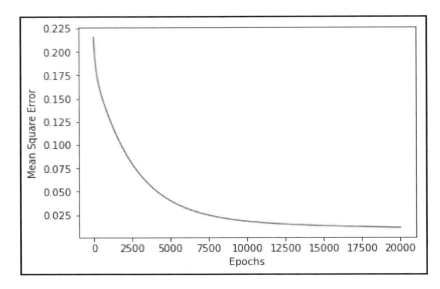

On the test dataset, we achieved an R^2 value of *0.768* and mean square error of *0.011*.

Logistic regression for classification

In the previous section, we learned how to predict. There's another common task in ML: the task of classification. Separating dogs from cats and spam from not spam, or even identifying the different objects in a room or scene—all of these are classification tasks.

Logistic regression is an old classification technique. It provides the probability of an event taking place, given an input value. The events are represented as categorical dependent variables, and the probability of a particular dependent variable being *1* is given using the logit function:

$$Y_{pred} = P(y = 1 | X = x) = \frac{1}{1 + exp(-(b + W^T X))}$$

Before going into the details of how we can use logistic regression for classification, let's examine the logit function (also called the **sigmoid** function because of its S-shaped curve). The following diagram shows the logit function and its derivative varies with respect to the input *X*, the Sigmoidal function (blue) and its derivative (orange):

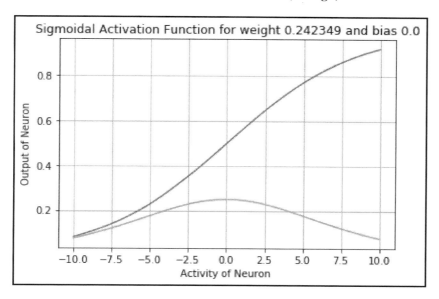

A few important things to note from this diagram are the following:

- The value of sigmoid (and hence Y_{pred}) lies between (*0, 1*)
- The derivative of the sigmoid is highest when $W^T X + b = 0.0$ and the highest value of the derivative is just *0.25* (the sigmoid at same place has a value *0.5*)
- The slope by which the sigmoid varies depends on the weights, and the position where we'll have the peak of derivative depends on the bias

I would suggest you play around with the `Sigmoid_function.ipynb` program available at this book's GitHub repository, to get a feel of how the sigmoid function changes as the weight and bias changes.

Cross-entropy loss function

Logistic regression aims to find weights W and bias b, so that each input vector, X_i, in the input feature space is classified correctly to its class, y_i. In other words, y_i and Y_{pred_i} should have a similar distribution for the given x_i. We first consider a binary classification problem; in this case, the data point y_i can have value *1* or *0*. Since logistic regression is a supervised learning algorithm, we give as input the training data pair (X_i, Y_i) and let Y_{pred_i} be the probability that $P(y=1|X=X_i)$; then, for p training data points, the total average loss is defined as follows:

$$loss = \frac{1}{p} \sum_{i=1}^{p} Y_i log(Y_{pred_i}) + (1 - Y_i)log(1 - Y_{pred_i})$$

Hence, for every data pair, for $Y_i = 1$, the first term will contribute to the loss term, with the contribution changing from infinity to *0* as Y_{pred_i} varies from *0* to *1*, respectively. Similarly, for $Y_i = 0$, the second term will contribute to the loss term, with the contribution changing from infinity to zero as Y_{pred_i} varies from *1* to *0*, respectively.

For multiclass classification, the loss term is generalized to the following:

$$loss = \sum_{i=1}^{p} \sum_{j=1}^{K} Y_{ij} log(Y_{pred_{ij}})$$

In the preceding, K is the number of classes. An important thing to note is that, while for binary classification the output Y_i and Y_{pred} were single values, for multiclass problems, both Y_i and Y_{pred} are now vectors of K dimensions, with one component for each category.

Classifying wine using logistic regressor

Let's now use what we've learned to classify wine quality. I can hear you thinking: *What wine quality? No way!* Let's see how our logistic regressor fares as compared to professional wine tasters. We'll be using the wine quality dataset (https://archive.ics.uci.edu/ml/datasets/wine+quality); details about the dataset are given in Chapter 1, *Principles and Foundation of AI and IoT*. The full code is in the file named Wine_quality_using_logistic_regressor.ipynb at the GitHub repository. Let's understand the code step by step:

1. The first step is loading all of the modules:

```
# Import the modules
import tensorflow as tf
import numpy as np
import pandas as pd
import matplotlib.pyplot as plt
from sklearn.preprocessing import MinMaxScaler
from sklearn.metrics import mean_squared_error, r2_score
from sklearn.model_selection import train_test_split
%matplotlib inline
```

2. We read the data; in the present code, we are analyzing only the red wine, so we read data from the winequality-red.csv file. The file contains the data values separated not by commas, but instead by semicolons, so we need to specify the separator argument:

```
filename = 'winequality-red.csv' # Download the file from UCI ML
Repo
df = pd.read_csv(filename, sep=';')
```

3. We separate from the data file input features and target quality. In the file, the target, wine quality is given on a scale from 0—10. Here, for simplicity, we divide it into three classes, so if the initial quality is less than five, we make it the third class (signifying bad); between five and eight, we consider it ok (second class); and above eight, we consider it good (the first class). We also normalize the input features and split the data into training and test datasets:

```
X, Y = df[columns[0:-1]], df[columns[-1]]
scaler = MinMaxScaler()
X_new = scaler.fit_transform(X)
Y.loc[(Y<3)]=3
Y.loc[(Y<6.5) & (Y>=3 )] = 2
Y.loc[(Y>=6.5)] = 1
Y_new = pd.get_dummies(Y) # One hot encode
```

```
X_train, X_test, Y_train, y_test = \
train_test_split(X_new, Y_new, test_size=0.4, random_state=333)
```

4. The main part of the code is the `LogisticRegressor` class; at first glance, you'll think that it's similar to the `LinearRegressor` class we made earlier. The class is defined in the Python file, `LogisticRegressor.py`. It is indeed, but there are a few important differences: the Y output is replaced by Y_{pred}, which instead of having a single value, now is a three-dimensional categorical value, each dimension specifying the probability of three categories. The weights here have dimensions of $d \times n$, where d is the number of input features and n the number of output categories. The bias too now is three-dimensional. Another important change is the change in the loss function:

```
class LogisticRegressor:
    def __init__(self, d, n, lr=0.001 ):
        # Place holders for input-output training data
        self.X = tf.placeholder(tf.float32, \
                shape=[None,d], name='input')
        self.Y = tf.placeholder(tf.float32, \
                name='output')
        # Variables for weight and bias
        self.b = tf.Variable(tf.zeros(n), dtype=tf.float32)
        self.W = tf.Variable(tf.random_normal([d,n]), \
                dtype=tf.float32)
        # The Logistic Regression Model
        h = tf.matmul(self.X, self.W) + self.b
        self.Ypred = tf.nn.sigmoid(h)
        # Loss function
        self.loss = cost = tf.reduce_mean(-
tf.reduce_sum(self.Y*tf.log(self.Ypred), \
                reduction_indices=1), name = 'cross-entropy-loss')
        # Gradient Descent with learning
        # rate of 0.05 to minimize loss
        optimizer = tf.train.GradientDescentOptimizer(lr)
        self.optimize = optimizer.minimize(self.loss)
        # Initializing Variables
        init_op = tf.global_variables_initializer()
        self.sess = tf.Session()
        self.sess.run(init_op)

    def fit(self, X, Y,epochs=500):
        total = []
        for i in range(epochs):
            _, l = self.sess.run([self.optimize,self.loss], \
                    feed_dict={self.X: X, self.Y: Y})
            total.append(l)
```

```
        if i%1000==0:
            print('Epoch {0}/{1}: Loss {2}'.format(i,epochs,l))
    return total

def predict(self, X):
    return self.sess.run(self.Ypred, feed_dict={self.X:X})

def get_weights(self):
    return self.sess.run([self.W, self.b])
```

5. Now we simply train our model and predict the output. The learned model gives us an accuracy of ~85% on the test dataset. Pretty impressive!

Using ML, we can also identify what ingredients make wine good quality. A company called IntelligentX recently started brewing beer based on user feedback; it uses AI to get the recipe for the tastiest beer. You can read about the work in this *Forbes* article: `https://www.forbes.com/sites/emmasandler/2016/07/07/you-can-now-drink-beer-brewed-by-artificial-intelligence/#21fd11cc74c3`.

Classification using support vector machines

Support Vector Machines (SVMs) is arguably the most used ML technique for classification. The main idea behind SVM is that we find an optimal hyperplane with maximum margin separating the two classes. If the data is linearly separable, the process of finding the hyperplane is straightforward, but if it isn't linearly separable, then kernel trick is used to make the data linearly separable in some transformed high-dimensional feature space.

SVM is considered a non-parametric supervised learning algorithm. The main idea of SVM is to find a **maximal margin separator**: a separating hyperplane that is farthest from the training samples presented.

Consider the following diagram; the red dots represent class 1 for which the output should be 1, and the blue dots represent the class 2 for which the output should be -1. There can be many lines which can separate the red dots from the blue ones; the diagram demonstrates three such lines: **A**, **B**, and **C** respectively. Which of the three lines do you think will be the best choice? Intuitively, the best choice is line B, because it's farthest from the examples of both classes, and hence ensures the least error in classification:

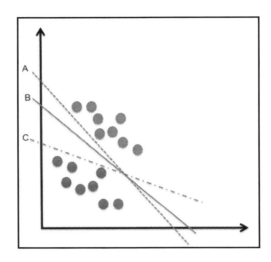

In the following section, we'll learn the basic maths behind finding the maximal-separator hyperplane. Though the maths here is mostly basic, if you don't like maths you can simply skip to the implementation section where we use SVM to classify wine again! Cheers!

Maximum margin hyperplane

From our knowledge of linear algebra, we know that the equation of a plane is given by the following:

$$W_0 + W^T X = 0$$

In SVM, this plane should separate the positive classes (*y= 1*) from the negative classes (*y=-1*), and there's an additional constrain: the distance (margin) of this hyperplane from the closest positive and negative training vectors (X_{pos} and X_{neg} respectively) should be maximum. Hence, the plane is called the maximum margin separator.

The vectors X_{pos} and X_{neg} are called **support vectors,** and they play an important role in defining the SVM model.

Mathematically, this means that the following is true:

$$W_0 + W^T X_{pos} = 1$$

And, so is this:

$$W_0 + W^T X_{neg} = -1$$

From these two equations, we get the following:

$$W^T (X_{pos} + X_{neg}) = 2$$

Dividing by the weight vector length into both sides, we get the following:

$$\frac{W^T (X_{pos} + X_{neg})}{\|W\|} = \frac{2}{\|W\|}$$

So we need to find a separator so that the margin between positive and negative support vectors is maximum, that is: $\frac{2}{\|W\|}$ is maximum, while at the same time all the points are classified correctly, such as the following:

$$y_i (W^T X_i + b) > 1$$

Using a little maths, which we'll not go into in this book, the preceding condition can be represented as finding an optimal solution to the following:

$$\arg\max_b \sum_j \alpha_j - \frac{1}{2} \sum_{j,k} \alpha_j \alpha_k y_j y_k (X_j X_k)$$

Subject to the constraints that:

$$\alpha_j \geq 0$$

$$\sum_j \alpha_j y_j = 0$$

From the values of alpha, we can get weights W from α, the vector of coefficients, using the following equation:

$$W = \sum_j \alpha_j X_j$$

This is a standard quadratic programming optimization problem. Most ML libraries have built-in functions to solve it, so you need not worry about how to do so.

 For the reader interested in knowing more about SVMs and the math behind it, the book *The Nature of Statistical Learning Theory* by Vladimir Vapnik, published by *Springer Science+Business Media*, 2013, is an excellent reference.

Kernel trick

The previous method works fine when the input feature space is linearly separable. What should we do when it isn't? One simple way is to transform the data (X) into a higher dimensional space where it's linearly separable and find a maximal margin hyperplane in that high-dimensional space. Let's see how; our hyperplane in terms of α is as follows:

$$W_0 + \sum_i \alpha_i X^T X^{(i)}$$

Let φ be the transform, then we can replace X by $\varphi(X)$ and hence its dot product $X^T X^{(i)}$ with a function $K(X^T, X^{(i)}) = \varphi(X)^T \varphi(X^{(i)})$ called **kernel**. So we now just preprocess the data by applying the transform φ and then find a linear separator in the transformed space as before.

The most commonly used kernel function is the **Gaussian kernel**, also called **radial basis function**, defined as follows:

$$K(X^i, X^j) = exp(-\gamma \|X^i - X^j\|^2)$$

Classifying wine using SVM

We'll use the `svm.SVC` function provided by the scikit library for the task. The reason to do so is that the TensorFlow library provides us, as of the time of writing, with only a linear implementation of SVM, and it works only for binary classification. We can make our own SVM using the maths we learned in previously in TensorFlow, and `SVM_TensorFlow.ipynb` in the GitHub repository contains the implementation in TensorFlow. The following code can be found in the `Wine_quality_using_SVM.ipynb`.

The SVC classifier of scikit is a support vector classifier. It can also handle multiclass support using a one-versus-one scheme. Some of the optional parameters of the method are as follows:

- `C`: It's a parameter specifying the penalty term (default value is `1.0`).

- `kernel`: It specifies the kernel to be used (default is `rbf`). The possible choices are `linear`, `poly`, `rbf`, `sigmoid`, `precomputed`, and `callable`.

- `gamma`: It specifies the kernel coefficient for `rbf`, `poly`, and `sigmoid` and the default value (the default is `auto`).

- `random_state`: It sets the seed of the pseudo-random number generator to use when shuffling the data.

Follow the given steps to create our SVM model:

1. Let's load all of the modules we'll need for the code. Note that we aren't importing TensorFlow here and instead have imported certain modules from the scikit library:

```
# Import the modules
import numpy as np
import pandas as pd
import matplotlib.pyplot as plt
from sklearn.preprocessing import MinMaxScaler, LabelEncoder
from sklearn.model_selection import train_test_split
from sklearn.metrics import confusion_matrix, accuracy_score
from sklearn.svm import SVC # The SVM Classifier from scikit
import seaborn as sns
%matplotlib inline
```

2. We read the data file, preprocess it, and separate it into test and training datasets. This time, for simplicity, we're dividing into two classes, good and bad:

```
filename = 'winequality-red.csv' #Download the file from UCI ML
Repo
df = pd.read_csv(filename, sep=';')

#categorize wine quality in two levels
bins = (0,5.5,10)
categories = pd.cut(df['quality'], bins, labels = ['bad','good'])
df['quality'] = categories

#PreProcessing and splitting data to X and y
X = df.drop(['quality'], axis = 1)
scaler = MinMaxScaler()
X_new = scaler.fit_transform(X)
y = df['quality']
labelencoder_y = LabelEncoder()
y = labelencoder_y.fit_transform(y)
X_train, X_test, y_train, y_test = train_test_split(X, y, \
        test_size = 0.2, random_state = 323)
```

3. Now we use the `SVC` classifier and train it on our training dataset with the `fit` method:

```
classifier = SVC(kernel = 'rbf', random_state = 45)
classifier.fit(X_train, y_train)
```

4. Let's now predict the output for the test dataset:

```
y_pred = classifier.predict(X_test)
```

5. The model gave an accuracy of `67.5%` and the confusion matrix is as follows:

```
print("Accuracy is {}".format(accuracy_score(y_test, y_pred)))
## Gives a value ~ 67.5%
cm = confusion_matrix(y_test, y_pred)
sns.heatmap(cm,annot=True,fmt='2.0f')
```

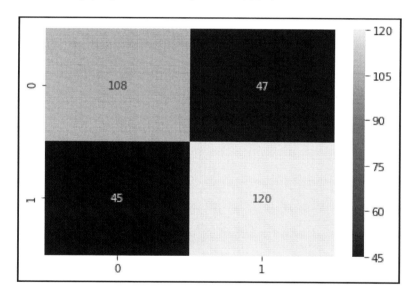

The preceding code uses the binary classification; we can change the code to work for more than two classes as well. For example, in the second step, we can replace the code with the following:

```
bins = (0,3.5,5.5,10)
categories = pd.cut(df['quality'], bins, labels =
['bad','ok','good'])
df['quality'] = categories
```

6. Then we have three categories just as our previous logistic classifier, and the accuracy is 65.9%. And the confusion matrix is as follows:

In the three-class case, the training data distribution is as follows:

- good 855
- ok 734
- bad 10

Since the number of samples in the bad class (corresponding to 0 in the confusion matrix) is only 10, the model isn't able to learn what parameters contribute to bad wine quality. Hence, data should be uniformly distributed among all classes of the classifiers that we explore in this chapter.

Naive Bayes

Naive Bayes is one of the simplest and fastest ML algorithms. This too belongs to the class of supervised learning algorithms. It's based on the Bayes probability theorem. One important assumption that we make in the case of the Naive Bayes classifier is that all of the features of the input vector are **independent and identically distributed** (**iid**). The goal is to learn a conditional probability model for each class C_k in the training dataset:

$$p(C_k|x_1, x_2, \ldots, x_n) = p(C_k|X)$$

Under the iid assumption, and using the Bayes theorem, this can be expressed in terms of the joint probability distribution $p(C_k, X)$:

$$p(C_k|X) \sim p(C_k, X) \sim p(C_k) \prod_{i=1}^{n} p(x_i|C_k)$$

We pick the class that maximizes this term *Maximum A Posteriori* (**MAP**):

$$\underset{k \in \{1,...,K\}}{\arg\max} \; p(C_k) \prod_{i=1}^{n} p(x_i|C_k)$$

There can be different Naive Bayes algorithms, depending upon the distribution of $p(x_i|C_k)$. The common choices are Gaussian in the case of real-valued data, Bernoulli for binary data, and MultiNomial when the data contains the frequency of a certain event (such as document classification).

Let's now see whether we can classify the wine using Naive Bayes. For the sake of simplicity and efficiency, we'll use the scikit built-in Naive Bayes distributions. Since the features values we have in our data are continuous-valued—we'll assume that they have a Gaussian distribution, and we'll use `GaussianNB` of scikit-learn.

Gaussian Naive Bayes for wine quality

The scikit-learn Naive Bayes module supports three Naive Bayes distributions. We can choose either of them depending on our input feature data type. The three Naive Bayes available in scikit-learn are as follows:

- `GaussianNB`
- `MultinomialNB`
- `BernoulliNB`

The wine data, as we have already seen, is a continuous data type. Hence, it will be good if we use Gaussian distribution for $p(x_i|C_k)$—that is, the `GaussianNB` module, and so we'll add `from sklearn.naive_bayes import GaussianNB` in the import cell of the Notebook. You can read more details about the `GaussianNB` module from the is scikit-learn link: `http://scikit-learn.org/stable/modules/generated/sklearn.naive_bayes.GaussianNB.html#sklearn.naive_bayes.GaussianNB`.

The first two steps will remain the same as in the SVM case. But now, instead of declaring an SVM classifier, we'll declare a GaussianNB classifier and we'll use its fit method to learn the training examples. The result from the learned model is obtained using the predict method. So follow these steps:

1. Import the necessary modules. Note that now we're importing GaussianNB from the scikit library:

```
# Import the modules
import numpy as np
import pandas as pd
import matplotlib.pyplot as plt
from sklearn.preprocessing import MinMaxScaler, LabelEncoder
from sklearn.model_selection import train_test_split
from sklearn.metrics import confusion_matrix, accuracy_score
from sklearn.naive_bayes import GaussianNB # The SVM Classifier
from scikit
import seaborn as sns
%matplotlib inline
```

2. Read the data file and preprocess it:

```
filename = 'winequality-red.csv' #Download the file from UCI ML
Repo
df = pd.read_csv(filename, sep=';')

#categorize wine quality in two levels
bins = (0,5.5,10)
categories = pd.cut(df['quality'], bins, labels = ['bad','good'])
df['quality'] = categories

#PreProcessing and splitting data to X and y
X = df.drop(['quality'], axis = 1)
scaler = MinMaxScaler()
X_new = scaler.fit_transform(X)
y = df['quality']
labelencoder_y = LabelEncoder()
y = labelencoder_y.fit_transform(y)
X_train, X_test, y_train, y_test = train_test_split(X, y, \
        test_size = 0.2, random_state = 323)
```

3. Now we declare a Gaussian Naive Bayes, train it on the training dataset, and use the trained model to predict the wine quality on the test dataset:

```
classifier = GaussianNB()
classifier.fit(X_train, y_train)
#Predicting the Test Set
y_pred = classifier.predict(X_test)
```

That's all, folks; our model is ready and kicking. The accuracy of this model is 71.25% for the binary classification case. In the following screenshot, you can a the heatmap of the confusion matrix:

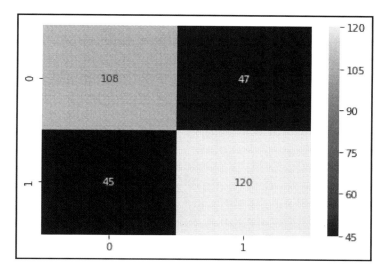

Before you conclude that Naive Bayes is best, let's be aware of some of its pitfalls:

- Naive Bayes makes the prediction based on the frequency-based probability; therefore, it's strongly dependent on the data we use for training.
- Another issue is that we made the iid assumption about input feature space; this isn't always true.

Decision trees

In this section, you'll learn about another ML algorithm that's very popular and fast—decision trees. In decision trees, we build a tree-like structure of decisions; we start with the root, choose a feature and split into branches, and continue till we reach the leaves, which represent the predicted class or value. The algorithm of decision trees involves two main steps:

- Decide which features to choose and what conditions to use for splitting
- Know when to stop

Let's understand it with an example. Consider a sample of 40 students; we have three variables: the gender (boy or girl; discrete), class (XI or XII; discrete), and height (5 to 6 feet; continuous). Eighteen students prefer to go to the library in their spare time and rest prefer to play. We can build a decision tree to predict who will be going to the library and who will be going to the playground in their leisure time. To build the decision tree, we'll need to separate the students who go to library/playground based on the highly significant input variable among the three input variables. The following diagram gives the split based on each input variable:

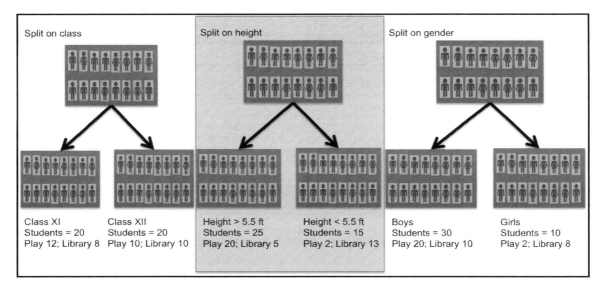

We consider all of the features and choose the one that gives us the maximum information. In the previous example, we can see that a split over the feature height generates the most homogeneous groups, with the group **Height > 5.5 ft** containing 80% students who play and 20% who go to the library in the leisure time and the group **Height < 5.5 ft** containing 13% students who play and 86% who go to the library in their spare time. Hence, we'll make our first split on the feature height. We'll continue the split in this manner and finally reach the decision (leaf node) telling us whether the student will play or go to the library in their spare time. The following diagram shows the decision tree structure; the black circle is the **Root Node**, the blue circles are the **Decision Nodes**, and the green circles are the **Leaf Nodes**:

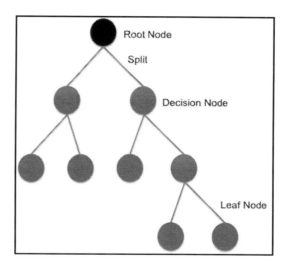

The decision trees belong to the family of greedy algorithms. To find the most homogeneous split, we define our cost function so that it tries to maximize the same class input values in a particular group. For regression, we generally use the mean square error cost function:

$$loss_{regression} = \sum (y - y_{pred})^2$$

Here, y and y_{pred} represent the given and predicted output values for the input values (*i*); we find the split that minimizes this loss.

For classification, we use either the *gini* impurity or cross-entropy as the loss function:

$$loss_{gini} = \sum c_k * (1 - c_k)$$

$$loss_{cross-entropy} = -\sum c_k log(c_k)$$

In the preceding, c_k defines the proportion of same class input values present in a particular group.

Some good resources to learn more about decision trees are as follows:

- L. Breiman, J. Friedman, R. Olshen, and C. Stone: *Classification and Regression Trees,* Wadsworth, Belmont, CA, 1984
- J.R. Quinlan: *C4. 5: programs for ML,* Morgan Kaufmann, 1993
- T. Hastie, R. Tibshirani and J. Friedman: *Elements of Statistical Learning,* Springer, 2009

Decision trees in scikit

The `scikit` library provides `DecisionTreeRegressor` and `DecisionTreeClassifier` to implement regression and classification. Both can be imported from `sklearn.tree`. `DecisionTreeRegressor` is defined as follows:

```
class sklearn.tree.DecisionTreeRegressor (criterion='mse', splitter='best',
max_depth=None, min_samples_split=2, min_samples_leaf=1,
min_weight_fraction_leaf=0.0, max_features=None, random_state=None,
max_leaf_nodes=None, min_impurity_decrease=0.0, min_impurity_split=None,
presort=False)
```

The different arguments are as follows:

- `criterion`: It defines which loss function to use to determine the split. The default value is mean square error (`mse`). The library supports the use of `friedman_mse` and mean absolute error (`mae`) as loss functions.
- `splitter`: We use this to decide whether to use the greedy strategy and go for the best split (default) or we can use random `splitter` to choose the best random split.

- `max_depth`: It defines the maximum depth of the tree.
- `min_samples_split`: It defines the minimum number of samples required to split an internal node. It can be integer or float (in this case it defines the percentage of minimum samples needed for the split).

`DecisionTreeClassifier` is defined as follows:

```
class sklearn.tree.DecisionTreeClassifier(criterion='gini', splitter='best',
max_depth=None, min_samples_split=2, min_samples_leaf=1,
min_weight_fraction_leaf=0.0, max_features=None, random_state=None,
max_leaf_nodes=None, min_impurity_decrease=0.0, min_impurity_split=None,
class_weight=None, presort=False)
```

The different arguments are as follows:

- `criterion`: It tells which loss function to use to determine the split. The default value for the classifier is the `gini`. The library supports the use of `entropy` as loss functions.
- `splitter`: We use this to decide how to choose the split (default value is the best split) or we can use random `splitter` to choose the best random split.
- `max_depth`: It defines the maximum depth of the tree. When the input feature space is large, we use this to restrict the maximum depth and take care of overfitting.
- `min_samples_split`: It defines the minimum number of samples required to split an internal node. It can be integer or float (in this case it tells the percentage of minimum samples needed for the split).

 We've listed only the commonly used preceding arguments; details regarding the remaining parameters of the two can be read on the scikit-learn website: http://scikit-learn.org/stable/modules/generated/ sklearn.tree.DecisionTreeRegressor.html and http://scikit-learn. org/stable/modules/generated/sklearn.tree. DecisionTreeClassifier.html

Decision trees in action

We'll use a decision tree regressor to predict electrical power output first. The dataset and its description have already been introduced in Chapter 1, *Principles and Foundations of IoT and AI*. The code is available at the GitHub repository in the file named ElectricalPowerOutputPredictionUsingDecisionTrees.ipynb:

```python
# Import the modules
import tensorflow as tf
import numpy as np
import pandas as pd
import matplotlib.pyplot as plt
from sklearn.preprocessing import MinMaxScaler
from sklearn.metrics import mean_squared_error, r2_score
from sklearn.model_selection import train_test_split
from sklearn.tree import DecisionTreeRegressor
%matplotlib inline

# Read the data
filename = 'Folds5x2_pp.xlsx' # The file can be downloaded from UCI ML repo
df = pd.read_excel(filename, sheet_name='Sheet1')
df.describe()

# Preprocess the data and split in test/train
X, Y = df[['AT', 'V','AP','RH']], df['PE']
scaler = MinMaxScaler()
X_new = scaler.fit_transform(X)
target_scaler = MinMaxScaler()
Y_new = target_scaler.fit_transform(Y.values.reshape(-1,1))
X_train, X_test, Y_train, y_test = \
  train_test_split(X_new, Y_new, test_size=0.4, random_state=333)


# Define the decision tree regressor
model = DecisionTreeRegressor(max_depth=3)
model.fit(X_train, Y_train)

# Make the prediction over the test data
Y_pred = model.predict(np.float32(X_test))
print("R2 Score is {} and MSE {}".format(\
  r2_score(y_test, Y_pred),\
  mean_squared_error(y_test, Y_pred)))
```

We get an R-square value of 0.90 and mean square error of 0.0047 on the test data; it's a significant improvement over the prediction results obtained using linear regressor (R-square: 0.77;mse: 0.012).

Let's also see the performance of decision trees in the classification task; we use it for the wine quality classification as before. The code is available in the `Wine_quality_using_DecisionTrees.ipynb` file in the GitHub repository:

```
# Import the modules
import numpy as np
import pandas as pd
import matplotlib.pyplot as plt
from sklearn.preprocessing import MinMaxScaler, LabelEncoder
from sklearn.metrics import mean_squared_error, r2_score
from sklearn.model_selection import train_test_split
from sklearn.tree import DecisionTreeClassifier
%matplotlib inline

# Read the data
filename = 'winequality-red.csv' #Download the file from
https://archive.ics.uci.edu/ml/datasets/wine+quality df =
pd.read_csv(filename, sep=';')




# categorize the data into three classes
bins = (0,3.5,5.5,10)
categories = pd.cut(df['quality'], bins, labels = ['bad','ok','good'])
df['quality'] = categories

# Preprocessing and splitting data to X and y X = df.drop(['quality'], axis
= 1) scaler = MinMaxScaler() X_new = scaler.fit_transform(X) y =
df['quality'] from sklearn.preprocessing import LabelEncoder labelencoder_y
= LabelEncoder() y = labelencoder_y.fit_transform(y) X_train, X_test,
y_train, y_test = train_test_split(X, y, test_size = 0.2, random_state =
323)


# Define the decision tree classifier
classifier = DecisionTreeClassifier(max_depth=3)
classifier.fit(X_train, y_train)

# Make the prediction over the test data
Y_pred = classifier.predict(np.float32(X_test))
print("Accuracy is {}".format(accuracy_score(y_test, y_pred)))
```

The decision tree generates a classification accuracy of around 70%. We can see that, for small data size, we can use both decision trees and Naive Bayes with almost equal success. Decision trees suffer from overfitting, which can be taken care of by restricting the maximum depth or setting a minimum number of training inputs. They, like Naive Bayes, are unstable—a little variation in the data can result in a completely different tree; this can be resolved by making use of bagging and boosting techniques. Last, but not least, since it's a greedy algorithm, there's no guarantee that it returns a globally optimal solution.

Ensemble learning

In our daily life, when we have to make a decision, we take guidance not from one person, but from many individuals whose wisdom we trust. The same can be applied in ML; instead of depending upon one single model, we can use a group of models (ensemble) to make a prediction or classification decision. This form of learning is called **ensemble learning**.

Conventionally, ensemble learning is used as the last step in many ML projects. It works best when the models are as independent of one another as possible. The following diagram gives a graphical representation of ensemble learning:

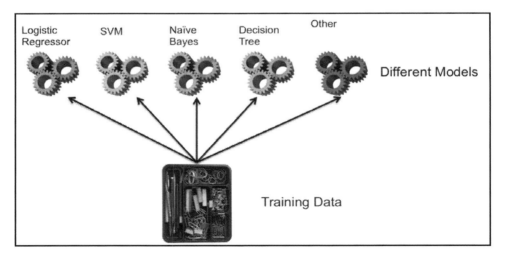

The training of different models can take place either sequentially or in parallel. There are various ways to implement ensemble learning: voting, bagging and pasting, and random forest. Let's see what each of these techniques and how we can implement them.

Voting classifier

The voting classifier follows the majority; it aggregates the prediction of all the classifiers and chooses the class with maximum votes. For example, in the following screenshot, the voting classifier will predict the input instance to belong to class **1**:

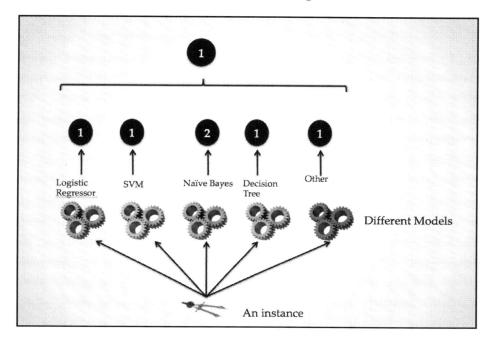

scikit has the VotingClassifier class to implement this. Using ensemble learning on wine quality classification, we reach an accuracy score of 74%, higher than any of the models considered alone. The complete code is in the Wine_quality_using_Ensemble_learning.ipynb file. The following is the main code to perform ensemble learning using voting:

```
# import the different classifiers
from sklearn.svm import SVC
from sklearn.naive_bayes import GaussianNB
from sklearn.tree import DecisionTreeClassifier
from sklearn.ensemble import VotingClassifier

# Declare each classifier
clf1 = SVC(random_state=22)
clf2 = DecisionTreeClassifier(random_state=23)
clf3 = GaussianNB()
X = np.array(X_train)
```

```
y = np.array(y_train)

#Employ Ensemble learning
eclf = VotingClassifier(estimators=[
('lr', clf1), ('rf', clf2), ('gnb', clf3)], voting='hard')
eclf = eclf.fit(X, y)

# Make prediction on test data
y_pred = eclf.predict(X_test)
```

Bagging and pasting

In voting, we used different algorithms for training on the same dataset. We can also achieve ensemble learning by using different models with the same learning algorithm, but we train them on different training data subsets. The training subset is sampled randomly. The sampling can be done with replacement (bagging) or without replacement (pasting):

- **Bagging**: In it, additional data for training is generated from the original dataset using combinations with repetitions. This helps in decreasing the variance of different models.
- **Pasting**: Since pasting is without replacement, each subset of the training data can be used at most once. It's more suitable if the original dataset is large.

The scikit library has a method for performing bagging and pasting; from sklearn.ensemble, we can import BaggingClassifier and use it. The following code estimates 500 decision tree classifiers, each with 1000 training samples using bagging (for pasting, keep bootstrap=False):

```
from sklearn.ensemble import BaggingClassifier
bag_classifier = BaggingClassifier(
        DecisionTreeClassifier(), n_estimators=500, max_samples=1000,\
        bootstrap=True, n_jobs=-1)
bag_classifier.fit(X_train, y_train)
y_pred = bag_classifier.predict(X_test)
```

This results in an accuracy of 77% for wine quality classification. The last argument to BaggingClassifier, n_jobs, defines how many CPU cores to use (that's the number of jobs to run in parallel); when its value is set to -1, then it uses all of the available CPU cores.

An ensemble of only decision trees is called **random forest**. And so what we've implemented previously is a random forest. We can directly implement random forest in scikit using the `RandomForestClassifier` class. The advantage of using the class is that it introduces extra randomness while building the tree. While splitting, it searches for the best feature to split among a random subset of features.

Improving your model – tips and tricks

In this chapter, we've learned a large number of ML algorithms, each with its own pros and cons. In this section, we'll look into some common problems and ways to resolve them.

Feature scaling to resolve uneven data scale

The data that's collected normally doesn't have the same scale; for example, one feature may be varying in the range 10–100 and another one may be only distributed in range 2–5. This uneven data scale can have an adverse effect on learning. To resolve this, we use the method of feature scaling (normalization). The choice of normalization has been found to drastically affect the performance of certain algorithms. Two common normalization methods (also called standardization in some books) are as follows:

- **Z-score normalization**: In z-score normalization, each individual feature is scaled so that it has the properties of a standard normal distribution, that is, a mean of *0* and variance of *1*. If μ is the mean and σ the variance, we can compute Z-score normalization by making the following linear transformation on each feature as follows:

$$x_{new} = \frac{x_{old} - \mu}{\sigma}$$

- **Min-max normalization**: The min-max normalization rescales the input features so that they lie in the range between *0* and *1*. It results in reducing the standard deviation in the data and hence suppresses the effect of outliers. To achieve min-max normalization, we find the maximum and minimum value of the feature (x_{max} and x_{min} respectively), and perform the following linear transformation:

$$x_{new} = \frac{x_{old} - x_{min}}{x_{max} - x_{min}}$$

We can use the `scikit` library `StandardScaler` or `MinMaxscaler` methods to normalize the data. In all of the examples in this chapter, we've used `MinMaxScaler`; you can try changing it to `StandardScalar` and observe if the performance changes. In the next chapter, we'll also learn how to perform these normalizations in TensorFlow.

Overfitting

Sometimes the model tries to overfit the training dataset; in doing so, it loses its ability to generalize and hence performs badly on the validation dataset; this in turn will affect its performance on unseen data values. There are two standard ways to take care of overfitting: regularization and cross-validation.

Regularization

Regularization adds a term in the loss function to ensure that the cost increases as the model increases the number of features. Hence, we force the model to stay simpler. If $L(X, Y)$ was the loss function earlier, we replace it with the following:

$$\mathcal{L}_{new} = \mathcal{L}_{old}(X, Y) + \lambda N(W)$$

In the preceding, N can be L_1 norm, L_2 norm, or a combination of the two, and λ is the regularization coefficient. Regularization helps in reducing the model variance, without losing any important properties of the data distribution:

- **Lasso regularization**: In this case, the N is L_1 norm. It uses the modulus of weight as the penalty term N:

$$N(W) = \sum_{j=1}^{p} |W_j|$$

- **Ridge regularization**: In this case, the N is $L2$ norm, given by the following:

$$N(W) = \sum_{j=1}^{p} W_j^2$$

Cross-validation

Using cross-validation can also help in reducing the problem of overfitting. In *k*-fold cross-validation, data is divided into *k*-subsets, called **folds**. Then it trains and evaluates the model *k*-times; each time, it picks one of the folds for validation and the rest for training the model. We can perform the cross-validation when the data is less and training time is small. scikit provides a `cross_val_score` method to implement the k-folds. Let `classifier` be the model we want to cross-validate, then we can use the following code to perform cross-validation on 10 folds:

```
from sklearn.model_selection import cross_val_score
accuracies = cross_val_score(estimator = classifier, X = X_train,\
    y = y_train, cv = 10)
print("Accuracy Mean {} Accuracy Variance \
    {}".format(accuracies.mean(),accuracies.std()))
```

The result of this is an average mean and variance value. A good model should have a high average and low variance.

No Free Lunch theorem

With so many models, one always wonders which one to use. Wolpert, in his famous paper *The Lack of A Priori Distinctions Between Learning*, explored this issue and showed that if we make no prior assumption about the input data, then there's no reason to prefer one model over any other. This is known as the **No Free Lunch theorem**.

This means that there's no model hat can be *a* priori guaranteed to work better. The only way we can ascertain which model is best is by evaluating them all. But, practically, it isn't possible to evaluate all of the models and so, in practice, we make reasonable assumptions about the data and evaluate a few relevant models.

Hyperparameter tuning and grid search

Different models have different hyperparameters; for example, in linear regressor, the learning rate was a hyperparameter; if we're using regularization, then the regularizing parameter λ is a hyperparameter. What should be their value? While there's a rule of thumb for some hyperparameters, most of the time we make either a guess or use grid search to perform a sequential search for the best hyperparameters. In the following, we present the code to perform hyperparameter search in the case of SVM using the `scikit` library; in the next chapter, we'll see how we can use TensorFlow to perform hyperparameter tuning:

```
Grid search for best model and parameters
from sklearn.model_selection import GridSearchCV
#parameters = {'kernel':('linear', 'rbf'), 'C':[1, 10]}
classifier = SVC()
parameters = [{'C': [1, 10], 'kernel': ['linear']},
    {'C': [1, 10], 'kernel': ['rbf'],
    'gamma': [0.1, 0.2, 0.3, 0.4, 0.5, 0.6, 0.7, 0.8, 0.9]}]
    grid_search = GridSearchCV(estimator = classifier,
    param_grid = parameters,
    scoring = 'accuracy',
    cv = 10,)
grid_search.fit(X_train, y_train)
best_accuracy = grid_search.best_score_
best_parameters = grid_search.best_params_
#here is the best accuracy
best_accuracy
```

GridSearchCV will provide us with the hyperparameters that produce the best results for the SVM classifier.

Summary

The goal of this chapter was to provide you with intuitive understanding of different standard ML algorithms so that you can make an informed choice. We covered the popular ML algorithms used for classification and regression. We also learnt how supervised and unsupervised learning are different from each other. Linear regression, logistic regression, SVM, Naive Bayes, and decision trees were introduced along with the fundamental principles involved in each. We used the regression methods to predict electrical power production of a thermal station and classification methods to classify wine as good or bad. Lastly, we covered the common problems with different ML algorithms and some tips and tricks to solve them.

In the next chapter, we'll study different deep learning models and learn how to use them to analyze our data and make predictions.

4
Deep Learning for IoT

In the last chapter, we learned about different **machine learning** (**ML**) algorithms. The focus of this chapter is neural networks based on multiple layered models, also known as deep learning models. They have become a buzzword in the last few years and an absolute favorite of investors in the field of artificial-intelligence-based startups. Achieving above human level accuracy in the task of object detection and defeating the world's Dan Nine Go master are some of the feats possible by **deep learning** (**DL**). In this chapter and a few subsequent chapters, we will learn about the different DL models and how to use DL on our IoT generated data. In this chapter, we will start with a glimpse into the journey of DL, and learn about four popular models, the **multilayered perceptron** (**MLP**), the **convolutional neural network** (**CNN**), **recurrent neural network** (**RNN**), and autoencoders. Specifically, you will learn about the following:

- The history of DL and the factors responsible for its present success
- Artificial neurons and how they can be connected to solve non-linear problems
- The backpropagation algorithm and using it to train the MLP model
- The different optimizers and activation functions available in TensorFlow
- How the CNN works and the concept behind kernel, padding, and strides
- Using CNN model for classification and recognition
- RNNs and modified RNN and long short-term memory and gated recurrent units
- The architecture and functioning of autoencoders

Deep learning 101

The human mind has always intrigued philosophers, scientists, and engineers alike. The desire to imitate and replicate the intelligence of the human brain by man has been written about over many years; Galatea by Pygmalion of Cyprus in Greek mythology, Golem in Jewish folklore, and Maya Sita in Hindu mythology are just a few examples. Robots with **Artificial Intelligence** (**AI**) are a favorite of (science) fiction writers since time immemorial.

AI, as we know today, was conceived parallel with the idea of computers. The seminal paper, *A Logical Calculus Of The Ideas Immanent In Nervous Activity*, in the year 1943 by McCulloch and Pitts proposed the first neural network model—the threshold devices that could perform logical operations such as AND, OR, AND-NOT. In his pioneering work, *Computing Machinery and Intelligence,* published in the year 1950, Alan Turing proposed a **Turing test**; a test to identify whether a machine has intelligence or not. Rosenblatt, in 1957, laid the base for networks that could learn from experience in his report, *The Perceptron—a perceiving and recognizing automaton*. These ideas were far ahead of their time; while the concepts looked theoretically possible, computational resources at that time severely limited the performance you could get through these models that could do logic and learn.

While these papers seem old and irrelevant, they are very much worth reading and give great insight into the vision these initial thinkers had. Following, are the links to these papers for interested readers:

- *A Logical Calculus Of The Ideas Immanent In Nervous Activity*, McCulloch and Pitts: `https://link.springer.com/article/10.1007%2FBF02478259`
- *Computing Machinery and Intelligence*, Alan Turing: `http://phil415.pbworks.com/f/TuringComputing.pdf`
- *The Perceptron—a perceiving and recognizing automaton*, Rosenblatt: `https://blogs.umass.edu/brain-wars/files/2016/03/rosenblatt-1957.pdf`

Another interesting paper one by Wang and Raj from Carnegie Melon University, *On the Origin of Deep Learning*; the 72-page paper covers in detail the history of DL, starting from the McCulloch Pitts model to the latest attention models: `https://arxiv.org/pdf/1702.07800.pdf`.

Two AI winters and a few successes later (with the breakthrough in 2012, when Alex Krizhvesky, Ilya Sutskever, and Geoffrey Hinton's AlexNet entry in the annual ImageNet challenge achieved an error rate of 16%), today we stand at a place where DL has outperformed most of the existing AI techniques. The following screenshot from Google Trends shows that, roughly around 2014, **Deep Learning** became popular and had been growing since then:

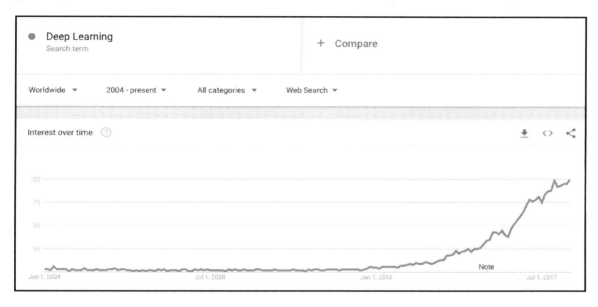

Deep learning in Google Trends from 2004 to April 2018

Let's see the reasons behind this growing trend and analyze whether it's just hype or whether there's more to it.

Deep learning—why now?

Most of the core concepts in the field of DL were already in place by the 80s and 90s, and therefore, the question arises why suddenly we see an increase in the applications of DL to solve different problems from image classification and image inpainting, to self-driving cars and speech generation. The major reason is twofold, outlined as follows:

- **Availability of large high-quality dataset**: The internet resulted in the generation of an enormous amount of datasets in terms of images, video, text, and audio. While most of it's unlabeled, by the effort of many leading researchers (for example, Fei Fei Li creating the ImageNet dataset), we finally have access to large labeled datasets. If DL is a furnace lighting your imagination, data is the fuel burning it. The greater the amount and variety of the data, the better the performance of the model.
- **Availability of parallel computing using graphical processing units**: In DL models, there are mainly two mathematical matrix operations that play a crucial role, namely, matrix multiplication and matrix addition. The possibility of parallelizing these processes for all the neurons in a layer with the help of **graphical processing units** (**GPUs**) made it possible to train the DL models in reasonable time.

Once the interest in DL grew, people came up with further improvements, like better optimizers for the gradient descent (the necessary algorithm used to calculate weight and bias update in DL models), for example, Adam and RMSprop; new regularization techniques such as dropout and batch normalization that help, not only in overfitting, but can also reduce the training time, and last, but not the least, availability of DL libraries such as TensorFlow, Theano, Torch, MxNet, and Keras, which made it easier to define and train complex architectures.

According to Andrew Ng, founder of `deeplearning.ai`, despite plenty of hype and frantic investment, we won't see another AI winter, because improvements in the computing devices *will keep the performance advances and breakthroughs coming for the foreseeable future*, Andrew Ng said this at EmTech Digital in 2016, and true to his prediction, we have seen advancements in the processing hardware with Google's **Tensor Processing Unit** (**TPUs**), Intel Movidius, and NVIDIA's latest GPUs. Moreover, there are cloud computing GPUs that are available today at as low as 0.40 cents per hour, making it affordable for all.

You can read the complete article *AI Winter Isn't Coming*, published in MIT Technology Review: `https://www.technologyreview.com/s/603062/ai-winter-isnt-coming/`. Here Andrew Ng answers different queries regarding the future of AI.

For DL, GPU processing power is a must; there are a large number of companies offering cloud computing services for the same. But in case you are starting in the field, you can use one of the following:

- **Google Colaboratory**: It provides a browser-based, GPU enabled Jupyter Notebook—like interface. It gives free access to the GPU computing power for 12 continuous hours.
- **Kaggle**: Kaggle too provides a Jupyter Notebook style interface with GPU computing power for roughly six continuous hours free of cost.

Artificial neuron

The fundamental component of all DL models is an artificial neuron. The artificial neuron is inspired by the working of biological neurons. It consists of some inputs connected via weights (also called **synaptic connections**), the weighted sum of all the inputs goes through a processing function (called the **activation function**) and generates a non-linear output.

The following screenshot shows **A biological Neuron** and **An Artificial Neuron**:

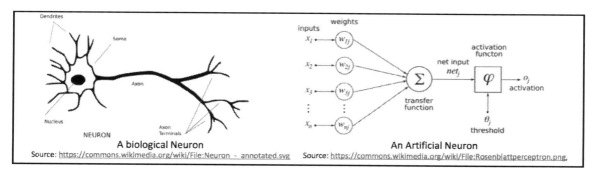

A biological neuron and an artificial neuron

If X_i is the ith input to the artificial neuron (j) connected via the synaptic connection w_{ij}, then, the net input to the neuron, commonly called the **activity of the neuron**, can be defined as the weighted sum of all its contains, and is given by the following:

$$h_j = \sum_{i=1}^{N} X_i W_{ij} - \theta_j$$

In the preceding equation, N is the total number of inputs to the jth neuron, and θ_j is the threshold of the jth neuron; the output of the neuron is then given by the following:

$$y_j = g(h_j)$$

In the preceding, g is the activation function. The following point lists different activation functions used in different DL models, along with their mathematical and graphical representations:

- Sigmoid: $g(h_j) = \dfrac{1}{1 + e^{-h_j}}$

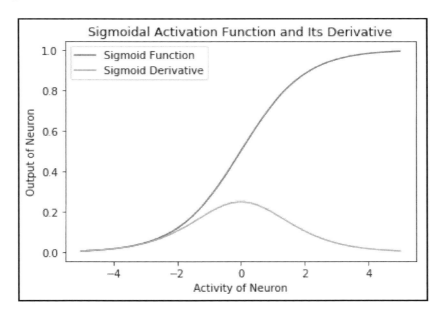

- Hyperbolic Tangent: $g(h_j) = tanh(h_j)$

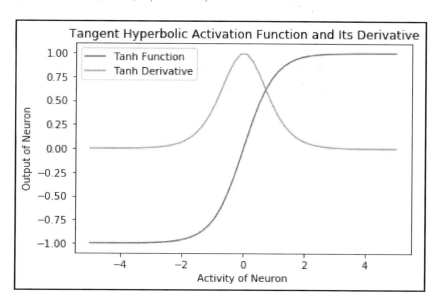

- ReLU: $g(h_j) = max(0, h_j)$

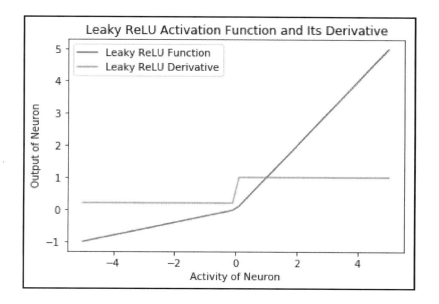

- Softmax: $g(h_j) = \dfrac{e^{h_j}}{\sum_{i=1}^{N} e^{h_i}}$

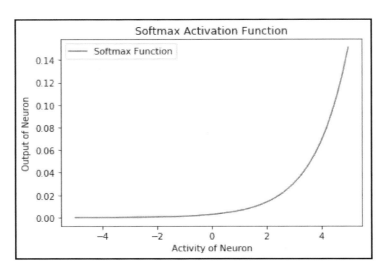

- Leaky ReLU: $g(h_j) = \begin{cases} h_j & for\ h_j \geq 0 \\ 0 & for\ h_j < 0 \end{cases}$

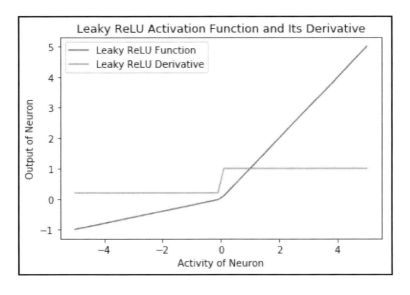

- **ELU:** $g(h_j) = \begin{cases} h_j & for \ h_j \geq 0 \\ a(e^{h_j} - 1) & for \ h_j < 0 \end{cases}$

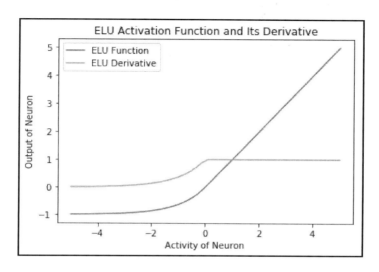

- **Threshold:** $g(h_j) = \begin{cases} 1 & for \ h_j \geq 0 \\ 0 & for \ h_j < 0 \end{cases}$

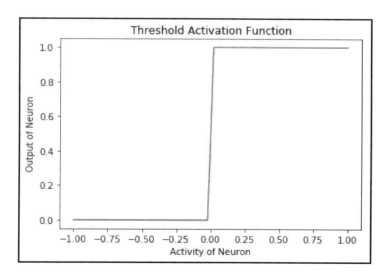

Modelling single neuron in TensorFlow

Can we use this single neuron and make it learn? The answer is yes, the process of learning involves adapting the weights such that a predefined loss function (*L*) reduces. If we update the weights in the direction opposite to the gradient of the loss function with respect to weights, it will ensure that loss function decreases with each update. This algorithm is called the **gradient descent** algorithm, and is at the heart of all DL models. Mathematically, if *L* is the loss function and η the learning rate, then the weight w_{ij} is updated and represented as:

$$w_{ij}^{new} = w_{ij}^{old} - \eta \frac{\partial L}{\partial w_{ij}}$$

If we have to model the single artificial neuron, we need first to decide the following parameters:

- **Learning rate parameter**: Learning rate parameter determines how fast we descent the gradient. Conventionally, it lies between *0* and *1*. If learning rate is too high, the network may either oscillate around the correct solution or completely diverge from the solution. On the other hand, when learning rate is too low, it will take a long time to converge to the solution finally.
- **Activation function**: The activation function decides how the output of the neuron varies with its activity. Since the weight update equation involves a derivative of the loss function, which in turn will depend on the derivative of the activation function, we prefer a continuous-differentiable function as the activation function for the neuron. Initially, sigmoid and hyperbolic tangent were used, but they suffered from slow convergence and vanishing gradients (the gradient becoming zero, and hence, no learning, while the solution hasn't been reached). In recent years, **rectified linear units (ReLU)** and its variants such as leaky ReLU and ELU are preferred since they offer fast convergence and at the same time, help in overcoming the vanishing gradient problem. In ReLU, we sometimes have a problem of **dead neurons**, that is some neurons never fire because their activity is always less than zero, and hence, they never learn. Both leaky ReLU and ELU overcome the problem of dead neurons by ensuring a non-zero neuron output, even when the activity is negative. The lists of the commonly used activation functions, and their mathematical and graphical representations is explained before this section. (You can play around with the `activation_functions.ipynb` code , which uses TensorFlow defined activation functions.)

- **Loss function**: Loss function is the parameter our network tries to minimize, and so choosing the right loss function is crucial for the learning. As you will delve deep into DL, you will find many cleverly defined loss functions. You will see how, by properly defining loss functions, we can make our DL model create new images, visualize dreams, or give a caption to an image, and much more. Conventionally, depending on the type of task regression or classification, people use **mean square error** (**MSE**) or **categorical-cross entropy** loss function. You will learn these loss functions as we progress through the book.

Now that we know the basic elements needed to model an artificial neuron, let's start with the coding. We will presume a regression task, and so we will use MSE loss function. If y_j is the output of our single neuron for the input vector X and $\hat{y}_j$ is the output we desire for output neuron j, then the MSE error is mathematically expressed as (mean of the square of the error $\hat{y}_j - y_j$), shown as follows:

$$\mathcal{L}_{MSE} = \frac{1}{2M} \sum_{j=1}^{M} (\hat{y}_j - y_j)^2$$

In the preceding, M is the total number of training sample (input-output pair).

Note that if you were to implement this artificial neuron without using TensorFlow (to be specific without using any of the DL libraries mentioned earlier), then you will need to calculate the gradient yourself, for example, you will write a function or a code that will first compute the gradient of loss function, and then you will have to write a code to update all of the weights and biases. For a single neuron with the MSE loss function, calculating derivative is still straightforward, but as the complexity of the network increases, calculating the gradient for the specific loss function, implementing it in code, and then finally updating weights and biases can become a very cumbersome act.

TensorFlow makes this whole process easier by using automatic differentiation. TensorFlow specifies all the operations in a TensorFlow graph; this allows it to use the chain rule and go complicated in the graph assigning the gradients.

And so, in TensorFlow we build the execution graph, and define our loss function, then it calculates the gradient automatically, and it supports many different gradients, calculating algorithms (optimizers), which we can conveniently use.

You can learn more about the concept of automatic differentiation through this link: `http:/ /www.columbia.edu/~ahd2125/post/2015/12/5/`.

Now with all this basic information, we build our single neuron in TensorFlow with the following steps:

1. The first step, in every Python code, is always importing the modules one will need in the rest of the program. We will import TensorFlow to build the single artificial neuron. Numpy and pandas are there for any supporting mathematical calculations and for reading the data files. Beside this, we are also importing some useful functions (for normalization of data, splitting it into train, validation, and shuffling the data) from scikit-learn, we have already used these functions in the earlier chapters and know that normalization and shuffling is an important step in any AI pipeline:

```
import tensorflow as tf
import numpy as np
import pandas as pd
import matplotlib.pyplot as plt
from sklearn.utils import shuffle
from sklearn.preprocessing import MinMaxScaler
from sklearn.model_selection import train_test_split
% matplotlib inline
```

As explained earlier, validation helps in knowing if the model has learned or it's overfitting or underfitting

2. In TensorFlow, we first build a model graph and then execute it. This might, when starting, seem complicated, but once you get the hang of it, it's very convenient and allows us to optimize the code for production. So, let's first define our single neuron graph. We define `self.X` and `self.y` as placeholders to pass on the data to the graph, as shown in the following code:

```
class ArtificialNeuron:
    def __init__(self,N=2, act_func=tf.nn.sigmoid, learning_rate=
0.001):
        self.N = N # Number of inputs to the neuron
        self.act_fn = act_func

        # Build the graph for a single neuron
        self.X = tf.placeholder(tf.float32, name='X',
```

```
        shape=[None,N])
            self.y = tf.placeholder(tf.float32, name='Y')
```

3. The weights and biases are defined as variables so that the automatic differentiation automatically updates them. TensorFlow provides a graphical interface to support TensorBoard to see the graph structure, as well as different parameters, and how they change during training. It's beneficial for debugging and understanding how your model is behaving. In the following code, we, therefore, add code lines to create histogram summaries for both weights and biases:

```
self.W = tf.Variable(tf.random_normal([N,1], stddev=2, seed = 0),
name = "weights")
        self.bias = tf.Variable(0.0, dtype=tf.float32, name="bias")
        tf.summary.histogram("Weights",self.W)
        tf.summary.histogram("Bias", self.bias)
```

4. Next, we perform the mathematical operations, the matrix multiplication, between input and weights, add the bias, and calculate the activity of the neuron and its output, denoted by `self.y_hat` shown as follows:

```
activity = tf.matmul(self.X, self.W) + self.bias
self.y_hat = self.act_fn(activity)
```

5. We define the loss function that we want our model to minimize, and use the TensorFlow optimizer to minimize it, and update weights and biases using the gradient descent optimizer, as shown in the following code:

```
error = self.y - self.y_hat

self.loss = tf.reduce_mean(tf.square(error))
self.opt =
tf.train.GradientDescentOptimizer(learning_rate=learning_rate).mini
mize(self.loss)
```

6. We complete the `init` function by defining a TensorFlow Session and initializing all the variables. We also add code to ensure that TensorBoard writes all the summaries at the specified place, shown as follows:

```
tf.summary.scalar("loss",self.loss)
init = tf.global_variables_initializer()

self.sess = tf.Session()
self.sess.run(init)

self.merge = tf.summary.merge_all()
```

```
self.writer =
tf.summary.FileWriter("logs/",graph=tf.get_default_graph())
```

7. We define the `train` function where the graph we previously built is executed, as shown in the following code:

```
def train(self, X, Y, X_val, Y_val, epochs=100):
epoch = 0
X, Y = shuffle(X,Y)
loss = []
loss_val = []
while epoch &amp;lt; epochs:
            # Run the optimizer for the whole training set batch
wise (Stochastic Gradient Descent)
            merge, _, l =
self.sess.run([self.merge,self.opt,self.loss], feed_dict={self.X:
X, self.y: Y})
            l_val = self.sess.run(self.loss, feed_dict={self.X:
X_val, self.y: Y_val})

            loss.append(l)
            loss_val.append(l_val)
            self.writer.add_summary(merge, epoch)

            if epoch % 10 == 0:
                print("Epoch {}/{} training loss: {} Validation
loss {}".\
                    format(epoch,epochs,l, l_val ))


            epoch += 1
        return loss, loss_val
```

8. To make a prediction, we also include a `predict` method, as shown in the following code:

```
def predict(self, X):
        return self.sess.run(self.y_hat, feed_dict={self.X: X})
```

9. Next, like in the previous chapter, we read the data, normalize it using scikit-learn functions, and split it into training and validation set, shown as follows:

```
filename = 'Folds5x2_pp.xlsx'
df = pd.read_excel(filename, sheet_name='Sheet1')
X, Y = df[['AT', 'V','AP','RH']], df['PE']
scaler = MinMaxScaler()
X_new = scaler.fit_transform(X)
target_scaler = MinMaxScaler()
```

```
Y_new = target_scaler.fit_transform(Y.values.reshape(-1,1))
X_train, X_val, Y_train, y_val = \
        train_test_split(X_new, Y_new, test_size=0.4,
random_state=333)
```

10. We use the artificial neuron we created to make the energy output prediction. Training Loss and Validation Loss are plotted as the artificial neuron learns, as shown in the following:

```
_, d = X_train.shape
model = ArtificialNeuron(N=d)

loss, loss_val = model.train(X_train, Y_train, X_val, y_val, 30000)

plt.plot(loss, label="Taining Loss")
plt.plot(loss_val, label="Validation Loss")
plt.legend()
plt.xlabel("Epochs")
plt.ylabel("Mean Square Error")
```

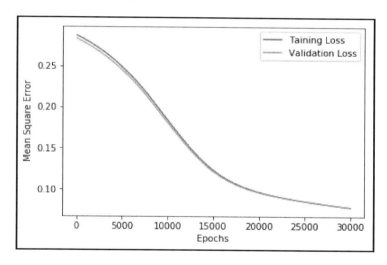

Mean square error for training and validation data as the single artificial neuron learns to predict the energy output

The complete code with data reading, data normalization, training, and so on is given in the single_neuron_tf.ipynb Jupyter Notebook.

Multilayered perceptrons for regression and classification

In the last section, you learned about a single artificial neuron and used it to predict the energy output. If we compare it with the linear regression result of Chapter 3, *Machine Learning for IoT*, we can see that though the single neuron did a good job, it was not as good as linear regression. The single neuron architecture had an MSE value of 0.078 on the validation dataset as compared 0.01 of linear regression. Can we make it better, with maybe more epochs, or different learning rate, or perhaps more single neurons. Unfortunately not, single neurons can solve only linearly separable problems, for example, they can provide a solution only if there exists a straight line separating the classes/decision.

The network with a single layer of neurons is called **simple perceptron**. The perceptron model was given by Rosenblatt in 1958 (http://citeseerx.ist.psu.edu/viewdoc/download?doi=10.1.1.335.3398amp;rep=rep1amp;type=pdf). The paper created lots of ripples in the scientific community and lots of research was initiated in the field. It was first implemented in hardware for the task of image recognition. Although perceptron seemed very promising initially, the book *Perceptrons* by Marvin Minsky and Seymour Papert proved that simple perceptron can solve only linearly separable problems (https://books.google.co.in/books?hl=enamp;lr=amp;id=PLQ5DwAAQBAJamp;oi=fnd amp;pg=PR5amp;dq=
Perceptrons:+An+Introduction+to+Computational+Geometryamp;ots=
zyEDwMrl__amp;sig=DfDDbbj3es52hBJU9znCercxj3M#v=onepageamp;q=
Perceptrons%3A%20An%20Introduction%20to%20Computational%20Geometry
amp;f=false).

So what do we do? We can use multiple layers of single neurons, in other words, use MLP. Just as in real life, we solve a complex problem by breaking it into small problems, each neuron in the first layer of the MLP breaks the problem into small linearly separable. Since the information flows here in one direction from the input layer to the output layer via hidden layers, this network is also called a **feedforward** network. In the following diagram, we see how the **XOR** problem is solved using two neurons in the first layer, and a single neuron in the **Output Layer**. The network breaks the non-linearly separable problem into three linearly separable problems:

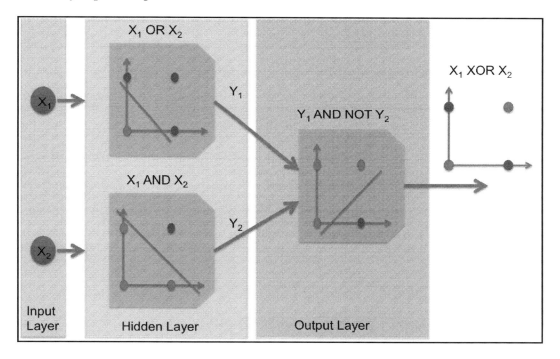

Previous diagram can be explained as XOR solved using MLP with one hidden layer with neurons and one neuron in the output layer. Red points represent zero and blue points represent one. We can see that the hidden neurons separate the problem into two linearly separable problems (AND and OR), the output neuron then implements another linearly separable logic the AND-NOT logic, combining them together we are able to solve the XOR, which is not linearly separable

The hidden neurons transform the problem into a form that output layer can use. The idea of multiple layers of neurons was given by McCulloch and Pitts earlier, but while Rosenblatt gave the learning algorithm for simple perceptrons, he had no way of training multiple layered percetrons. The major difficulty was that, while for the output neurons we know what should be the desired output and so can calculate the error, and hence, the loss function and weight updates using gradient descent, there was no way to know the desired output of hidden neurons. Hence, in the absence of any learning algorithm, MLPs were never explored much. This changed in 1982 when Hinton proposed the backpropagation algorithm (https://www.researchgate.net/profile/Yann_Lecun/publication/2360531_A_Theoretical_Framework_for_Back-Propagation/links/0deec519dfa297eac1000000/A-Theoretical-Framework-for-Back-Propagation.pdf), which can be used to calculate the error, and hence, the weight updates for the hidden neurons. They employed a neat and straightforward mathematical trick of differentiation using the chain rule, and solved the problem of passing the errors at the output layer back to the hidden neurons, and in turn, boosted life back to neural networks. Today, backpropagation algorithm is at the heart of almost all DL models.

The backpropagation algorithm

Let's first gain a little understanding of the technique behind the backpropagation algorithm. If you remember from the previous section, the loss function at the output neuron is as follows:

$$\mathcal{L}_{MSE} = \frac{1}{2M} \sum_{j=1}^{M} (\hat{y}_j - y_j)^2$$

You can see that it's unchanged, and so the weight connecting hidden neuron k to the output neuron j would be given as follows:

$$w_{kj}^{new} - w_{kj}^{old} = \triangle w_{kj} = -\eta \frac{\partial L}{\partial w_{kj}}$$

Applying the chain rule of differentiation, this reduces to the following:

$$\triangle w_{kj} = \eta \frac{1}{2M} \frac{(\partial \hat{y}_j - y_j)^2}{\partial y_j} \frac{\partial y_i}{\partial h_j} \frac{\partial h_j}{\partial w_{kj}} = \eta \frac{1}{M} (\hat{y}_j - y_j) g'(h_j) O_k$$

In the preceding equation, O_k is the output of the hidden neuron k. Now the weight update connecting input neuron i to the hidden neuron k of hidden layer n can be written as the following:

$$w_{ik}^{new} - w_{ik}^{old} = \triangle w_i k = -\eta \frac{\partial L}{\partial w_i k}$$

Again applying the chain rule, it reduces to the following:

$$\triangle w_{kj} = \eta \frac{1}{2M} \sum_i \left\{ \frac{(\partial \hat{y}_j - y_j)^2}{\partial y_j} \frac{\partial y_i}{\partial h_j} \frac{\partial h_j}{\partial O_k} \right\} \frac{\partial O_k}{\partial w_{ik}} = \eta \frac{1}{M} \sum_i \left\{ (\hat{y}_j - y_j) g'(h_j) w_k j \right\} g'(h_k) O_i$$

Here, O_i is the output of the hidden neuron i in the $n\text{-}1^{th}$ hidden layer. Since we are using TensorFlow, we need not bother with calculating these gradients, but still, it's a good idea to know the expressions. From these expressions, you can see why it's important that the activation function is differentiable. The weight updates depend heavily on the derivative of the activation function, as well as the inputs to the neurons. Therefore, a smooth derivative function like that in the case of ReLU and ELU result in faster convergence. If the derivative becomes too large, we have the problem of exploding gradients, and if the derivative becomes almost zero, we have the problem of vanishing gradients. In both cases, the network does not learn optimally.

Universal approximation theorem: in 1989 Hornik et al. and George Cybenko independently proved the universal approximation theorem. The theorem, in its simplest form, states that a large enough feedforward multilayered perceptron, under mild assumptions on activation function, with a single hidden layer, can approximate any Borel measurable function with any degree of accuracy we desire.

In simpler words, it means that the neural network is a universal approximator, and we can approximate any function, listed as follows:

- We can do so using a single hidden layer feedforward network.

- We can do so provided the network is large enough (that is add more hidden neurons if needed).

- Cybenko proved it for sigmoid activation function at the hidden layer, and linear activation function at the output layer. Later, Hornik et al showed that it's actually the property of MLPs and can be proved for other activation functions too

The theorem gives a guarantee that MLP can solve any problem, but does not give any measure on how large the network should be. Also, it does not guarantee learning and convergence.

You can refer to the papers using the following links:

- Hornik et al.: https://www.sciencedirect.com/science/article/pii/0893608089900208
- Cybenko: https://pdfs.semanticscholar.org/05ce/b32839c26c8d2cb38d5529cf7720a68c3fab.pdf

Now we can describe the steps involved in the backpropagation algorithm, listed as follows:

1. Apply the input to the network
2. Propagate the input forward and calculate the output of the network
3. Calculate the loss at the output, and then using the preceding expressions, calculate weight updates for output layer neuron

4. Using the weighted errors at output layers, calculate the weight updates for hidden layer
5. Update all the weights
6. Repeat the steps for other training examples

Energy output prediction using MLPs in TensorFlow

Let's now see how good an MLP is for predicting energy output. This will be a regression problem. We will be using a single hidden layer MLP and will predict the net hourly electrical energy output from a combined cycle power plant. The description of the dataset is provided in `Chapter 1`, *Principles and foundations of IoT and AI*.

Since it's a regression problem, our loss function remains the same as before. The complete code implementing the `MLP` class is given as follows:

```
class MLP:
    def __init__(self,n_input=2,n_hidden=4, n_output=1,
act_func=[tf.nn.elu, tf.sigmoid], learning_rate= 0.001):
        self.n_input = n_input # Number of inputs to the neuron
        self.act_fn = act_func
        seed = 123

        self.X = tf.placeholder(tf.float32, name='X', shape=[None,n_input])
        self.y = tf.placeholder(tf.float32, name='Y')

        # Build the graph for a single neuron
        # Hidden layer
        self.W1 = tf.Variable(tf.random_normal([n_input,n_hidden],\
                stddev=2, seed = seed), name = "weights")
        self.b1 = tf.Variable(tf.random_normal([1, n_hidden], seed =
seed),\
                    name="bias")
        tf.summary.histogram("Weights_Layer_1",self.W1)
        tf.summary.histogram("Bias_Layer_1", self.b1)


        # Output Layer
        self.W2 = tf.Variable(tf.random_normal([n_hidden,n_output],\
                stddev=2, seed = 0), name = "weights")
        self.b2 = tf.Variable(tf.random_normal([1, n_output], seed =
seed),\
                    name="bias")
        tf.summary.histogram("Weights_Layer_2",self.W2)
```

```
        tf.summary.histogram("Bias_Layer_2", self.b2)


        activity = tf.matmul(self.X, self.W1) + self.b1
        h1 = self.act_fn[0](activity)

        activity = tf.matmul(h1, self.W2) + self.b2
        self.y_hat = self.act_fn[1](activity)


        error = self.y - self.y_hat

        self.loss = tf.reduce_mean(tf.square(error))\
                + 0.6*tf.nn.l2_loss(self.W1)
        self.opt = tf.train.GradientDescentOptimizer(learning_rate\
                =learning_rate).minimize(self.loss)


        tf.summary.scalar("loss",self.loss)
        init = tf.global_variables_initializer()

        self.sess = tf.Session()
        self.sess.run(init)

        self.merge = tf.summary.merge_all()
        self.writer = tf.summary.FileWriter("logs/",\
                graph=tf.get_default_graph())


    def train(self, X, Y, X_val, Y_val, epochs=100):
        epoch = 0
        X, Y = shuffle(X,Y)
        loss = []
        loss_val = []
        while epoch &lt; epochs:
            # Run the optimizer for the training set
            merge, _, l = self.sess.run([self.merge,self.opt,self.loss],\
                    feed_dict={self.X: X, self.y: Y})
            l_val = self.sess.run(self.loss, feed_dict=\
                    {self.X: X_val, self.y: Y_val})

            loss.append(l)
            loss_val.append(l_val)
            self.writer.add_summary(merge, epoch)

            if epoch % 10 == 0:
                print("Epoch {}/{} training loss: {} Validation loss {}".\
                    format(epoch,epochs,l, l_val ))
```

```
        epoch += 1
    return loss, loss_val

def predict(self, X):
    return self.sess.run(self.y_hat, feed_dict={self.X: X})
```

Before using it, let's see the differences between previous code and the code we made earlier for the single artificial neuron. Here the dimensions of weights of hidden layer is `#inputUnits x #hiddenUnits`; the bias of the hidden layer will be equal to the number of hidden units (`#hiddenUnits`). The output layer weights have the dimensions `#hiddenUnits x #outputUnits`; the bias of output layer is of the dimension of the number of units in the output layer (`#outputUnits`).

 In defining the bias, we have used only the column dimensions, not row. This is because TensorFlow like `numpy` broadcasts the matrices according to the operation to be performed. And by not fixing the row dimensions of bias, we are able to maintain the flexibility of the number of input training samples (batch-size) we present to the network.

Following screenshot shows matrix multiplication and addition dimensions while calculating activity:

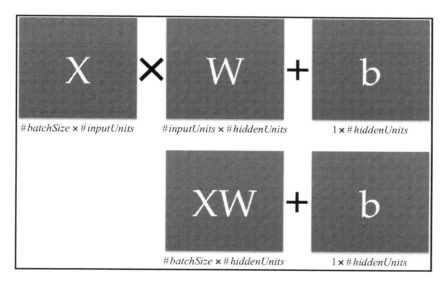

The matrix multiplication and addition dimensions while calculating activity

The second difference that you should note is in the definition of loss, we have added here the 12 regularization term to reduce overfitting as discussed in `Chapter 3`, *Machine Learning for IoT*, shown as follows:

```
self.loss = tf.reduce_mean(tf.square(error)) + 0.6*tf.nn.l2_loss(self.W1)
```

After reading the data from the `csv` file and separating it into training and validation like before, we define the `MLP` class object with 4 neurons in the input layer, 15 neurons in the hidden layer, and 1 neuron in the output layer:

```
_, d = X_train.shape
_, n = Y_train.shape
model = MLP(n_input=d, n_hidden=15, n_output=n)
```

In the following code we train the model on training dataset for 6000 epochs:

```
loss, loss_val = model.train(X_train, Y_train, X_val, y_val, 6000)
```

This trained network gives us an MSE of 0.016 and an R^2 value of 0.67. Both are better than what we obtained from a single neuron, and comparable to the ML methods we studied in `Chapter 3`, *Machine Learning for IoT*. The complete code can be accessed in the file named `MLP_regresssion.ipynb`.

You can play around with hyperparameters namely: the number of hidden neurons, the activation functions, the learning rate, the optimizer, and the regularization coefficient, and can obtain even better results.

Wine quality classification using MLPs in TensorFlow

MLP can be used to do classification tasks as well. We can reuse the MLP class from the previous section with minor modifications to perform the task of classification.

We will need to make the following two major changes:

- The target in the case of classification will be one-hot encoded
- The loss function will now be categorical cross-entropy loss:
  ```
  tf.reduce_mean(tf.nn.softmax_cross_entropy_with_logits(logits=s
  elf.y_hat, labels=self.y))
  ```

So let's now see the complete code, which is also available at GitHub in the file `MLP_classification`. We will be classifying the red wine quality, to make it convenient, we use only two wine classes:

1. We import the necessary modules namely: TensorFlow, Numpy, Matplotlib, and certain functions from scikit-learn, as shown in the following code:

   ```
   import tensorflow as tf
   import numpy as np
   import pandas as pd
   import matplotlib.pyplot as plt
   from sklearn.utils import shuffle
   from sklearn.preprocessing import MinMaxScaler
   from sklearn.model_selection import train_test_split
   % matplotlib inline
   ```

2. We defined our `MLP` class, it's very similar to the `MLP` class you saw earlier, the only difference is in the definition of the loss function:

   ```
   class MLP:
       def __init__(self,n_input=2,n_hidden=4, n_output=1,
   act_func=[tf.nn.relu, tf.nn.sigmoid], learning_rate= 0.001):
           self.n_input = n_input # Number of inputs to the neuron
           self.act_fn = act_func
           seed = 456

           self.X = tf.placeholder(tf.float32, name='X',
   shape=[None,n_input])
           self.y = tf.placeholder(tf.float32, name='Y')

           # Build the graph for a single neuron
           # Hidden layer
           self.W1 = tf.Variable(tf.random_normal([n_input,n_hidden],\
               stddev=2, seed = seed), name = "weights")
           self.b1 = tf.Variable(tf.random_normal([1, n_hidden],\
               seed = seed), name="bias")
           tf.summary.histogram("Weights_Layer_1",self.W1)
           tf.summary.histogram("Bias_Layer_1", self.b1)
   ```

```
            # Output Layer
            self.W2 =
tf.Variable(tf.random_normal([n_hidden,n_output],\
                stddev=2, seed = seed), name = "weights")
            self.b2 = tf.Variable(tf.random_normal([1, n_output],\
                seed = seed), name="bias")
            tf.summary.histogram("Weights_Layer_2",self.W2)
            tf.summary.histogram("Bias_Layer_2", self.b2)


            activity1 = tf.matmul(self.X, self.W1) + self.b1
            h1 = self.act_fn[0](activity1)

            activity2 = tf.matmul(h1, self.W2) + self.b2
            self.y_hat = self.act_fn[1](activity2)


            self.loss =
tf.reduce_mean(tf.nn.softmax_cross_entropy_with_logits(\
                logits=self.y_hat, labels=self.y))
            self.opt = tf.train.AdamOptimizer(learning_rate=\
                learning_rate).minimize(self.loss)


            tf.summary.scalar("loss",self.loss)
            init = tf.global_variables_initializer()

            self.sess = tf.Session()
            self.sess.run(init)

            self.merge = tf.summary.merge_all()
            self.writer = tf.summary.FileWriter("logs/",\
                graph=tf.get_default_graph())



    def train(self, X, Y, X_val, Y_val, epochs=100):
        epoch = 0
        X, Y = shuffle(X,Y)
        loss = []
        loss_val = []
        while epoch &amp;lt; epochs:
            # Run the optimizer for the training set
            merge, _, l =
self.sess.run([self.merge,self.opt,self.loss],\
                feed_dict={self.X: X, self.y: Y})
            l_val = self.sess.run(self.loss, feed_dict={self.X:
X_val, self.y: Y_val})
```

```
                    loss.append(l)
                    loss_val.append(l_val)
                    self.writer.add_summary(merge, epoch)

                    if epoch % 10 == 0:
                        print("Epoch {}/{} training loss: {} Validation
        loss {}".\
                            format(epoch,epochs,l, l_val ))


                    epoch += 1
            return loss, loss_val

        def predict(self, X):
            return self.sess.run(self.y_hat, feed_dict={self.X: X})
```

3. Next, we read the data, normalize it, and preprocess it so that wine quality is one-hot encoded with two labels. We also divide the data into training and validation set, shown as follows:

```
filename = 'winequality-red.csv'
#Download the file from
https://archive.ics.uci.edu/ml/datasets/wine+quality
df = pd.read_csv(filename, sep=';')
columns = df.columns.values
# Preprocessing and Categorizing wine into two categories
X, Y = df[columns[0:-1]], df[columns[-1]]
scaler = MinMaxScaler()
X_new = scaler.fit_transform(X)
#Y.loc[(Y&amp;lt;3.5)]=3
Y.loc[(Y&amp;lt;5.5) ] = 2
Y.loc[(Y&amp;gt;=5.5)] = 1
Y_new = pd.get_dummies(Y) # One hot encode
X_train, X_val, Y_train, y_val = \
 train_test_split(X_new, Y_new, test_size=0.2, random_state=333)
```

4. We define an MLP object and train it, demonstrated in the following code:

```
_, d = X_train.shape
_, n = Y_train.shape
model = MLP(n_input=d, n_hidden=5, n_output=n)
loss, loss_val = model.train(X_train, Y_train, X_val, y_val, 10000)
```

5. Following, you can see the results of training, the cross-entropy loss decreases as the network learns:

```
plt.plot(loss, label="Taining Loss")
plt.plot(loss_val, label="Validation Loss")
```

```
plt.legend()
plt.xlabel("Epochs")
plt.ylabel("Cross Entropy Loss")
```

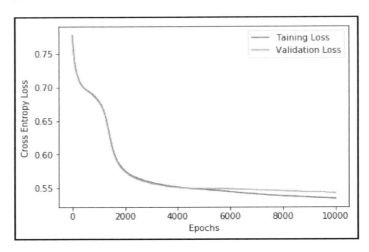

6. The trained network, when tested on the validation dataset, provides an accuracy of 77.8%. The `confusion_matrix` on the validation set is shown as follows:

```
from sklearn.metrics import confusion_matrix, accuracy_score
import seaborn as sns
cm = confusion_matrix(np.argmax(np.array(y_val),1),
np.argmax(Y_pred,1))
sns.heatmap(cm,annot=True,fmt='2.0f')
```

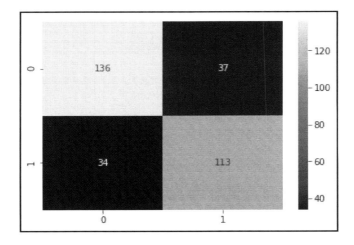

These results are again comparable to the results we obtained using ML algorithms. We can make it even better by playing around with the hyperparameters.

Convolutional neural networks

MLPs were fun, but as you must have observed while playing with MLP codes in the previous section, the time to learn increases as the complexity of input space increases; moreover, the performance of MLPs is just second to the ML algorithms. Whatever you can do with MLP, there's a high probability you can do it slightly better using ML algorithms you learned in Chapter 3, *Machine Learning for IoT*. Precisely for this reason, despite backpropagation algorithm being available in the 1980s, we observed the second AI winter roughly from 1987 to 1993.

This all changed, and the neural networks stopped playing the second fiddle to ML algorithms, in the 2010s with the development of deep neural networks. Today DL has achieved human level or more than human level performance in varied tasks of computer vision like recognizing traffic signals (http://people.idsia.ch/~juergen/cvpr2012.pdf), faces (https://www.cv-foundation.org/openaccess/content_cvpr_2014/papers/Taigman_DeepFace_Closing_the_2014_CVPR_paper.pdf), handwritten digits, (https://cs.nyu.edu/~wanli/dropc/dropc.pdf) and so on. The list is continuously growing.

CNN has been a major part of this success story. In this section, you will learn about CNN, the maths behind CNN, and some of the popular CNN architectures.

Different layers of CNN

CNN consists of three main types of neuron layers: convolution layers, pooling layers, and fully connected layers. Fully connected layers are nothing but layers of MLP, they are always the last few layers of the CNN, and perform the final task of classification or regression. Let's see how the convolution layer and max pooling layers work.

The convolution layer

This is the core building block of CNNs. It performs the mathematical operation similar to convolution (cross-correlation to be precise) on its input, normally a 3D image. It's defined by kernels (filters). The basic idea is that these filters stride through the entire image and extract specific features from the image.

Before going into further details, let's first see the convolution operation on a two-dimensional matrix for simplicity. The following diagram shows the operation when one pixel placed at position [2, 2] of a 5×5 **2D image** matrix is convolved with a 3×3 filter:

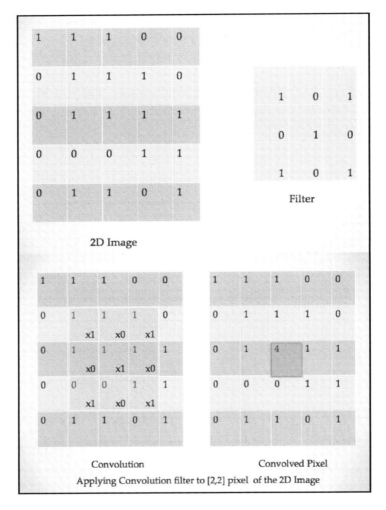

Applying Convolution filter to [2,2] pixel of the 2D Image

Convolution operation at a single pixel

The convolution operation involves placing the filter with the pixel at the center, then performing element-wise multiplication between the filter elements and the pixel, along with its neighbors. Finally, summing the product. Since convolution operation is performed on a pixel, the filters are conventionally odd-sized like 5×5, 3×3, or 7×7, and so on. The size of the filters specify how much neighboring area it's covering.

The important parameters when designing the convolution layers are as follows:

- The size of the filters (k×k).
- The number of filters in the layer, also called **channels**. The input color image is present in the three RGB channels. The number of channels are conventionally increased in the higher layers. Resulting in deeper information in higher layers.
- The number of pixels the filter strides (s) through the image. Conventionally, the stride is of one pixel so that the filter covers the entire image starting from top-left to bottom-right.
- The padding to be used while convolving. Traditionally, there are two options, either valid or same. In **valid** padding, there's no padding at all, and thus the size of the convolved image is less than that of the original. In **same**, the padding of zeros is done around the boundary pixels, so that the size of the convolved image is the same as that of the original image. The following screenshot shows the complete **Convolved Image**. The green square of size 3×3 is the result when padding is valid, the complete 5×5 matrix on the right will be the result when padding is the same:

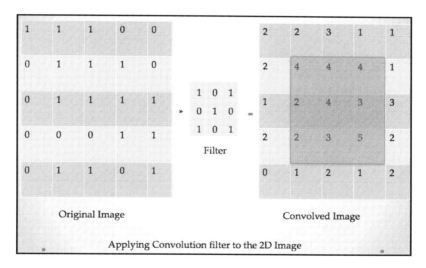

Applying Convolution filter to the 2D Image

Convolution operation applied on a 5×5 image

The green square on the right will be the result of **valid** padding. For the **same** padding, we will get the complete 5×5 matrix shown on the right-hand side.

Pooling layer

The convolution layer is followed conventionally by a pooling layer. The purpose of the pooling layer is to progressively reduce the size of the representation, and thus, reduce the number of parameters and computations in the network. Thus, it down samples the information as it propagates through the network in feed forward manner.

Here again, we have a filter, traditionally people prefer a filter of size 2×2, and it moves with a stride of two pixels in both directions. The pooling process replaces the four elements under the 2×2 filter by either the maximum value of the four (**Max Pooling**) or the average value of the four (**Average Pooling**). In the following diagram, you can see the result of pooling operation on a **2D single channel slice of an image**:

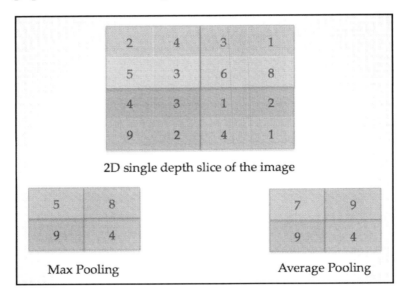

Max pooling and average pooling operation on a two-dimensional single depth slice of an image

Multiple convolution pooling layers are stacked together to form a deep CNN. As the image propagates through the CNN, each convolutional layer extracts specific features. The lower layers extract the gross feature like shape, curves, lines, and so on, while the higher layers extract more abstract features like eyes, lips, and so on. The image, as it propagates through the network, reduces in dimensions, but increases in depth. The output from the last convolutional layer is flattened and passed to fully connected layers, as shown in the following diagram:

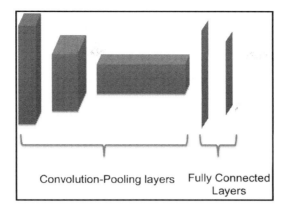

Convolution-Pooling layers   Fully Connected
                                    Layers

The basic architecture of a CNN network

The values of filter matrix are also called **weights** and they are shared by the whole image. This sharing reduces the number of training parameters. The weights are learned by the network using the backpropagation algorithm. Since we will be using the auto-differentiation feature of TensorFlow, we are not calculating the exact expression for weight update for convolution layers.

Some popular CNN model

The following is a list of some of the popular CNN models available:

- **LeNet**: LeNet was the first successful CNN applied to recognize handwritten digits. It was developed by Yann LeCun in the 1990s. You can know more about LeNet architecture and its related publications at Yann LeCun's home page (http://yann.lecun.com/exdb/lenet/).

- **VGGNet**: This was the runner-up in ILSVRC 2014, developed by Karen Simonyan and Andrew Zisserman. Its first version contains 16 Convolution+FC layers and was called **VGG16**, later they brought VGG19 with 19 layers. The details about its performance and publications can be accessed from the University of Oxford site (http://www.robots.ox.ac.uk/~vgg/research/very_deep/).

- **ResNet**: Developed by Kaiming He et al., ResNet was the winner of ILSVRC 2015. It made use of new feature called **residual learning** and **batch normalization**. It's a very deep network with more than 100 layers. It's known that adding more layers will improve the performance, but adding layers also introduced the problem of vanishing gradients. ResNet solved this issue by making use of identity shortcut connection, where the signal skips one or more layers. You can read the original paper for more information (https://arxiv.org/abs/1512.03385).

- **GoogleNet**: This was the winning architecture of ILSVRC 2014. It has 22 layers, and introduced the idea of inception layer. The basic idea is to cover a bigger area, while at the same time, keep a fine resolution for small information on the images. As a result instead of one size filters, at each layer, we have filter ranging from 1×1 (for fine detailing) to 5×5. The result of all the filters are concatenated and passed to next layer, the process is repeated in the next inception layer.

LeNet to recognize handwritten digits

In the chapters ahead, we will be using some of these popular CNNs and their variants to solve image and video processing tasks. Right now, let's use the LeNet architecture proposed by Yann LeCun to recognize handwritten digits. This architecture was used by the US Postal Service to recognize handwritten ZIP codes on the letters they received (http://yann.lecun.com/exdb/publis/pdf/jackel-95.pdf).

LeNet consists of five layers with two convolutional max pool layers and three fully connected layers. The network also uses dropout feature, that is while training, some of the weights are turned off. This forces the other interconnections to compensate for them, and hence helps in overcoming overfitting:

1. We import the necessary modules, shown as follows

```
# Import Modules
import numpy as np
import pandas as pd
import matplotlib.pyplot as plt
%matplotlib inline
```

2. Next, we create the class object `LeNet`, which will have the necessary CNN architecture and modules to train and make the prediction. In the __init__ method, we define all the needed placeholders to hold input images and their output labels. We also define the loss, since this is a classification problem, we use cross-entropy loss, as shown in the following code:

```
# Define your Architecture here
import tensorflow as tf
from tensorflow.contrib.layers import flatten
class my_LeNet:
    def __init__(self, d, n, mu = 0, sigma = 0.1, lr = 0.001):
        self.mu = mu
        self.sigma = sigma
        self.n = n
        # place holder for input image dimension 28 x 28
        self.x = tf.placeholder(tf.float32, (None, d, d, 1))
        self.y = tf.placeholder(tf.int32, (None,n))
        self.keep_prob = tf.placeholder(tf.float32) # probability
to keep units


        self.logits = self.model(self.x)
        # Define the loss function
        cross_entropy =
tf.nn.softmax_cross_entropy_with_logits(labels=self.y,\
                        logits=self.logits)
        self.loss = tf.reduce_mean(cross_entropy)
        optimizer = tf.train.AdamOptimizer(learning_rate = lr)
        self.train = optimizer.minimize(self.loss)
        correct_prediction = tf.equal(tf.argmax(self.logits, 1),
tf.argmax(self.y, 1))
        self.accuracy = tf.reduce_mean(tf.cast(correct_prediction,
tf.float32))
        init = tf.global_variables_initializer()
        self.sess = tf.Session()
        self.sess.run(init)
        self.saver = tf.train.Saver()
```

3. The `model` method is the one where the convolutional network architecture graph is actually build. We use the TensorFlow `tf.nn.conv2d` function to build the convolutional layers. The function takes an argument the filter matrix defined as weights and computes the convolution between the input and the filter matrix. We also use biases to give us a high degree of freedom. After the two convolution layers, we flatten the output and pass it to the fully connected layers, shown as follows:

```
def model(self,x):
    # Build Architecture
    keep_prob = 0.7
    # Layer 1: Convolutional. Filter 5x5 num_filters = 6
Input_depth =1
    conv1_W = tf.Variable(tf.truncated_normal(shape=(5, 5, 1, 6), mean \
                    = self.mu, stddev = self.sigma))
    conv1_b = tf.Variable(tf.zeros(6))
    conv1 = tf.nn.conv2d(x, conv1_W, strides=[1, 1, 1, 1],
padding='VALID') + conv1_b
    conv1 = tf.nn.relu(conv1)

    # Max Pool 1
    self.conv1 = tf.nn.max_pool(conv1, ksize=[1, 2, 2, 1],\
                strides=[1, 2, 2, 1], padding='VALID')


    # Layer 2: Convolutional. Filter 5x5 num_filters = 16
Input_depth =6
    conv2_W = tf.Variable(tf.truncated_normal(shape=(5, 5, 6, 16),
\
                    mean = self.mu, stddev = self.sigma))
    conv2_b = tf.Variable(tf.zeros(16))
    conv2 = tf.nn.conv2d(self.conv1, conv2_W, strides=[1, 1, 1,
1],\
                    padding='VALID') + conv2_b
    conv2 = tf.nn.relu(conv2)

    # Max Pool 2.
    self.conv2 = tf.nn.max_pool(conv2, ksize=[1, 2, 2, 1], \
                strides=[1, 2, 2, 1], padding='VALID')

    # Flatten.
    fc0 = flatten(self.conv2)
    print("x shape:",fc0.get_shape())

    # Layer 3: Fully Connected. Input = fc0.get_shape[-1]. Output =
120.
```

```
fc1_W = tf.Variable(tf.truncated_normal(shape=(256, 120), \
            mean = self.mu, stddev = self.sigma))
fc1_b = tf.Variable(tf.zeros(120))
fc1 = tf.matmul(fc0, fc1_W) + fc1_b
fc1 = tf.nn.relu(fc1)

# Dropout
x = tf.nn.dropout(fc1, keep_prob)

# Layer 4: Fully Connected. Input = 120. Output = 84.
fc2_W = tf.Variable(tf.truncated_normal(shape=(120, 84), \
              mean = self.mu, stddev = self.sigma))
fc2_b = tf.Variable(tf.zeros(84))
fc2 = tf.matmul(x, fc2_W) + fc2_b
fc2 = tf.nn.relu(fc2)

# Dropout
x = tf.nn.dropout(fc2, keep_prob)

# Layer 6: Fully Connected. Input = 120. Output = n_classes.
fc3_W = tf.Variable(tf.truncated_normal(shape=(84, self.n), \
              mean = self.mu, stddev = self.sigma))
fc3_b = tf.Variable(tf.zeros(self.n))
logits = tf.matmul(x, fc3_W) + fc3_b
#logits = tf.nn.softmax(logits)
return logits
```

4. The `fit` method performs the batch-wise training, and `predict` method provides the output for given input, as shown in the following code:

```
def fit(self,X,Y,X_val,Y_val,epochs=10, batch_size=100):
    X_train, y_train = X, Y
    num_examples = len(X_train)
    l = []
    val_l = []
    max_val = 0
    for i in range(epochs):
        total = 0
        for offset in range(0, num_examples, batch_size): # Learn
Batch wise
            end = offset + batch_size
            batch_x, batch_y = X_train[offset:end],
y_train[offset:end]
            _, loss = self.sess.run([self.train,self.loss], \
                        feed_dict={self.x: batch_x, self.y:
batch_y})
            total += loss
            l.append(total/num_examples)
```

```
            accuracy_val = self.sess.run(self.accuracy, \
                            feed_dict={self.x: X_val, self.y:
Y_val})
            accuracy = self.sess.run(self.accuracy,
feed_dict={self.x: X, self.y: Y})
            loss_val = self.sess.run(self.loss,
feed_dict={self.x:X_val,self.y:Y_val})
            val_l.append(loss_val)
            print("EPOCH {}/{} loss is {:.3f} training_accuracy
{:.3f} and \
                    validation accuracy is {:.3f}".\
                    format(i+1,epochs,total/num_examples,
accuracy, accuracy_val))
            # Saving the model with best validation accuracy
            if accuracy_val &gt; max_val:
                save_path = self.saver.save(self.sess,
"/tmp/lenet1.ckpt")
                    print("Model saved in path: %s" % save_path)
                max_val = accuracy_val

    #Restore the best model
    self.saver.restore(self.sess, "/tmp/lenet1.ckpt")
    print("Restored model with highest validation accuracy")
    accuracy_val = self.sess.run(self.accuracy, feed_dict={self.x:
X_val, self.y: Y_val})
    accuracy = self.sess.run(self.accuracy, feed_dict={self.x: X,
self.y: Y})
    return l,val_l, accuracy, accuracy_val

def predict(self, X):
    return self.sess.run(self.logits,feed_dict={self.x:X})
```

5. We use the handwritten digits dataset and download it from Kaggle (https://www.kaggle.com/c/digit-recognizer/data). The dataset is available in .csv format. We load the .csv files and preprocess the data. The following are the sample training diagrams:

```
def load_data():
    # Read the data and create train, validation and test dataset
    data = pd.read_csv('train.csv')
    # This ensures always 80% of data is training and
    # rest Validation unlike using np.random
    train = data.sample(frac=0.8, random_state=255)
    val = data.drop(train.index)
    test = pd.read_csv('test.csv')
    return train, val, test
```

```
def create_data(df):
    labels = df.loc[:]['label']
    y_one_hot = pd.get_dummies(labels).astype(np.uint8)
    y = y_one_hot.values # One Hot encode the labels
    x = df.iloc[:,1:].values
    x = x.astype(np.float)
    # Normalize data
    x = np.multiply(x, 1.0 / 255.0)
    x = x.reshape(-1, 28, 28, 1) # return each images as 96 x 96 x
1
    return x,y

train, val, test = load_data()
X_train, y_train = create_data(train)
X_val, y_val = create_data(val)
X_test = (test.iloc[:,:].values).astype(np.float)
X_test = np.multiply(X_test, 1.0 / 255.0)
X_test = X_test.reshape(-1, 28, 28, 1) # return each images as 96 x
96 x 1

# Plot a subset of training data
x_train_subset = X_train[:12]


# visualize subset of training data
fig = plt.figure(figsize=(20,2))
for i in range(0, len(x_train_subset)):
    ax = fig.add_subplot(1, 12, i+1)
    ax.imshow(x_train_subset[i].reshape(28,28), cmap='gray')
fig.suptitle('Subset of Original Training Images', fontsize=20)
plt.show()
```

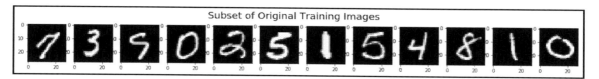

Here we will be training the model:

```
n_train = len(X_train)
# Number of validation examples
n_validation = len(X_val)

# Number of testing examples.
n_test = len(X_test)

# What's the shape of an handwritten digits?
```

```
image_shape = X_train.shape[1:-1]

# How many unique classes/labels there are in the dataset.
n_classes = y_train.shape[-1]
print("Number of training examples =", n_train)
print("Number of Validation examples =", n_validation)
print("Number of testing examples =", n_test)
print("Image data shape =", image_shape)
print("Number of classes =", n_classes)

# The result
## &amp;gt;&amp;gt;&amp;gt; Number of training examples = 33600
## &amp;gt;&amp;gt;&amp;gt; Number of Validation examples = 8400
## &amp;gt;&amp;gt;&amp;gt; Number of testing examples = 28000
## &amp;gt;&amp;gt;&amp;gt; Image data shape = (28, 28)
## &amp;gt;&amp;gt;&amp;gt; Number of classes = 10

# Define the data values
d = image_shape[0]
n = n_classes
from sklearn.utils import shuffle
X_train, y_train = shuffle(X_train,y_train)
```

6. We create the `LeNet` object and train it on the training data. The obtain is 99.658% on the training dataset and 98.607% on the validation dataset:

```
# Create the Model
my_model = my_LeNet(d, n)

### Train model  here.
loss, val_loss, train_acc, val_acc = my_model.fit(X_train, y_train,
\
    X_val, y_val, epochs=50)
```

Impressive! You can predict the output for the test dataset and make a submission at Kaggle.

Recurrent neural networks

The models that we have studied till now respond only present input. You present them an input, and based on what they have learned, they give you a corresponding output. But this is not the way we humans work. When you are reading a sentence, you do not interpret each word individually, you take the previous words into account to conclude its semantic meaning.

RNNs are able to address this issue. They use the feedback loops, which preserves the information. The feedback loop allows the information to be passed from the previous steps to the present. The following diagram shows the basic architecture of an RNN and how the feedback allows the passing of information from one step of the network to the next (**Unroll**):

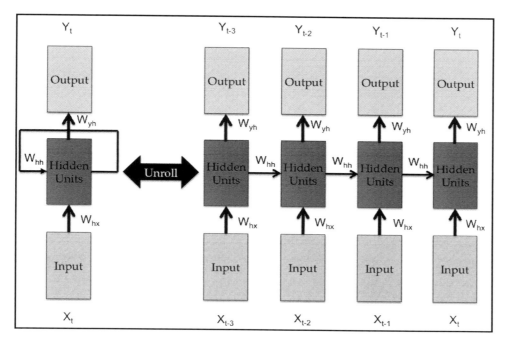

Recurrent neural network

In the preceding diagram, X represents the inputs. It's connected to the neurons in the hidden layer by weights W_{hx}, the output of the hidden layer, h, is fed back to the hidden layer via weights W_{hh}, and also contributes to the output, O, via weights W_{yh}. We can write the mathematical relationships as the following:

$$h_t = g(W_{hx} X_t + W_{hh} h_{t-1} + b_h)$$

$$O_t = g(W_{yh} h_t)$$

Where g is the activation function, b_h and b_y are the biases of hidden and output neurons, respectively. In the a preceding relation all X, h, and O are vectors; W_{hx}, W_{hh}, and W_{yh} are matrices. The dimensions of the input X and the output O depends upon the dataset you are working on, and the number of units in hidden layer h are decided by you; you will find many papers where researchers have used 128 number of hidden units. The preceding architecture shows only one hidden layer, but we can have as many hidden layers as we want. RNNs have been applied in the field of natural language processing, they have also been applied to analyze the time series data, like stock prices.

RNNs learn via an algorithm called as **backpropagation through time (BPTT)**, it's a modification of backpropagation algorithm that takes into account the time series nature of data. Here, the loss is defined as the sum of all the loss functions at times $t=1$ to $t=T$ (number of time steps to be unrolled), for example:

$$\mathcal{L} = \sum_{t=1}^{T} \mathcal{L}^{(t)}$$

Where $L^{(t)}$ is the loss at time t, we apply the chain rule of differentiation like before, and derive the weight updates for weights W_{hx}, W_{hh}, and W_{yh}.

We are not deriving the expression for weight updates in this book, because we will not be coding it. TensorFlow provides an implementation for RNN and BPTT. But for the readers interested in going into the mathematical details, following are some references:

- *On the difficulty of training Recurrent Neural Networks*, Razvan Pascanu, Tomas Mikolov, and Yoshua Bengio (https://arxiv.org/pdf/1211.5063.pdf)
- *Learning Long-Term Dependencies with Gradient Descent is Difficult*, Yoshua Bengio, Patrice Simard, and Paolo Frasconi (www.iro.umontreal.ca/~lisa/pointeurs/ieeetrnn94.pdf)
- Also, it will be incomplete not to mention Colah's blog (http://colah.github.io/posts/2015-08-Understanding-LSTMs/) and Andrej Karpathy's blog (http://karpathy.github.io/2015/05/21/rnn-effectiveness/) for an excellent explanation of RNNs and some of their cool applications

We present the RNN with one input each timestep and predict the corresponding output. BPTT works by unrolling all input timesteps. The errors are calculated and accumulated for each timestep, later the network is rolled back to update the weights. One of the disadvantages of BPTT is that when the number of time steps increases, the computation also increases. This makes the overall model computationally expensive. Moreover, due to multiple gradient multiplications, the network is prone to the vanishing gradient problem.

To solve this issue, a modified version of BPTT, the truncated-BPTT is often used. In the truncated-BPTT, the data is processed one timestep at a time and the BPTT weight update is performed periodically for a fixed number of time steps.

We can enumerate the steps of the truncated-BPTT algorithm as follows:

1. Present the sequence of K_1 time steps of input and output pairs to the network
2. Calculate and accumulate the errors across K_2 time steps by unrolling the network
3. Update the weights by rolling up the network

The performance of the algorithm depends on two hyperparameters K_1 and K_2. The number of forwarding pass timesteps between updates is represented by K_1, it affects how fast or slow the training will be training and the frequency of the weight updates. K_2 on the other hand, represents the number of timesteps that apply to BPTT, it should be large enough to capture the temporal structure of the input data.

Long short-term memory

Hochreiter and Schmidhuber in 1997 proposed a modified RNN model, called the **long short-term memory** (**LSTM**) as a solution to overcome the vanishing gradient problem. The hidden layer in the RNNs is replaced by an LSTM cell.

The LSTM cell consists of three gates: forget gate, input gate, and the output gate. These gates control the amount of long-term memory and the short-term memory generated and retained by the cell. The gates all have the `sigmoid` function, which squashes the input between *0* and *1*. Following, we see how the outputs from various gates are calculated, in case the expressions seem daunting to you, do not worry, we will be using the TensorFlow `tf.contrib.rnn.BasicLSTMCell` and `tf.contrib.rnn.static_rnn` to implement the LSTM cell, shown in the following diagram:

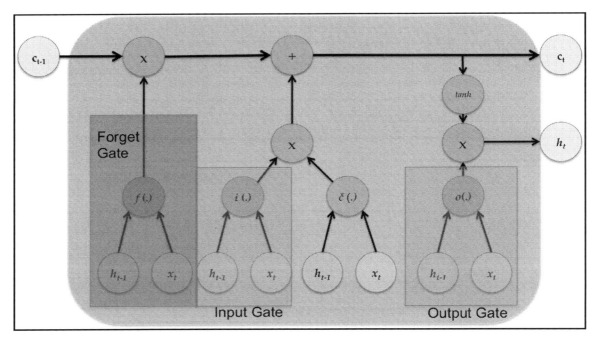

The basic LSTM cell, *x* is the input to the cell, *h* the short-term memory and *c* the long-term memory. The subscript refers to the time

At each time step, t, the LSTM cell takes three inputs: the input x_t, the short-term memory h_{t-1}, and the long-term memory c_{t-1}, and outputs the long-term memory c_t at and short-term memory h_t. The subscript to x, h, and c refer to the timestep.

The **Forget Gate** $f(.)$ controls the amount of short-term memory, h, to be remembered for further flow in the present time step. Mathematically we can represent Forget Gate $f(.)$ as:

$$f(.) = \sigma(W_{fx}x_t + W_{fh}h_{t-1} + b_f)$$

Where σ represents the sigmoid activation function, W_{fx} and W_{fh} are the weights controlling the influence of input x_t, short-term memory h_{t-1}, and b_f the bias of the forget gate.

The **Input Gate** $i(.)$ controls the amount of input and working memory influencing the output of the cell. We can express it as follows:

$$i(.) = \sigma(W_{ix}x_t + W_{ih}h_{t-1} + b_i)$$

The **Output Gate** $o(.)$ controls the amount of information that's used for updating the short-term memory, and given by the following:

$$o(.) = \sigma(W_{ox}x_t + W_{oh}h_{t-1} + b_o)$$

Beside these three gates, the LSTM cell also computes the candidate hidden state $\tilde{c}$, which along with the input and forget gate, is used to compute the amount of long term memory c_i:

$$\tilde{c}(.) = tanh(W_{\tilde{c}x}x_t + W_{\tilde{c}h}h_{t-1} + b_{\tilde{c}})$$

$$c_t = c_{t-1} \circ f(.) + i(.) \circ \tilde{c}(.)$$

The circle represents the element wise multiplication. The new value of the short-term memory is then computed as the following:

$$h_t = tanh(c_t) \circ o(.)$$

Let's now see how we can implement LSTM in TensorFlow in the following steps:

1. We are using the following modules:

```
import tensorflow as tf
from tensorflow.contrib import rnn
import numpy as np
```

2. We define a class LSTM where we construct the graph and define the LSTM layer with the help of TensorFlow `contrib`. To take care of memory, we first clear the default graph stack and reset the global default graph using `tf.reset_default_graph()`. The input goes directly to the LSTM layer with `num_units` number of hidden units. It's followed by a fully connected output layer with the `out_weights` weights and `out_bias` bias. Create the placeholders for input `self.x` and `self.y` label. The input is reshaped and fed to the LSTM cell. To create the LSTM layer, we first define the LSTM cell with `num_units` hidden units and forget bias set to `1.0`. This adds the biases to the forget gate in order to reduce the scale of forgetting in the beginning of the training. Reshape the output from the LSTM layer and feed it to the fully connected layer, shown as follows:

```
class LSTM:
    def __init__(self, num_units, n_classes, n_input,\
            time_steps, learning_rate=0.001,):
        tf.reset_default_graph()
        self.steps = time_steps
        self.n = n_input
        # weights and biases of appropriate shape
        out_weights = tf.Variable(tf.random_normal([num_units,
n_classes]))
        out_bias = tf.Variable(tf.random_normal([n_classes]))
        # defining placeholders
        # input placeholder
        self.x = tf.placeholder("float", [None, self.steps,
self.n])
        # label placeholder
        self.y = tf.placeholder("float", [None, n_classes])
        # processing the input tensor from
[batch_size,steps,self.n] to
        # "steps" number of [batch_size,self.n] tensors
        input = tf.unstack(self.x, self.steps, 1)

        # defining the network
        lstm_layer = rnn.BasicLSTMCell(num_units, forget_bias=1)
        outputs, _ = rnn.static_rnn(lstm_layer, input,
dtype="float32")
        # converting last output of dimension
[batch_size,num_units] to
        # [batch_size,n_classes] by out_weight multiplication
        self.prediction = tf.matmul(outputs[-1], out_weights) +
out_bias

        # loss_function
        self.loss =
```

```
tf.reduce_mean(tf.squared_difference(self.prediction, self.y))
        # optimization
        self.opt =
tf.train.AdamOptimizer(learning_rate=learning_rate).minimize(self.l
oss)

        # model evaluation
        correct_prediction = tf.equal(tf.argmax(self.prediction,
1), tf.argmax(self.y, 1))
        self._accuracy = tf.reduce_mean(tf.cast(correct_prediction,
tf.float32))

        init = tf.global_variables_initializer()
        gpu_options = tf.GPUOptions(allow_growth=True)

        self.sess =
tf.Session(config=tf.ConfigProto(gpu_options=gpu_options))
        self.sess.run(init)
```

3. We create the methods to train and predict, as shown in the following code:

```
def train(self, X, Y, epochs=100,batch_size=128):
    iter = 1
    #print(X.shape)
    X = X.reshape((len(X),self.steps,self.n))
    while iter &amp;lt; epochs:
        for i in range(int(len(X)/batch_size)):
            batch_x, batch_y = X[i:i+batch_size,:],
Y[i:i+batch_size,:]
            #print(batch_x.shape)
            #batch_x = batch_x.reshape((batch_size, self.steps,
self.n))
            #print(batch_x.shape)
            self.sess.run(self.opt, feed_dict={self.x: batch_x,
self.y: batch_y})
            if iter % 10 == 0:
                acc = self.sess.run(self._accuracy,
feed_dict={self.x: X, self.y: Y})
                los = self.sess.run(self.loss, feed_dict={self.x:
X, self.y: Y})
                print("For iter ", iter)
                print("Accuracy ", acc)
                print("Loss ", los)
                print("_____")
            iter = iter + 1

def predict(self,X):
    # predicting the output
```

```
    test_data = X.reshape((-1, self.steps, self.n))
    out = self.sess.run(self.prediction,
feed_dict={self.x:test_data})
    return out
```

In the coming chapters, we will be using the RNN for handling time series production and text processing.

Gated recurrent unit

Gated recurrent unit (GRU) is another modification of RNN. It has a simplified architecture compared to LSTM and overcomes the vanishing gradient problem. It takes only two inputs, the input x_t at time t and memory h_{t-1} from time t-1. There are only two gates, **Update Gate** and **Reset Gate**, shown in the following diagram:

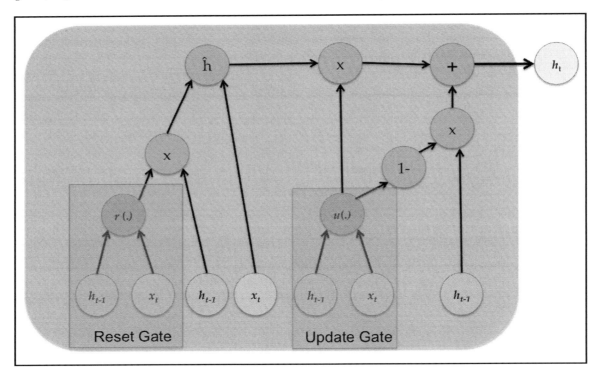

The architecture of a basic GRU cell

The update gate controls how much previous memory to keep, and the reset gate determines how to combine the new input with previous memory. We can define the complete GRU cell by the following four equations:

- $u(.) = \sigma(W_{ux}x_t + W_{uh}h_{t-1} + b_u)$
- $r(.) = \sigma(W_{rx}x_t + W_{rh}h_{t-1} + b_r)$
- $\tilde{h} = tanh(W_{\tilde{h}x}x_t + W_{\tilde{h}h}(r_t \circ h_{t-1}) + b_{\tilde{h}})$
- $h_t = (u_t \circ \tilde{h}_t) + (1 - u_t) \circ h_{t-1}$

Both GRU and LSTM give a comparable performance, but GRU has fewer training parameters.

Autoencoders

The models we have learned up to now were learning using supervised learning. In this section, we will learn about autoencoders. They are feedforward, non-recurrent neural network, and learn through unsupervised learning. They are the latest buzz, along with generative adversarial networks, and we can find applications in image reconstruction, clustering, machine translation, and much more. They were initially proposed in the 1980s by Geoffrey E. Hinton and the PDP group (http://www.cs.toronto.edu/~fritz/absps/clp.pdf).

The autoencoder basically consists of two cascaded neural networks—the first network acts as an encoder; it takes the input x and encodes it using a transformation h to encoded signal y, shown in the following equation:

$$y = h(x)$$

The second neural network uses the encoded signal y as its input and performs another transformation f to get a reconstructed signal r, shown as follows:

$$r = f(y) = f(h(x))$$

The loss function is the MSE with error e defined as the difference between the original input x and the reconstructed signal r:

$$e = X - r$$

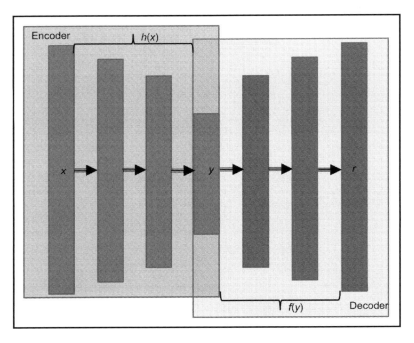

Basic architecture of an autoencoder

The preceding diagram shows an autoencoder with **Encoder** and **Decoder** highlighted separately. Autoencoders may have weight sharing, that is, weights of decoder and encoder are shared. This is done by simply making them a transpose of each other; this helps the network learn faster as the number of training parameters is less. There are a large variety of autoencoders for example: sparse autoencoders, denoising autoencoders, convolution autoencoders, and variational autoencoders.

Denoising autoencoders

A denoising autoencoder learns from a corrupted (noisy) input; we feed the encoder network the noisy input and the reconstructed image from the decoder is compared with the original denoised input. The idea is that this will help the network learn how to denoise an input. The network does not just make a pixel-wise comparison, instead, in order to denoise the image, the network is forced to learn the information of neighboring pixels as well.

Once the autoencoder has learned the encoded features y, we can remove the decoder part of the network and use only the encoder part to achieve dimensionality reduction. The dimensionally reduced input can be fed to some other classification or regression model.

Variational autoencoders

Another very popular autoencoder is **variational autoencoders** (**VAE**). They are a mix of the best of both worlds: DL and the Bayesian inference.

VAEs have an additional stochastic layer; this layer, after the encoder network, samples the data using a Gaussian distribution, and the one after the decoder network samples the data using Bernoulli's distribution.

VAEs can be used to generate images. VAEs allow one to set complex priors in the latent and learn powerful latent representations. We will learn more about them in a later chapter.

Summary

In this chapter, we covered some basic and useful deep neural network models. We started with a single neuron, saw its power and its limitations. The multilayered perceptron was built for both regression and classification tasks. The backpropagation algorithm was introduced. The chapter progressed to CNN, with an introduction to the convolution layers and pooling layers. We learned about some of the successful CNN and used the first CNN LeNet to perform handwritten digits recognition. From the feed forward MLPs and CNNs, we moved forward to RNNs. LSTM and GRU networks were introduced. We made our own LSTM network in TensorFlow and finally learned about autoencoders.

In the next chapter, we will start with a totally new type of AI model genetic algorithms. Like neural networks, they too are inspired by nature. We will be using what we learned in this chapter and the coming few chapters in the case studies we'll do in later chapters.

Genetic Algorithms for IoT

5

In the previous chapter, we looked at different deep learning-based algorithms; these algorithms have shown their success in the fields of recognition, detection, reconstruction, and even in the generation of vision, speech, and text data. While, at present, **deep learning** (**DL**) is on top in terms of both application and employability, it has close competition with evolutionary algorithms. The algorithms are inspired by the natural process of evolution, the world's best optimizers. Yes, even we are the result of years of genetic evolution. In this chapter, you will be introduced to the fascinating world of evolutionary algorithms and learn about a specific type of evolutionary algorithm, genetic algorithms, in more detail. In this chapter, you will learn about the following:

- What is optimization
- Different methods to solve an optimization problem
- Understand the intuition behind genetic algorithms
- The advantages of genetic algorithms
- Understand and implement the processes of cross-over, mutation, and fitness function selection
- Use a genetic algorithm to find a lost password
- Various uses of genetic algorithms in optimizing your models
- The Distributed Evolutionary Algorithms in the Python genetic algorithm library

Optimization

Optimization is not a new word; we have used it earlier with respect to both machine learning and DL algorithms, where we used the TensorFlow auto differentiator to find the optimum model weights and biases using a form of gradient descent algorithm. In this section, we will learn a little more about optimization, optimization problems, and different techniques used to perform optimization.

In its most basic terms, **optimization** is the process of making something better. The idea is to find the best solution, and obviously when we talk about the best solution, it means there exists more than one solution. In optimization, we try to adjust our variable parameters/processes/inputs so that we can find the minimum or maximum output. Normally, the variables constitute the inputs, we have a function called an **objective function**, **loss function**, or **fitness function**, and as output we expect the cost/loss or fitness. The cost or loss should be minimized, and if we define fitness, then it should be maximized. Here, we vary the inputs (variables) to achieve a desired (optimized) output.

I hope you can appreciate that calling it loss/cost or fitness is just a matter of choice, the function which calculates the cost and needs to be minimized, if we just add a negative sign to it then we expect the modified function to be maximized. As an example, minimizing $2 - x^2$ over the interval $-2 < x < 2$ is the same as maximizing $x^2 - 2$ over the same interval.

Our daily lives are full of many such optimization tasks. What will be the best route to take to the office? Which project should I do first? Preparing for an interview what topics to read such that your success rate in the interview is maximized. The following diagram shows the basic relationship between **Input Variables**, the **Function** to be optimized, and the **Output/Cost**:

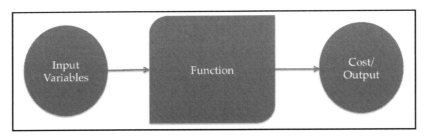

Relationship between input, the function to be optimized, and the output

The aim is to minimize the cost, such that the constraints specified by the function are satisfied by the input variables. The mathematical relationship between the cost function, constraints, and input variables determines the complexity of the optimization problem. One of the key issues is whether the cost function and constraints are convex or non-convex. If the cost function and constraints are convex, we can be confident that there does exist a feasible solution, and if we search in a sufficiently large domain, we will find one. The following figure shows an example of a convex cost function:

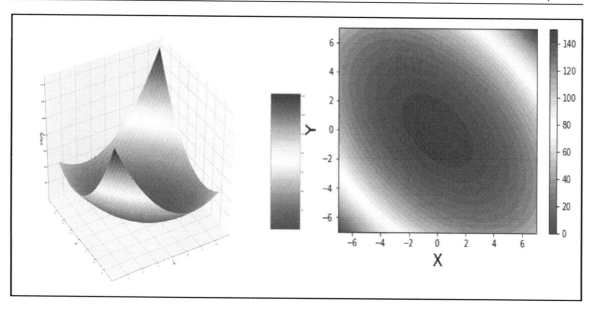

A convex cost function. The one on the left is the surface plot and the one on the right shows the contour plot of the same cost function. The darkest red point in the image corresponds to the optimum solution point.

If, on other hand, the cost function or constraints are non-convex, the optimization problem becomes harder and we cannot be sure that there does exist a solution, or that we can even find one.

There are various methods to solve optimization problems in mathematics and computer programming. Let's find out a little about each of them next.

Deterministic and analytic methods

When the objective function is smooth with a continuous second derivative, then we know from the knowledge of calculus that at a local minimum the following are true:

- The gradient of the objective function at minima x^*, that is, $f(x^*) = 0$
- The second derivative (Hessian $H(x^*) = \nabla^2 f(x)$) is positively definite

In such conditions, for some problems, it is possible to find the solution analytically by determining the zeros of the gradient and verifying the positive definiteness of the Hessian matrix at the zeros. So, in these cases, we can explore the search space iteratively for the minima of the objective function. There are various search methods; let's see them.

Gradient descent method

We learned about gradient descent and how it works in earlier chapters, and we saw that the search direction is the direction of the gradient descent, $-\nabla f(x)$. It is also called the **Cauchy method** because it was given by Cauchy, in 1847, and since then it has been very popular. We start from an arbitrary point on the objective function surface and change the variables (in earlier chapters, these were the weights and biases) along the direction of the gradient. Mathematically, it is represented as follows:

$$x_{n+1} = x_n - \alpha_n \nabla f(x_n)$$

Here α_n is the step size (variation/learning rate) at iteration n. Gradient descent algorithms have worked well in training DL models, but they have some severe drawbacks:

- The performance of the optimizer used depends greatly on the learning rate and other constants. If you change them even slightly, there is a big possibility that the network may not converge. And it is because of this that sometimes researchers call training a model an art, or alchemy.
- Since these methods are based on derivatives, they do not work for discrete data.
- We cannot reliably apply it when the objective function is non-convex, which is the case in many DL networks (especially models using a non-linear activation function). The presence of many hidden layers can result in many local minima, and there is a strong possibility that the model gets stuck in a local minimum. Here, you can see an example of the objective function with many local minima:

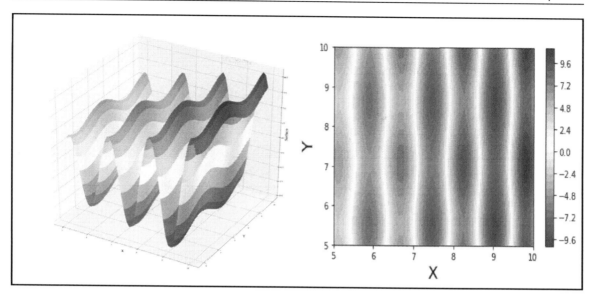

A cost function with many local minima. The one on the left is the surface plot and the one on the right shows the contour plot of the same cost function. The dark red points in the image correspond to minima.

There are many variants of the gradient descent method, and the most popular of them are available in the TensorFlow optimizers, including the following:

- Stochastic gradient optimizer
- Adam optimizer
- Adagrad optimizer
- RMSProp optimizer

You can learn more about the different optimizers available in TensorFlow from the TensorFlow documentation at `https://www.tensorflow.org/api_guides/python/train`.

A nice source is a blog (`http://ruder.io/optimizing-gradient-descent/index.html#gradientdescentoptimizationalgorithms`) by Sebastian Ruder based on his arXiv paper at `https://arxiv.org/abs/1609.04747`.

Newton-Raphson method

This method is based on the second order Taylor series expansion of the objective function, $f(x)$, around the point $\overset{*}{x}$:

$$f(x) = f(x_*) + \nabla f(x_*)(x - x_*)^T + \frac{(x - x_*)}{2!} H(x - x_*)^T + \dots$$

Here, x^* is the point about which the Taylor series is expanded, x is a point near x^*, the superscript T represents the transpose, and H is the Hessian matrix with elements given by the following:

$$h_{mn} = \frac{\partial^2 f}{\partial x_m \partial x_n}$$

Taking the gradient of the Taylor series expansion and equating to **0**, we get this:

$$\nabla f(x) = \nabla f(x_*) + (x - x_*)H = 0$$

Assuming the initial guess as x_0, the next point x_{n+1} can be obtained from the previous point x_n using this:

$$x_{n+1} = x_n - H^{-1}\nabla f(x_n)$$

The method uses both the first and the second partial derivatives of the objective function to find the minima. At iteration k, it approximates the objective function by a quadratic function around $x(k)$ and moves toward its minima.

Since computing the Hessian matrix is computationally expensive and not normally known, a large number of algorithms exist around approximating the Hessian; these techniques are called **quasi-Newton methods**. They can be represented as follows:

$$x_{n+1} = x_n - \alpha_n A_n \nabla f(x_n)$$

α_n is the step size (variation/learning rate) at iteration n, and A_n is the approximation to the Hessian matrix at iteration n. We construct a sequence of approximations to the Hessian, such that the following is true:

$$\lim_{n \to \infty} A_n = H^{-1}$$

Two popular quasi-Newton methods are as follows:

- Davidon-Fletcher-Powell algorithm
- Broyden-Fletcher-Goldfarb-Shanno algorithm

 When the approximation A_n to the Hessian is the identity matrix, the Newton method becomes the gradient descent method.

The major disadvantage of the Newton method is that it is not scalable to problems with a high-dimensional input feature space.

Natural optimization methods

Natural optimization methods are inspired by some natural processes, that is, a process, existing in nature, that is remarkably successful at optimizing some natural phenomena. These algorithms do not require taking objective function derivatives, and thus can be employed even for discrete variables and non-continuous objective functions.

Simulated annealing

Simulated annealing is a stochastic method. It is inspired by the physical process of annealing, in which a solid is first heated to a high enough temperature so that it melts, and then the temperature is decreased slowly; this allows the particles of the solid to arrange themselves in the lowest possible energy state and thus produce a highly structured lattice.

We start with some random values assigned to each variable; this represents the initial state. At each step, we pick a variable (or group of variables) at random and then select a random value. If, upon the assignment of that value to the variable, there is an improvement in the objective function, the algorithm accepts the assignment, there is a new current assignment, and the state of the system changes. Otherwise, it accepts the assignment with some probability P, which depends on the temperature T and the difference between the values of the objective function in the current state and the new state. If the change is not accepted, the current state remains unchanged. The probability P that we will change from state i to state j is as follows:

$$P(i \Rightarrow j) = exp\left(\frac{f(x_i) - f(x_j)}{T}\right)$$

Here, T represents a variable analogous to temperature in the physical system. As the temperature approaches 0, the simulated annealing algorithm reduces to the gradient descent algorithm.

Particle Swarm Optimization

Particle Swarm Optimization (PSO) was developed by Edward and Kennedy in 1995. It is based on the social behavior of animals, such as a flock of birds. You must have noticed in the sky, birds fly in a V shape. Those who have studied bird behavior tell us that birds fly like this when in search of food or a better location, with the one leading being nearest to the desired source.

Now, when they fly, the leading bird does not remain the same; instead, it changes as they move. The bird in the flock that sees the food sends a sound signal, and all other birds then collect around that bird in a V fashion. This is a continuous repetitive process, and has served birds well for millions of years.

PSO takes inspiration from this bird behavior and uses it to solve optimization problems. In PSO, every single solution is a bird (called a **particle**) in the search space. Each particle has a fitness value, which is evaluated by the fitness function to be optimized; they also have velocities, which direct the flying of the particles. The particles fly through the problem search space by following the current optimum particle.

The particles are moved around in the search space guided by two best fitness values, one their own best known position in the search space (**pbest**: particle best), the other the entire swarm's best known fitness value (**gbest**: global best). As improved positions are discovered, they are used to guide the movements of the particles of the swarm. This process is repeated and it is hoped that an optimum solution will eventually be discovered.

Genetic algorithms

When we look around the world and see different species, a question naturally arises: why are these sets of features stable and not others; why should the majority of animals have two legs or four legs, and why not three? Is it possible that the world that we see today is the result of many iterations in a grand optimization algorithm?

Let's imagine there is a cost function that measures survivability, which should be maximized. The characteristics of the organisms of the natural world fit into a topological landscape. The level of survivability (measured through adaptation) represents the elevation of the landscape. The highest points correspond to the most-fit conditions, and the constraints are provided by the environment and through interaction between different species.

Then, the process of evolution can be thought of as a grand optimization algorithm that selects which characteristics produce a species of organism fit for survival. The peaks of the landscape are populated by living organisms. Some peaks are broad and hold a wide range of characteristics encompassing many organisms, while other peaks are very narrow and allow only very specific characteristics.

We can extend this analogy to include valleys between the peaks separating different species. And, we can think that humankind might be at the global maximum peak of this landscape, since we have intelligence and the ability to alter the environment and ensure better survivability, even in extreme environments.

Thus, the world with different life forms can be thought of as a big search space, with different species as the result of many iterations of a grand optimization algorithm. This idea forms the basis of genetic algorithms.

Since the main theme of this chapter is genetic algorithms, let's dive into them.

Introduction to genetic algorithms

According to the work of Charles Darwin, the famous biologist, the animal and plant species that we see today have emerged due to millions of years of evolution. The process of evolution is guided by the principle of *survival of the fittest*, selecting the organisms that have a better chance of survivability. The plants and animals that we see today are the results of millions of years of adaptation to the constraints imposed by the environment. At any given time, a large number of varied organisms may coexist and compete for the same environmental resources.

The organisms that are most capable of both acquiring the resources and procreation are the ones whose descendants will have more chances of survival. Organisms that are less capable, on the other hand, will tend to have few or no descendants. Over time, the entire population will evolve, containing on average organisms that are more fit than the previous generations.

What makes this possible? What decides that a person will be tall, and a plant will have a particular shape of leaf? All this is encoded like a set of rules in the program on the blueprint of life itself—genes. Every living organism on Earth has this set of rules and they describe how that organism is designed (created). Genes reside in chromosomes. Each being has a different number of chromosomes and they contain thousands of genes. For example, we homo sapiens have 46 chromosomes and these chromosomes contain about 20,000 genes. Each gene represents a specific rule: a person will have blue eyes, will have brown hair, will be a female, and so on. These genes pass from parents to offspring through the process of reproduction.

There are two ways by which genes pass from parents to offspring:

- **Asexual reproduction**: In this, the child is the duplicate copy of the parent. It happens during a biological process called **mitosis**; lower organisms such as bacteria and fungi reproduce via mitosis. Only one parent is needed in this:

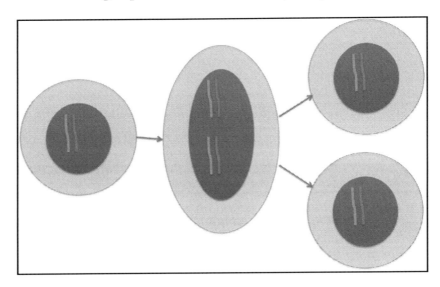

The process of mitosis: the chromosomes of the parent first double, and the cell divides into two

- **Sexual reproduction**: This happens via a biological process called **meiosis**. In this, two parents are involved initially; each parent cell undergoes a process of crossover, where a part of one chromosome gets interchanged with a part of another chromosome. This modifies the genetic sequence; the cells then divide into two, but with only half the number of chromosomes each. The cells containing half the number of chromosomes (haploid) from the two parents then meet together to form a zygote, which later through mitosis and cell differentiation results in the production of an **offspring** similar to, yet different from, the parents:

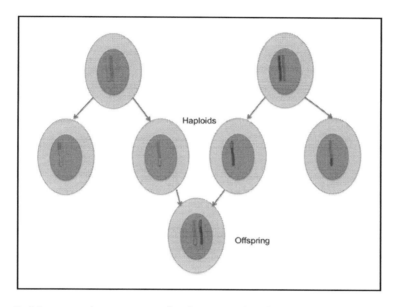

The process of meiosis: parents' cell chromosomes undergo crossover, a part of one chromosome overlaps and changes position with part of another chromosome. The cells then divide into two, with each divided cell containing only one chromosome (haploids). The two haploids from two parents then meet together to complete the total number of chromosomes.

Another interesting thing that happens in the natural process of selection and evolution is the phenomenon of mutation. Here, the genes undergo a sudden change and generate a completely new gene, which was not present in either parent. This phenomenon generates further diversity.

Sexual reproduction through generations is supposed to bring about evolution and ensure that organisms with the fittest characteristics have more descendants.

The genetic algorithm

Let's now learn how can we implement the genetic algorithm. This method was developed by John Holland in 1975. It was shown that it can be used to solve an optimization problem by his student Goldberg, who used genetic algorithms to control gas pipeline transmission. Since then, genetic algorithms have remained popular, and have inspired various other evolutionary programs.

To apply genetic algorithms to solving optimization problems using the computer, as the first step we will need to **encode the problem variables into genes**. The genes can be a string of real numbers or a binary bit string (series of 0s and 1's). This represents a potential solution (individual) and many such solutions together form the population at time *t*. For instance, consider a problem where we need to find two variables, a and b, such that the two lie in the range (0, 255). For binary gene representation, these two variables can be represented by a 16-bit chromosome, with the higher 8 bits representing gene a and the lower 8 bits for b. The encoding will need to be later decoded to get the real values of the variables a and b.

The second important requirement for genetic algorithms is defining a proper **fitness function**, which calculates the fitness score of any potential solution (in the preceding example, it should calculate the fitness value of the encoded chromosome). This is the function that we want to optimize by finding the optimum set of parameters of the system or the problem at hand. The fitness function is problem-dependent. For example, in the natural process of evolution, the fitness function represents the organism's ability to operate and to survive in its environment.

Once we have decided the encoding of the problem solution in genes and decided upon the fitness function, the genetic algorithm will then follow these steps:

1. **Population Initialization**: We need to create an initial population, where all chromosomes are (usually) randomly generated to yield an entire range of possible solutions (the search space). Occasionally, the solutions may be seeded in areas where optimal solutions are likely to be found. The population size depends on the nature of the problem, but typically contains several hundred potential solutions encoded into chromosomes.

2. **Parent Selection**: For each successive generation, based on the fitness function (or randomly), we next select a certain proportion of the existing population. This selected proportion of the population will then breed to form a new generation. This is done by the method of tournament selection: a fixed number of individuals are randomly selected (tournament size) and the individual with the best fitness score is chosen as one of the parents.

3. **Reproduction**: We next generate the successive generation from those selected in step 2, through genetic operators such as crossover and mutation. These genetic operators ultimately result in a child (next generation) population of chromosomes that is different from the initial generation but at the same time shares many of the characteristics of its parents.

4. **Evaluation**: The offspring generated are then evaluated using the fitness function, and they replace the least-fit individuals in the population to keep the population size unchanged.

5. **Termination**: During the *Evaluation* step, if any of the offspring achieve the objective fitness score or the maximum number of generations is reached, then the genetic algorithm process is terminated. Otherwise, steps 2 to 4 are repeated to produce the next generation.

Two operators that are important for the success of genetic algorithms are crossover and mutation.

Crossover

To perform the crossover operation, we select a random position on the chromosome of two parents, then the genetic information is swapped between them about this point, with a probability P_x. This results in two new offspring. When the crossover takes place over a random point, it is called a **one-point crossover** (or **Single Point Crossover**):

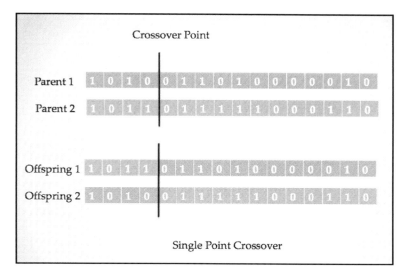

One-point crossover: a random point is selected in the parent's chromosomes and the corresponding gene bits are swapped

We can also have more than one point where parents' genes are swapped; this is called a **Multi-Point Crossover**:

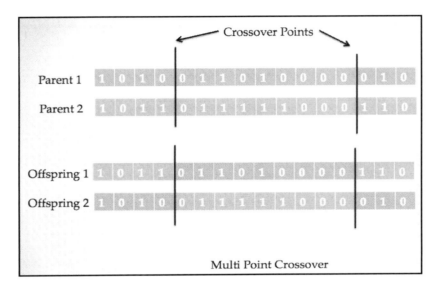

Multi-point crossover: there is more than one point where the genes of the parents are swapped. This is an example of a double-point crossover.

There exist a lot of crossovers people have tried, for example, uniform crossover, order-based crossover, and cyclic crossover.

Mutation

While the crossover operation ensures variety and can help speed up the search, it does not generate new solutions. This is the work of the mutation operator, which helps in maintaining and introducing diversity in the population. The mutation operator is applied to certain genes (bits) of the child chromosomes with a probability, P_m.

We can have a bit flip mutation; if we consider our earlier example, then in the 16-bit chromosome, the bit flip mutation will cause a single bit to change its state (from *0* to *1* or from *1* to *0*).

There is a possibility that we set the gene to a random value for all possible values. This is called **random resetting**.

The probability P_m plays an important role; if we assign a very low value to P_m it can lead to genetic drift, but on the other hand, a high P_m may result in a loss of good solutions. We choose a mutation probability such that the algorithm learns to sacrifice short-term fitness in order to gain longer-term fitness.

Pros and cons

Genetic algorithms sound cool, right! Now, before we try and build a code around them, let's point out certain advantages and disadvantages of genetic algorithms.

Advantages

Genetic algorithms offer some intriguing advantages and can produce results when the tradition gradient-based approaches fail:

- They can be used to optimize either continuous or discrete variables.
- Unlike gradient descent, we do not require derivative information, which also means that there is no need for the fitness function to be continuous and differentiable.
- It can simultaneously search from a wide sampling of the cost surface.
- We can deal with a large number of variables without a significant increase in computation time.
- The generation of the population and calculating their fitness values can be performed in parallel, and hence genetic algorithms are well suited for parallel computers.
- They can work even when the topological surface is extremely complex because crossover and mutation operators help them in jumping out of a local minimum.
- They can provide more than one optimum solution.
- We can use them with numerically generated data, experimental data, or even analytical functions. They specifically work well for large-scale optimization problems.

Disadvantages

Despite the previously mentioned advantages, we still do not find genetic algorithms to be a ubiquitous solution to all optimization problems. This is for the following reasons:

- If the optimization function is a well-behaved convex function, then gradient-based methods will give a faster convergence
- The large population of solutions that helps genetic algorithms cover the search space more extensively also results in slow convergence
- Designing a fitness function can be a daunting task

Coding genetic algorithms using Distributed Evolutionary Algorithms in Python

Now that we understand how genetic algorithms work, let's try solving some problems with them. They have been used to solve NP-hard problems such as the traveling salesman problem. To make the task of generating a population, performing the crossover, and performing mutation operations easy, we will make use of **Distributed Evolutionary Algorithms in Python** (DEAP). It supports multiprocessing and we can use it for other evolutionary algorithms as well. You can download DEAP directly from PyPi using this:

```
pip install deap
```

It is compatible with Python 3.

To learn more about DEAP, you can refer to its GitHub repository (https://github.com/DEAP/deap) and its user's guide (http://deap.readthedocs.io/en/master/).

Guess the word

In this program, we use genetic algorithms to guess a word. The genetic algorithm will know the number of letters in the word and will guess those letters until it finds the right answer. We decide to represent the genes as a single alphanumeric character; strings of these characters thus constitute a chromosome. And our fitness function is the sum of the characters matching in the individual and the right word:

1. As the first step, we import the modules we will need. We use the `string` module and the `random` module to generate random characters from (a—z, A—Z, and 0—9). From the DEAP module, we use `creator`, `base`, and `tools`:

   ```
   import string
   import random

   from deap import base, creator, tools
   ```

2. In DEAP, we start with creating a class that inherits from the `deep.base` module. We need to tell it whether we are going to have a minimization or maximization of the function; this is done using the weights parameter. A value of +1 means we are maximizing (for minimizing, we give the value `-1.0`). The following code line will create a class, `FitnessMax`, that will maximize the function:

   ```
   creator.create("FitnessMax", base.Fitness, weights=(1.0,))
   ```

3. We also define an `Individual` class, which will inherit the class list, and tell the DEAP creator module to assign `FitnessMax` as its `fitness` attribute:

   ```
   creator.create("Individual", list, fitness=creator.FitnessMax)
   ```

4. Now, with the `Individual` class defined, we use the `toolbox` of DEAP defined in the base module. We will use it to create a population and define our gene pool. All the objects that we will need from now onward—an individual, the population, the functions, the operators, and the arguments—are stored in a container called `toolbox`. We can add or remove content to/from the `toolbox` container using the `register()` and `unregister()` methods:

   ```
   toolbox = base.Toolbox()
   # Gene Pool
   toolbox.register("attr_string", random.choice, \
                    string.ascii_letters + string.digits )
   ```

5. Now that we have defined how the gene pool will be created, we create an individual and then a population by repeatedly using the `Individual` class. We will pass the class to the toolbox responsible for creating a `N` parameter , telling it how many genes to produce:

```
#Number of characters in word
# The word to be guessed
word = list('hello')
N = len(word)
# Initialize population
toolbox.register("individual", tools.initRepeat, \
        creator.Individual, toolbox.attr_string, N )
toolbox.register("population",tools.initRepeat, list,\
        toolbox.individual)
```

6. We define the `fitness` function. Note the comma in the return statement. This is because the fitness function in DEAP is returned as a tuple to allow multi-objective `fitness` functions:

```
def evalWord(individual, word):
    return sum(individual[i] == word[i] for i in\
            range(len(individual))),
```

7. Add the fitness function to the container. Also, add the crossover operator, mutation operator, and parent selector operator. You can see that, for this, we are using the register function. In the first statement, we register the fitness function that we have defined, along with the additional arguments it will take. The next statement registers the crossover operation; it specifies that here we are using a two-point crossover (`cxTwoPoint`). Next, we register the mutation operator; we choose the `mutShuffleIndexes` option, which shuffles the attributes of the input individual with a probability `indpb=0.05`. And finally, we define how the parents are selected; here, we have defined the method of selection as tournament selection with a tournament size of 3:

```
toolbox.register("evaluate", evalWord, word)
toolbox.register("mate", tools.cxTwoPoint)
toolbox.register("mutate", tools.mutShuffleIndexes, indpb=0.05)
toolbox.register("select", tools.selTournament, tournsize=3)
```

8. Now we have all the ingredients, so we will write down the code of the genetic algorithm, which will perform the steps we mentioned earlier in a repetitive manner:

```
def main():
    random.seed(64)
    # create an initial population of 300 individuals
    pop = toolbox.population(n=300)
    # CXPB is the crossover probability
    # MUTPB is the probability for mutating an individual
    CXPB, MUTPB = 0.5, 0.2

    print("Start of evolution")

    # Evaluate the entire population
    fitnesses = list(map(toolbox.evaluate, pop))
    for ind, fit in zip(pop, fitnesses):
        ind.fitness.values = fit

    print(" Evaluated %i individuals" % len(pop))

    # Extracting all the fitnesses of individuals in a list
    fits = [ind.fitness.values[0] for ind in pop]
    # Variable keeping track of the number of generations
    g = 0

    # Begin the evolution
    while max(fits) < 5 and g < 1000:
        # A new generation
        g += 1
        print("-- Generation %i --" % g)

        # Select the next generation individuals
        offspring = toolbox.select(pop, len(pop))
        # Clone the selected individuals
        offspring = list(map(toolbox.clone, offspring))

        # Apply crossover and mutation on the offspring
        for child1, child2 in zip(offspring[::2], offspring[1::2]):
            # cross two individuals with probability CXPB
            if random.random() < CXPB:
            toolbox.mate(child1, child2)
            # fitness values of the children
            # must be recalculated later
            del child1.fitness.values
            del child2.fitness.values
        for mutant in offspring:
            # mutate an individual with probability MUTPB
```

```
            if random.random() < MUTPB:
                toolbox.mutate(mutant)
                del mutant.fitness.values

        # Evaluate the individuals with an invalid fitness
        invalid_ind = [ind for ind in offspring if not
ind.fitness.valid]
        fitnesses = map(toolbox.evaluate, invalid_ind)
        for ind, fit in zip(invalid_ind, fitnesses):
        ind.fitness.values = fit

        print(" Evaluated %i individuals" % len(invalid_ind))

        # The population is entirely replaced by the offspring
        pop[:] = offspring

        # Gather all the fitnesses in one list and print the stats
        fits = [ind.fitness.values[0] for ind in pop]

        length = len(pop)
        mean = sum(fits) / length
        sum2 = sum(x*x for x in fits)
        std = abs(sum2 / length - mean**2)**0.5

        print(" Min %s" % min(fits))
        print(" Max %s" % max(fits))
        print(" Avg %s" % mean)
        print(" Std %s" % std)

    print("-- End of (successful) evolution --")

    best_ind = tools.selBest(pop, 1)[0]
    print("Best individual is %s, %s" % (''.join(best_ind),\
            best_ind.fitness.values))
```

9. Here, you can see the result of this genetic algorithm. In seven generations, we reached the right word:

```
Start of evolution
  Evaluated 300 individuals
-- Generation 1 --
  Evaluated 178 individuals
  Min 0.0
  Max 2.0
  Avg 0.22
  Std 0.4526956299030656
-- Generation 2 --
  Evaluated 174 individuals
  Min 0.0
  Max 2.0
  Avg 0.51
  Std 0.613650280425803
-- Generation 3 --
  Evaluated 191 individuals
  Min 0.0
  Max 3.0
  Avg 0.9766666666666667
  Std 0.6502221842484989
-- Generation 4 --
  Evaluated 167 individuals
  Min 0.0
  Max 4.0
  Avg 1.45
  Std 0.6934214687571574
-- Generation 5 --
  Evaluated 191 individuals
  Min 0.0
  Max 4.0
  Avg 1.9833333333333334
  Std 0.7765665171481163
-- Generation 6 --
  Evaluated 168 individuals
  Min 0.0
  Max 4.0
  Avg 2.48
  Std 0.7678541528180985
-- Generation 7 --
  Evaluated 192 individuals
  Min 1.0
  Max 5.0
  Avg 3.013333333333333
  Std 0.6829999186595044
-- End of (successful) evolution --
Best individual is hello, (5.0,)
```

DEAP has options to select various crossover tools, different mutation operators, and even how the tournament selection takes place. The complete list of all evolutionary tools offered by DEAP and their description is available at `http://deap.readthedocs.io/en/master/api/tools.html`.

Genetic algorithm for CNN architecture

In `Chapter 4`, *Deep Learning for IoT*, we learned about different DL models, such as MLP, CNN, RNN, and so on. Now, we will see how we can use genetic algorithms with these DL models. Genetic algorithms can be used to find the optimized weights and biases, and people have tried them. But the most common use of genetic algorithms in DL models has been to find optimum hyperparameters.

Here, we use genetic algorithms to find the optimum CNN architecture. The solution here is based on the paper *Genetic CNN* by Lingxi Xie and Alan Yuille (`https://arxiv.org/abs/1703.01513`). The first step will be finding the right representation of the problem. The authors presented a binary string representation for the network architecture. The family of the network is encoded into fixed-length binary strings. The network is composed of S stages where the *s-th* stage $s= 1, 2,....S$, contains K_s nodes denoted by v_{s,k_s}, here $k_s = 1, 2,..., K_s$. The nodes in each stage are ordered and for proper representation they allow only connections from a lower-numbered node to a higher-numbered node. Each node represents a convolution layer operation, followed by batch normalization and ReLU activation. Each bit of the bit string represents the presence or absence of the connection between one convolution layer (node) and the other, the ordering of bits being as follows: the first bit represents the connection between $(v_{s,1}, v_{s,2})$, the following two bits represent the connection between $(v_{s,1}, v_{s,3})$ and $(v_{s,2}, v_{s,3})$, the following three bits will be $(v_{s,1}, v_{s,3})$, $(v_{s,1}, v_{s,4})$, and $(v_{s,2}, v_{s,4})$, and so on.

To understand it better, let's consider a two-stage network (each stage will have the same number of filters and filter size). Stage S_1 let's say consists of four nodes (that is $K_s = 4$), thus the total number of bits required to encode it is $(4 \times 3 \times \frac{1}{2} =)$ 6. The number of convolutional filters in stage *1* is 32; also we ensure that convolutional operation does not change the spatial dimensions of the image (for example, padding is the same). The following diagram shows the respective bit string encoded and corresponding convolution layer connections. The connections in red are default connections and are not encoded in the bit string. The first bit encodes the connection between (*a1*, *a2*), the next two bits encode the connection between (*a1*, *a3*) and (*a2*, *a3*), and the last three bits encode the connection between (*a1*, *a4*), (*a2*, *a4*), and (*a3*, *a4*):

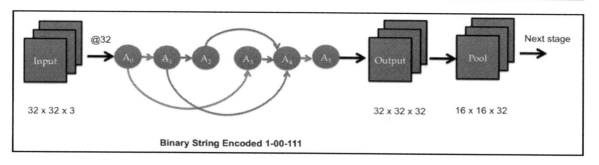

Bit string encoded and corresponding convolution layer connections

Stage *1* takes a **32 × 32 × 3** input; all the convolution nodes in this stage have 32 filters. The red connections are default connections not encoded in the bit string. The green connection represents the connections according to the encoded bit string 1-00-111. The output of stage *1* goes to the pooling layer and reduces by half in the spatial dimension.

Stage 2 has five nodes, and thus will need (5×4×½ =) 10 bits. It will take the input from stage *1* with dimensions **16 × 16 × 32**. Now, if we take the number of convolution filters in stage 2 as *64*, then after the pooling the output would be 8 × 8 × 64.

The code presented here is taken from `https://github.com/aqibsaeed/Genetic-CNN`. Since we need to represent a graph structure, the network is built using **directed acyclic graph (DAG)**. To represent DAG, we define a class, DAG, in which we define methods for adding a new node, deleting an existing node, adding an edge (connection) between two nodes, and deleting an edge between two nodes. Besides these, the methods are defined to find a node predecessor, the nodes it is connected to, and a list of leaves of the graph. The complete code is in `dag.py`, which you can access from the GitHub link.

The main code is given in the `Genetic_CNN.ipynb` Jupyter Notebook. We use the DEAP library to run the genetic algorithm, and TensorFlow to construct a CNN from the graph constructed by the genetic algorithm. The fitness function is the accuracy. The code is built to find the CNN that will give the highest accuracy on the MNIST dataset (the handwritten digits, which we used in `Chapter 4`, *Deep Learning for IoT*; here, we access them directly from the TensorFlow library):

1. The first step is to import the modules. Here, we will need DEAP and TensorFlow, and we also will import the DAG class we created in `dag.py` and the standard Numpy and Random modules:

```
import random
import numpy as np
```

```
from deap import base, creator, tools, algorithms
from scipy.stats import bernoulli
from dag import DAG, DAGValidationError

import tensorflow as tf
from tensorflow.examples.tutorials.mnist import input_data
```

2. We read the data directly from the TensorFlow examples library:

```
mnist = input_data.read_data_sets("mnist_data/", one_hot=True)
train_imgs   = mnist.train.images
train_labels = mnist.train.labels
test_imgs    = mnist.test.images
test_labels  = mnist.test.labels

train_imgs = np.reshape(train_imgs, [-1,28,28,1])
test_imgs = np.reshape(test_imgs, [-1,28,28,1])
```

3. Now, we build the bit data structure that will hold the network information. The network we are designing is a three-stage network, with three nodes in stage 1 (3 bits), four nodes in stage 2 (6 bits), and five nodes in stage 3 (10 bits). Thus, one Individual will be represented by a binary string of *3 + 6 + 10 = 19* bits:

```
STAGES = np.array(["s1","s2","s3"]) # S
NUM_NODES = np.array([3,4,5]) # K

L =  0 # genome length
BITS_INDICES, l_bpi = np.empty((0,2),dtype = np.int32), 0 # to keep
track of bits for each stage S
for nn in NUM_NODES:
    t = nn * (nn - 1)
    BITS_INDICES = np.vstack([BITS_INDICES,[l_bpi, l_bpi + int(0.5
* t)]])
    l_bpi = int(0.5 * t)
    L += t
L = int(0.5 * L)

TRAINING_EPOCHS = 20
BATCH_SIZE = 20
TOTAL_BATCHES = train_imgs.shape[0] // BATCH_SIZE
```

4. Now comes the part where we build the graph according to the encoded bit string. This will help build the population for the genetic algorithm. First, we define the functions we will need to build a CNN (`weight_variable`: creates the weight variable for a convolutional node; `bias_variable`: creates the bias variable for a convolutional node; `apply_convolution`: the function that performs the convolution operation; `apply_pool`: the function that will perform the pooling operation after each stage; and finally the last fully connected layer using the `linear_layer` function):

```
def weight_variable(weight_name, weight_shape):
    return tf.Variable(tf.truncated_normal(weight_shape, stddev =
0.1),name = ''.join(["weight_", weight_name]))

def bias_variable(bias_name,bias_shape):
    return tf.Variable(tf.constant(0.01, shape = bias_shape),name =
''.join(["bias_", bias_name]))

def linear_layer(x,n_hidden_units,layer_name):
    n_input = int(x.get_shape()[1])
    weights = weight_variable(layer_name,[n_input, n_hidden_units])
    biases = bias_variable(layer_name,[n_hidden_units])
    return tf.add(tf.matmul(x,weights),biases)

def
apply_convolution(x,kernel_height,kernel_width,num_channels,depth,l
ayer_name):
    weights = weight_variable(layer_name,[kernel_height,
kernel_width, num_channels, depth])
    biases = bias_variable(layer_name,[depth])
    return tf.nn.relu(tf.add(tf.nn.conv2d(x,
weights,[1,2,2,1],padding = "SAME"),biases))

def apply_pool(x,kernel_height,kernel_width,stride_size):
    return tf.nn.max_pool(x, ksize=[1, kernel_height, kernel_width,
1],
            strides=[1, 1, stride_size, 1], padding = "SAME")
```

5. Now, we can build the network based on the encoded bit string. So, we generate the DAG using the `generate_dag` function:

```
def generate_dag(optimal_indvidual,stage_name,num_nodes):
    # create nodes for the graph
    nodes = np.empty((0), dtype = np.str)
    for n in range(1, (num_nodes + 1)):
        nodes = np.append(nodes,''.join([stage_name,"_",str(n)]))
    # initialize directed asyclic graph (DAG) and add nodes to it
```

```
        dag = DAG()
        for n in nodes:
            dag.add_node(n)

        # split best indvidual found via genetic algorithm to identify
    vertices connections and connect them in DAG
        edges = np.split(optimal_indvidual,np.cumsum(range(num_nodes -
    1)))[1:]
        v2 = 2
        for e in edges:
            v1 = 1
            for i in e:
                if i:
    dag.add_edge(''.join([stage_name,"_",str(v1)]),''.join([stage_name,
    "_",str(v2)]))
                v1 += 1
            v2 += 1

        # delete nodes not connected to anyother node from DAG
        for n in nodes:
            if len(dag.predecessors(n)) == 0 and len(dag.downstream(n))
    == 0:
                dag.delete_node(n)
                nodes = np.delete(nodes, np.where(nodes == n)[0][0])
        return dag, nodes
```

6. The graph generated is used to build the TensorFlow graph
   using the `generate_tensorflow_graph` function. This function makes use
   of the `add_node` function to add a convolution layer,
   and the `sum_tensors` function to combine the input of more than one
   convolution layer:

```
    def
    generate_tensorflow_graph(individual,stages,num_nodes,bits_indices)
    :
        activation_function_pattern = "/Relu:0"
        tf.reset_default_graph()
        X = tf.placeholder(tf.float32, shape = [None,28,28,1], name =
    "X")
        Y = tf.placeholder(tf.float32,[None,10],name = "Y")
        d_node = X
        for stage_name,num_node,bpi in
    zip(stages,num_nodes,bits_indices):
            indv = individual[bpi[0]:bpi[1]]

            add_node(''.join([stage_name,"_input"]),d_node.name)
            pooling_layer_name =
```

```
''.join([stage_name,"_input",activation_function_pattern])

        if not has_same_elements(indv):
            # ------------------ Temporary DAG to hold all
connections implied by genetic algorithm solution ------------ #

            # get DAG and nodes in the graph
            dag, nodes = generate_dag(indv,stage_name,num_node)
            # get nodes without any predecessor, these will be
connected to input node
            without_predecessors = dag.ind_nodes()
            # get nodes without any successor, these will be
connected to output node
            without_successors = dag.all_leaves()

            # --------------------------------------------------
----------------------------------------- #

            # ------------------------- Initialize tensforflow
graph based on DAG ------------------------- #

            for wop in without_predecessors:
add_node(wop,''.join([stage_name,"_input",activation_function_patte
rn]))

            for n in nodes:
                predecessors = dag.predecessors(n)
                if len(predecessors) == 0:
                    continue
                elif len(predecessors) > 1:
                    first_predecessor = predecessors[0]
                    for prd in range(1,len(predecessors)):
                        t =
sum_tensors(first_predecessor,predecessors[prd],activation_function
_pattern)
                        first_predecessor = t.name
                    add_node(n,first_predecessor)
                elif predecessors:
add_node(n,''.join([predecessors[0],activation_function_pattern]))

            if len(without_successors) > 1:
                first_successor = without_successors[0]
                for suc in range(1,len(without_successors)):
                    t =
sum_tensors(first_successor,without_successors[suc],activation_func
tion_pattern)
                    first_successor = t.name
add_node(''.join([stage_name,"_output"]),first_successor)
```

```
            else:
add_node(''.join([stage_name,"_output"]),''.join([without_successor
s[0],activation_function_pattern]))

            pooling_layer_name =
''.join([stage_name,"_output",activation_function_pattern])
            # --------------------------------------------------
------------------------------------ #

        d_node =
apply_pool(tf.get_default_graph().get_tensor_by_name(pooling_layer_
name),
                                kernel_height = 16, kernel_width =
16,stride_size = 2)

    shape = d_node.get_shape().as_list()
    flat = tf.reshape(d_node, [-1, shape[1] * shape[2] * shape[3]])
    logits = linear_layer(flat,10,"logits")
    xentropy =  tf.nn.softmax_cross_entropy_with_logits(logits =
logits, labels = Y)
    loss_function = tf.reduce_mean(xentropy)
    optimizer = tf.train.AdamOptimizer().minimize(loss_function)
    accuracy = tf.reduce_mean(tf.cast(
tf.equal(tf.argmax(tf.nn.softmax(logits),1), tf.argmax(Y,1)),
tf.float32))
    return  X, Y, optimizer, loss_function, accuracy

# Function to add nodes
def add_node(node_name, connector_node_name, h = 5, w = 5, nc = 1,
d = 1):
    with tf.name_scope(node_name) as scope:
        conv =
apply_convolution(tf.get_default_graph().get_tensor_by_name(connect
or_node_name),
                    kernel_height = h, kernel_width = w,
num_channels = nc , depth = d,
                    layer_name = ''.join(["conv_",node_name]))

def sum_tensors(tensor_a,tensor_b,activation_function_pattern):
    if not tensor_a.startswith("Add"):
        tensor_a = ''.join([tensor_a,activation_function_pattern])
    return
tf.add(tf.get_default_graph().get_tensor_by_name(tensor_a),
tf.get_default_graph().get_tensor_by_name(''.join([tensor_b,activat
ion_function_pattern])))

def has_same_elements(x):
    return len(set(x)) <= 1
```

7. The fitness function evaluates the accuracy of the generated CNN architecture:

```
def evaluateModel(individual):
    score = 0.0
    X, Y, optimizer, loss_function, accuracy =
generate_tensorflow_graph(individual,STAGES,NUM_NODES,BITS_INDICES)
    with tf.Session() as session:
        tf.global_variables_initializer().run()
        for epoch in range(TRAINING_EPOCHS):
            for b in range(TOTAL_BATCHES):
                offset = (epoch * BATCH_SIZE) %
(train_labels.shape[0] - BATCH_SIZE)
                batch_x = train_imgs[offset:(offset + BATCH_SIZE),
:, :, :]
                batch_y = train_labels[offset:(offset +
BATCH_SIZE), :]
                _, c = session.run([optimizer,
loss_function],feed_dict={X: batch_x, Y : batch_y})
            score = session.run(accuracy, feed_dict={X: test_imgs, Y:
test_labels})
            #print('Accuracy: ',score)
    return score,
```

8. So, now we are ready to implement the genetic algorithm: our fitness function will be a max function (`weights=(1.0,)`), we initialize the binary string using Bernoulli's distribution (`bernoulli.rvs`), the individuals are created of length L= 19, and the population is generated with each population consisting of 20 individuals. This time, we chose an ordered crossover, where a substring is selected from the first parent and copied into the offspring in the same location; the remaining positions are filled from the second parent, ensuring the nodes in the sub-string are not repeated. We kept the same mutation operator as before, `mutShuffleIndexes`; the tournament selection method is `selRoulette`, which makes the selection using the roulette wheel selection method (we choose k individuals and from them select the ones with the highest fitness). This time, instead of coding the genetic algorithm, we make use of the DEAP eaSimple algorithm, which is the basic genetic algorithm:

```
population_size = 20
num_generations = 3
creator.create("FitnessMax", base.Fitness, weights = (1.0,))
creator.create("Individual", list , fitness = creator.FitnessMax)
toolbox = base.Toolbox()
toolbox.register("binary", bernoulli.rvs, 0.5)
toolbox.register("individual", tools.initRepeat,
creator.Individual, toolbox.binary, n = L)
toolbox.register("population", tools.initRepeat, list ,
```

```
toolbox.individual)
toolbox.register("mate", tools.cxOrdered)
toolbox.register("mutate", tools.mutShuffleIndexes, indpb = 0.8)
toolbox.register("select", tools.selRoulette)
toolbox.register("evaluate", evaluateModel)
popl = toolbox.population(n = population_size)

import time
t = time.time()
result = algorithms.eaSimple(popl, toolbox, cxpb = 0.4, mutpb =
0.05, ngen = num_generations, verbose = True)
t1 = time.time() - t
print(t1)
```

9. The algorithm will take some time; on i7 with NVIDIA 1070 GTX GPU it took about 1.5 hours. The best three solutions are the following:

```
best_individuals = tools.selBest(popl, k = 3)
for bi in best_individuals:
    print(bi)
```

```
[0, 1, 0, 1, 0, 0, 0, 0, 1, 1, 1, 0, 0, 0, 1, 0, 1, 0, 0]
[1, 0, 0, 0, 1, 0, 1, 0, 0, 0, 1, 0, 1, 1, 1, 1, 1, 1, 0]
[0, 1, 0, 1, 0, 0, 0, 0, 1, 1, 1, 0, 1, 1, 1, 1, 1, 1, 0]
```

Genetic algorithm for LSTM optimization

In a genetic CNN, we use genetic algorithms to estimate the optimum CNN architecture; in genetic RNN, we will now use a genetic algorithm to find the optimum hyperparameters of the RNN, the window size, and the number of hidden units. We will find the parameters that reduce the **root-mean-square error** (**RMSE**) of the model.

The hyperparameters window size and number of units are again encoded in a binary string with 6 bits for window size and 4 bits for the number of units. Thus, the complete encoded chromosome will be of 10 bits. The LSTM is implemented using Keras.

The code we implement is taken from `https://github.com/aqibsaeed/Genetic-Algorithm-RNN`:

1. The necessary modules are imported. This time, we are using Keras to implement the LSTM model:

```
import numpy as np
import pandas as pd
from sklearn.metrics import mean_squared_error
from sklearn.model_selection import train_test_split as split

from keras.layers import LSTM, Input, Dense
from keras.models import Model

from deap import base, creator, tools, algorithms
from scipy.stats import bernoulli
from bitstring import BitArray

np.random.seed(1120)
```

2. The dataset we need for LSTM has to be time series data; we use the wind-power forecasting data from Kaggle (`https://www.kaggle.com/c/GEF2012-wind-forecasting/data`):

```
data = pd.read_csv('train.csv')
data = np.reshape(np.array(data['wp1']),(len(data['wp1']),1))

train_data = data[0:17257]
test_data = data[17257:]
```

3. Define a function to prepare the dataset depending upon the chosen `window_size`:

```
def prepare_dataset(data, window_size):
    X, Y = np.empty((0,window_size)), np.empty((0))
    for i in range(len(data)-window_size-1):
        X = np.vstack([X,data[i:(i + window_size),0]])
        Y = np.append(Y,data[i + window_size,0])
    X = np.reshape(X, (len(X),window_size,1))
    Y = np.reshape(Y, (len(Y),1))
    return X, Y
```

4. The `train_evaluate` function creates the LSTM network for a given individual and returns its RMSE value (fitness function):

```
def train_evaluate(ga_individual_solution):
    # Decode genetic algorithm solution to integer for window_size
and num_units
    window_size_bits = BitArray(ga_individual_solution[0:6])
    num_units_bits = BitArray(ga_individual_solution[6:])
    window_size = window_size_bits.uint
    num_units = num_units_bits.uint
    print('\nWindow Size: ', window_size, ', Num of Units: ',
num_units)
    # Return fitness score of 100 if window_size or num_unit is
zero
    if window_size == 0 or num_units == 0:
        return 100,
    # Segment the train_data based on new window_size; split into
train and validation (80/20)
    X,Y = prepare_dataset(train_data,window_size)
    X_train, X_val, y_train, y_val = split(X, Y, test_size = 0.20,
random_state = 1120)
    # Train LSTM model and predict on validation set
    inputs = Input(shape=(window_size,1))
    x = LSTM(num_units, input_shape=(window_size,1))(inputs)
    predictions = Dense(1, activation='linear')(x)
    model = Model(inputs=inputs, outputs=predictions)
    model.compile(optimizer='adam',loss='mean_squared_error')
    model.fit(X_train, y_train, epochs=5,
batch_size=10,shuffle=True)
    y_pred = model.predict(X_val)
    # Calculate the RMSE score as fitness score for GA
    rmse = np.sqrt(mean_squared_error(y_val, y_pred))
    print('Validation RMSE: ', rmse,'\n')
    return rmse,
```

5. Next, we use DEAP tools to define Individual (again, since the chromosome is represented by a binary encoded string (10 bits), we use Bernoulli's distribution), create the population, use ordered crossover, use mutShuffleIndexes mutation, and use the roulette wheel selection for selecting the parents:

```
population_size = 4
num_generations = 4
gene_length = 10

# As we are trying to minimize the RMSE score, that's why using
-1.0.
# In case, when you want to maximize accuracy for instance, use 1.0
```

```
creator.create('FitnessMax', base.Fitness, weights = (-1.0,))
creator.create('Individual', list , fitness = creator.FitnessMax)

toolbox = base.Toolbox()
toolbox.register('binary', bernoulli.rvs, 0.5)
toolbox.register('individual', tools.initRepeat,
creator.Individual, toolbox.binary, n = gene_length)
toolbox.register('population', tools.initRepeat, list ,
toolbox.individual)

toolbox.register('mate', tools.cxOrdered)
toolbox.register('mutate', tools.mutShuffleIndexes, indpb = 0.6)
toolbox.register('select', tools.selRoulette)
toolbox.register('evaluate', train_evaluate)

population = toolbox.population(n = population_size)
r = algorithms.eaSimple(population, toolbox, cxpb = 0.4, mutpb =
0.1, ngen = num_generations, verbose = False)
```

6. We get the best solution, as follows:

```
best_individuals = tools.selBest(population,k = 1)
best_window_size = None
best_num_units = None

for bi in best_individuals:
    window_size_bits = BitArray(bi[0:6])
    num_units_bits = BitArray(bi[6:])
    best_window_size = window_size_bits.uint
    best_num_units = num_units_bits.uint
    print('\nWindow Size: ', best_window_size, ', Num of Units: ',
best_num_units)
```

7. And finally, we implement the best LSTM solution:

```
X_train,y_train = prepare_dataset(train_data,best_window_size)
X_test, y_test = prepare_dataset(test_data,best_window_size)

inputs = Input(shape=(best_window_size,1))
x = LSTM(best_num_units, input_shape=(best_window_size,1))(inputs)
predictions = Dense(1, activation='linear')(x)
model = Model(inputs = inputs, outputs = predictions)
model.compile(optimizer='adam',loss='mean_squared_error')
model.fit(X_train, y_train, epochs=5, batch_size=10,shuffle=True)
y_pred = model.predict(X_test)

rmse = np.sqrt(mean_squared_error(y_test, y_pred))
print('Test RMSE: ', rmse)
```

Yay! Now, you have the best LSTM network for predicting wind power.

Summary

This chapter introduced an interesting nature-inspired algorithm family: genetic algorithms. We covered various standard optimization algorithms, varying from deterministic models, to gradient-based algorithms, to evolutionary algorithms. The biological process of evolution through natural selection was covered. We then learned how to convert our optimization problems into a form suitable for genetic algorithms. Crossover and mutation, two very crucial operations in genetic algorithms, were explained. While it is not possible to extensively cover all the crossover and mutation methods, we did learn about the popular ones.

We applied what we learned on three very different optimization problems. We used it to guess a word. The example was of a five-letter word; had we used simple brute force, it would take a search of a 61^5 search space. We used genetic algorithms to optimize the CNN architecture; again note that, with *19* possible bits, the search space is 2^{19}. Then, we used it to find the optimum hyperparameters for an LSTM network.

In the next chapter, we will talk about another intriguing learning paradigm: reinforcement learning. This is another natural learning paradigm, in the sense that in nature we normally do not have supervised learning; rather, we learn through our interactions with the environment. In the same manner, here the agent is not told anything except the rewards and punishments it receives from the environment after its action.

Reinforcement Learning for IoT 6

Reinforcement learning (RL) is very different from both supervised and unsupervised learning. It's the way most living beings learn—interacting with the environment. In this chapter, we'll study different algorithms employed for RL. As you progress through the chapter, you'll do the following:

- Learn what RL is and how it's different from supervised learning and unsupervised learning
- Lear different elements of RL
- Learn about some fascinating applications of RL in the real world
- Understand the OpenAI interface for training RL agents
- Learn about Q-learning and use it to train an RL agent
- Learn about Deep Q-Networks and employ them to train an agent to play Atari
- Learn about the policy gradient algorithm and use it to

Introduction

Have you ever observed infants and how they learn to turn over, sit up, crawl, and even stand? Have you watched how baby birds learn to fly—the parents throw them out of the nest, they flutter for some time, and they slowly learn to fly. All of this learning involves a component of the following:

- **Trial and error**: The baby tries different ways and is unsuccessful many times before finally succeeding in doing it.
- **Goal-oriented**: All of the efforts are toward reaching a particular goal. The goal for the human baby can be to crawl, and for baby bird to fly.
- **Interaction with the environment**: The only feedback that they get is from the environment.

This YouTube video is a beautiful video of a child learning to crawl and the stages in between `https://www.youtube.com/watch?v=f3xWaOkXCSQ`.

The human baby learning to crawl or baby bird learning to fly are both examples of RL in nature.

RL (in Artificial Intelligence) can be defined as a computational approach to goal-directed learning and decision-making, from interaction with the environment, under some idealized conditions. Let's elaborate upon this since we'll be using various computer algorithms to perform the learning—it's a computational approach. In all of the examples that we'll consider, the agent (learner) has a specific goal, which it's trying to achieve—it's a goal-directed approach. The agent in RL isn't given any explicit instructions, it learns only from its interaction with the environment. This interaction with the environment, as shown in the following diagram, is a cyclic process. The **Agent** can sense the state of the **Environment**, and the **Agent** can perform specific well-defined actions on the **Environment**; this causes two things: first, a change in the state of the environment, and second, a reward is generated (under ideal conditions). This cycle continues:

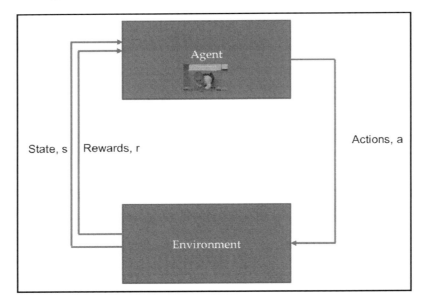

The interaction between agent and environment

Unlike supervised learning, the **Agent** isn't presented with any examples. The **Agent** doesn't know what the correct action is. And unlike unsupervised learning, the agent goal isn't to find some inherent structure in the input (the learning may find some structure, but that isn't the goal); instead, its goal is to maximize the rewards (in the long run).

RL terminology

Before learning different algorithms, let's accustom ourselves to the RL terminology. For illustration purposes, let's consider two examples: an agent finding a route in a maze and an agent steering the wheel of a **Self-Driving Car** (**SDC**). The two are illustrated in the following diagram:

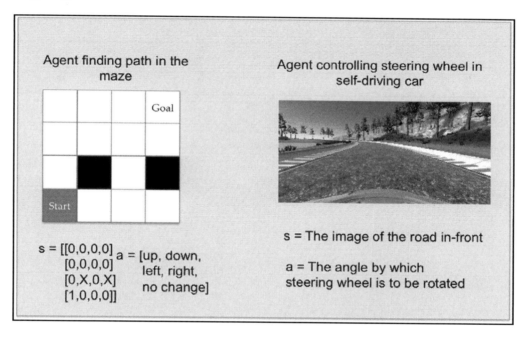

Two example RL scenarios

Before going further, let's acquaint ourselves with common RL terms:

- **States s**: The states can be thought of as a set of tokens (or representation) that can define all of the possible states the environment can be in. The state can be continuous or discrete. For example, in the case of an agent finding a path through a maze, the state can be represented by a 4×4 array, with a **0** representing an empty block, **1** representing a block occupied by the agent, and **X** the state that can't be occupied; the states here are discrete in nature. In the case of an agent steering the wheel, the state is the view in front of the SDC. The image contains continuous valued pixels.

- **Actions $a(s)$**: Actions are the set of all possible things that the agent can do in a particular state. The set of possible actions, a, depends on the present state, s. Actions may or may not result in the change of state. They can be discrete or continuous. The agent in the maze can perform five discrete actions **[up, down, left, right, no change]**. The SDC agent, on another hand, can rotate the steering wheel in a continuous range of angles.

- **Reward $r(s, a, s')$**: It's a scalar value returned by the environment when the agent selects an action. It defines the goal; the agent gets a higher reward if the action brings it near the goal, and a low (or even negative) reward otherwise. How we define a reward is totally up to us—in the case of the maze, we can define the reward as the Euclidean distance between the agent's current position and goal. The SDC agent reward can be that the car is on the road (positive reward) or off the road (negative reward).

- **Policy $\pi(s)$**: It defines a mapping between each state and the action to take in that state. The policy can be deterministic—that is, for each state a well-defined policy. Like for the maze agent, a policy can be that if the top block is empty, move up. The policy can also be stochastic—that is, where an action is taken by some probability. It can be implemented as a simple look-up table, or it can be a function dependent on the present state. The policy is the core of the RL agent. In this chapter, we'll learn about different algorithms that help the agent to learn the policy.

- **Value function $V(s)$**: It defines the goodness of a state in the long run. It can be thought of as the total amount of reward the agent can expect to accumulate over the future, starting from the state s. You can think of it as long-term goodness as opposed to the immediate goodness of rewards. What do you think is more important, maximizing the reward or maximizing the value function? Yes, you guessed right: just as in chess, we sometimes lose a pawn to win the game a few steps later, and so the agent should try to maximize the value function. There are two ways in which the value function is normally considered:

  - **Value function $V^\pi(s)$**: It's the goodness of state following the policy π. Mathematically, at state s, it's the expected cumulative reward from following the policy, π:

$$V^\pi(s) = E\left[\sum_{t \geqslant 0} \gamma^t r_t | s_0 = s, \pi\right]$$

- **Value-state function (or Q-function) $Q^\pi(s, a)$**: It's the goodness of a state s, taking action a, and thereafter following policy π. Mathematically, we can say that for a state-action pair (s, a), it's the expected cumulative reward from taking action a in state s and then following policy π:

$$Q^\pi(s, a) = E\left[\sum_{t \geqslant 0} \gamma^t r_t | s_0 = s, a_0 = a, \pi\right]$$

γ is the discount factor, and its value determines how much importance we give to the immediate rewards as compared to rewards received later on. A high value of discount factor decides how far into the future an agent can see. An ideal choice of γ in many successful RL algorithms has been a value of 0.97.

- **Model of the environment**: It's an optional element. It mimics the behavior of the environment, and it contains the physics of the environment; in other words, it defines how the environment will behave. The model of the environment is defined by the transition probability to the next state.

An RL problem is mathematically formulated as a **Markov Decision Process** (**MDP**), and it follows the Markov property— that is, *the current state completely characterizes the state of the world.*

Deep reinforcement learning

RL algorithms can be classified into two, based on what they iterate/approximate:

- **Value-based methods**: In these methods, the algorithms take the action that maximizes the value function. The agent here learns to predict how good a given state or action would be. Hence, here, the aim is to find the optimal value. An example of the value-based method is Q-learning. Consider, for example, our RL agent in a maze: assuming that the value of each state is the negative of the number of steps needed to reach from that box to the goal, then, at each time step, the agent will choose the action that takes it to a state with optimal value, as in the following diagram. So, starting from a value of **-6**, it'll move to **-5, -4, -3, -2, -1**, and eventually reach the goal with the value **0**:

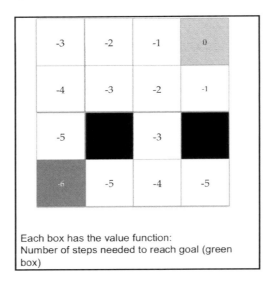

The maze world with the value of each box

- **Policy-based methods**: In these methods, the algorithms predict the best policy which maximizes the value function. The aim is to find the optimal policy. An example of the policy-based method is policy gradients. Here, we approximate the policy function, which allows us to map each state to the best corresponding action.

We can use neural networks as a function approximator to get an approximate value of either policy or value. When we use deep neural networks as a policy approximator or value approximator, we call it **deep reinforcement learning** (**DRL**). DRL has, in the recent past, given very successful results, hence, in this chapter, our will focus will be on DRL.

Some successful applications

In the last few years, RL has been successfully used in a variety of tasks, especially in game-playing and robotics. Let's acquaint ourselves with some success stories of RL before learning its algorithms:

- **AlphaGo Zero**: Developed by Google's DeepMind team, the AlphaGo Zero *Mastering the game of Go without any human knowledge*, starts from an absolutely blank slate (**tabula rasa**). The AlphaGo Zero uses one neural network to approximate both the move probabilities and value. This neural network takes as input the raw board representation. It uses a Monte Carlo Tree search guided by the neural network to select the moves. The reinforcement learning algorithm incorporates look-ahead search inside the training loop. It was trained for 40 days using a 40-block residual CNN and, over the course of training, it played about 29 million games (a big number!). The neural network was optimized on Google Cloud using TensorFlow, with 64 GPU workers and 19 CPU parameter servers. You can access the paper here: https://www.nature.com/articles/nature24270.

- **AI-controlled sailplanes**: Microsoft developed a controller system that can run on many different autopilot hardware platforms such as Pixhawk and Raspberry Pi 3. It can keep the sailplane in the air without using a motor, by autonomously finding and catching rides on naturally occurring thermals. The controller helps the sailplane to operate on its own; it detects and uses thermals to travel without the aid of a motor or a person. They implemented it as a partially observable MDP. They employ the Bayesian reinforcement learning and use the Monte Carlo tree search to search for the best action. They've divided the whole system into level planners—a high-level planer that makes a decision based on experience and a low-level planner that uses Bayesian reinforcement learning to detect and latch onto thermals in real time. You can see the sailplane in action at Microsoft News: https://news.microsoft.com/features/science-mimics-nature-microsoft-researchers-test-ai-controlled-soaring-machine/.

- **Locomotion behavior**: In the paper *Emergence of Locomotion Behaviours in Rich Environments* (`https://arxiv.org/pdf/1707.02286.pdf`), DeepMind researchers provided the agents with rich and diverse environments. The environments presented a spectrum of challenges at different levels of difficulty. The agent was provided with difficulties in increasing order; this led the agent to learn sophisticated locomotion skills without performing any reward engineering.

Simulated environments

Since RL involves trial and error, it makes sense to train our RL agent first in a simulated environment. While a large number of applications exist that can be used for the creation of an environment, some popular ones include the following:

- **OpenAI gym**: It contains a collection of environments that we can use to train our RL agents. In this chapter, we'll be using the OpenAI gym interface.
- **Unity ML-Agents SDK**: It allows developers to transform games and simulations created using the Unity editor into environments where intelligent agents can be trained using DRL, evolutionary strategies, or other machine learning methods through a simple-to-use Python API. It works with TensorFlow and provides the ability to train intelligent agents for two-dimensional/three-dimensional and VR/AR games. You can learn more about it here: `https://github.com/Unity-Technologies/ml-agents`.
- **Gazebo**: In Gazebo, we can build three-dimensional worlds with physics-based simulation. Gazebo along with **Robot Operating System (ROS)** and the OpenAI gym interface is gym-gazebo and can be used to train RL agents. To know more about this, you can refer to the whitepaper: `http://erlerobotics.com/whitepaper/robot_gym.pdf`.
- **Blender learning environment**: It's a Python interface for the Blender game engine, and it also works over OpenAI gym. It has it's base Blender. A free three-dimensional modeling software with an integrated game engine, this provides an easy-to-use, powerful set of tools for creating games. It provides an interface to the Blender game engine, and the games themselves are designed in Blender. We can then create the custom virtual environment to train an RL agent on a specific problem (`https://github.com/LouisFoucard/gym-blender`).

OpenAI gym

OpenAI gym is an open source toolkit to develop and compare RL algorithms. It contains a variety of simulated environments that can be used to train agents and develop new RL algorithms. To start, you'll first have to install `gym`. For Python 3.5+, you can install `gym` using `pip`:

```
pip install gym
```

OpenAI gym supports various environments, from simple text-based to three-dimensional. The environments supported in the latest version can be grouped as follows:

- **Algorithms**: It contains environments that involve performing computations such as addition. While we can easily perform the computations on a computer, what makes these problems interesting as an RL problem is that the agent learns these tasks purely by example.
- **Atari**: This environment provides a wide variety of classical Atari/arcade games.
- **Box2D**: It contains robotics tasks in two dimensions such as a car racing agent or bipedal robot walk.
- **Classic control**: This contains the classical control theory problems, such as balancing a cart pole.
- **MuJoCo**: This is proprietary (you can get a one-month free trial). It supports various robot simulation tasks. The environment includes a physics engine, hence, it's used for training robotic tasks.
- **Robotics**: This environment too uses the physics engine of MuJoCo. It simulates goal-based tasks for fetch and shadow-hand robots.
- **Toy text**: It's a simple text-based environment—very good for beginners.

To get a complete list of environments under these groups, you can visit: `https://gym.openai.com/envs/#atari`. The best part of the OpenAI interface is that all of the environments can be accessed with the same minimum interface. To get a list of all available environments in your installation, you can use the following code:

```
from gym import envs
print(envs.registry.all())
```

This will provide a list of all installed environments along with their environment ID, which is a string. It's also possible to add your own environment in the `gym` registry. To create an environment, we use the `make` command with the environment name passed as a string. For example, to create a game using the Pong environment, the string we need will be `Pong-v0`. The `make` command creates the environment, and the `reset` command is used to activate the environment. The `reset` command returns the environment in an initial state. The state is represented as an array:

```
import gym
env = gym.make('Pong-v0')
obs = env.reset()
env.render()
```

The state space of `Pong-v0` is given by an array of the size 210×160×3, which actually represents the raw pixel values for the Pong game. On the other hand, if you create a **Go9×9-v0** environment, the state is defined by a 3×9×9 array. We can visualize the environment using the `render` command. The following diagram shows the rendered environment for the **Pong-v0** and **Go9x9-v0** environments at the initial state:.

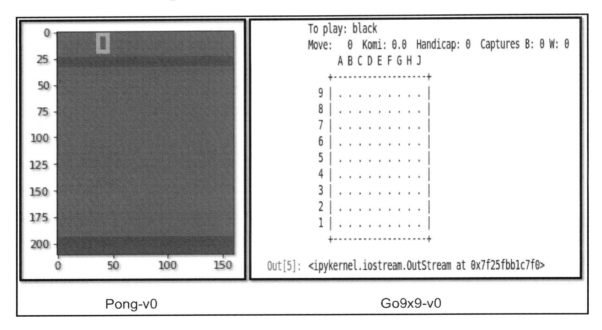

The rendered environments for Pong-v0 and Go9x9-v0

The `render` commands pop up a window. If you want to display the environment inline, then you can use Matplotlib inline and change the `render` command to `plt.imshow(env.render(mode='rgb_array'))`. This will show the environment inline in the Jupyter Notebook.

The environment contains the `action_space` variable, which determines the possible actions in the environment. We can select a random action using the `sample()` function. The selected action can affect the environment using the `step` function. The `step` function performs the selected action on the environment; it returns the changed state, the reward, a Boolean informing whether the game is over or not, and some information about the environment that can be useful for debugging, but isn't used while working with RL agents. The following code shows a game of Pong with the agent playing a random move. We're storing the state at each time step in an array, `frames`, so that we can later see the game:

```
frames = [] # array to store state space at each step
for _ in range(300):
    frames.append(env.render(mode='rgb_array'))
    obs,reward,done, _ = env.render(env.action_space.sample())
    if done:
        break
```

These frames can be displayed as a continuously playing GIF-style image in the Jupyter Notebook with the help of the animation function in Matplotlib and IPython:

```
import matplotlib.animation as animation
from JSAnimation.Ipython_display import display_animation
from IPython.display import display

patch = plt.imshow(frames[0])
plt.axis('off')

def animate(i)
    patch.set_data(frames[i])

anim = animation.FuncAnimation(plt.gcf(), animate, \
        frames=len(frames), interval=100)

display(display_animation(anim, default_mode='loop')
```

Normally, to train an agent, we'll need a very large number of steps, and so it won't be feasible to store the state space at each step. We can either choose to store after every 500th (or any other number you wish) step in the preceding algorithm. Instead, we can use the OpenAI gym wrapper to save the game as a video. To do so, we need to first import wrappers, then create the environment, and finally use Monitor. By default, it will store the video of 1, 8, 27, 64, and so on and then every 1,000[th] episode (episode numbers with perfect cubes); each training, by default, is saved in one folder. The code to do it is as follows:

```
import gym
from gym import wrappers
env = gym.make('Pong-v0')
env = wrappers.Monitor(env, '/save-mov', force=True)
# Follow it with the code above where env is rendered and agent
# selects a random action
```

If you want to use the same folder in the next training, you can choose the `force=True` option in the `Monitor` method call. In the end, we should close the environment using the `close` function:

```
env.close()
```

The preceding codes are available in the `OpenAI_practice.ipynb` Jupyter Notebook in the folder for `Chapter 6`, *Reinforcement Learning for IoT*, in GitHub.

Q-learning

In his doctoral thesis, *Learning from delayed rewards*, Watkins introduced the concept of Q-learning in the year 1989. The goal of Q-learning is to learn an optimal action selection policy. Given a specific state, *s*, and taking a specific action, *a*, Q-learning attempts to learn the value of the state *s*. In its simplest version, Q-learning can be implemented with the help of look-up tables. We maintain a table of values for every state (row) and action (column) possible in the environment. The algorithm attempts to learn the value—that is, how good it is to take a particular action in the given state.

We start by initializing all of the entries in the Q-table to *0*; this ensures all states a uniform (and hence equal chance) value. Later, we observe the rewards obtained by taking a particular action and, based on the rewards, we update the Q-table. The update in Q-value is performed dynamically with the help of **the Bellman Equation,** given by the following:

$$Q(s_t, a_t) = (1 - \alpha)Q(s_t, a_t) + \alpha(r_t + \gamma max_a Q(s_{t+1}, a_t))$$

Here, α is the learning rate. This shows the basic Q-learning algorithm:

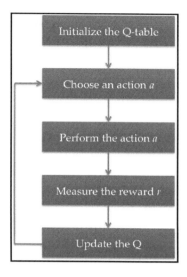

Simple Q-learning algorithm

 If you're interested, you can read the 240 pages Watkins doctoral thesis here: http://www.cs.rhul.ac.uk/~chrisw/new_thesis.pdf.

At the end of learning, we'll have a good Q-table, with optimal policy. An important question here is: how do we choose the action at the second step? There are two alternatives; first, we choose the action randomly. This allows our agent to explore all of the possible actions with equal probability but, at the same time, ignoring the information it has already learned. The second way is we choose the action for which the value is maximum; initially, all of the actions have the same Q-value but, as the agent will learn, some actions will get high value and others low value. In this case, the agent is exploiting the knowledge it has already learned. So what's better: exploration or exploitation? This is called the **exploration-exploitation trade-off**. A natural way to solve this problem is by relying on what the agent has learned, but at the same time sometimes just explore. This is achieved via the use of the **epsilon greedy algorithm**. The basic idea is that the agent chooses the actions randomly with the probability, ε, and exploits the information learned in previous episodes by a probability, *(1-ε)*. The algorithm chooses the best option (greedy) most of the time *(1-ε)* but sometimes *(ε)* it makes a random choice. Let's now try to implement what we learned in a simple problem.

Taxi drop-off using Q-tables

The simple Q-learning algorithm involves maintaining a table of the size $m \times n$, where m is the total number of states and n the total number of possible actions. Therefore, we choose a problem from the toy-text group since their `state` space and `action` space is small. For illustrative purposes, we choose the `Taxi-v2` environment. The goal of our agent is to choose the passenger at one location and drop them off at another. The agent receives *+20* points for a successful drop-off and loses *1* point for every time step it takes. There's also a 10-point penalty for illegal pick-up and drop-off. The state space has walls shown by | and four location marks, **R**, **G**, **Y**, and **B** respectively. The taxi is shown by box: the pick-up and drop-off location can be either of these four location marks. The pick-up point is colored blue, and the drop-off is colored purple. The `Taxi-v2` environment has a state space of size *500* and action space of size *6*, making a Q-table with *500×6=3000* entries:

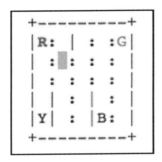

Taxi drop-off environment

In the taxi drop-off environment, the taxi is denoted by the yellow box. The location mark, **R**, is the pick-up position, and **G** is the drop-off location:

1. We start by importing the necessary modules and creating our environment. Since, here, we just need to make a look-up table, using TensorFlow won't be necessary. As mentioned previously, the `Taxi-v2` environment has *500* possible states and *6* possible actions:

```
import gym
import numpy as np
env = gym.make('Taxi-v2')
obs = env.reset()
env.render()
```

2. We initialize the Q-table of the size (*300×6*) with all zeros, and define the hyperparameters: γ, the discount factor, and α, the learning rate. We also set the values for maximum episodes (one episode means one complete run from reset to done=True) and maximum steps in an episode the agent will learn for:

```
m = env.observation_space.n # size of the state space
n = env.action_space.n # size of action space
print("The Q-table will have {} rows and {} columns, resulting in \
        total {} entries".format(m,n,m*n))

# Intialize the Q-table and hyperparameters
Q = np.zeros([m,n])
gamma = 0.97
max_episode = 1000
max_steps = 100
alpha = 0.7
epsilon = 0.3
```

3. Now, for each episode, we choose the action with the highest value, perform the action, and update the Q-table based on the received rewards and future state using the Bellman Equation:

```
for i in range(max_episode):
    # Start with new environment
    s = env.reset()
    done = False
    for _ in range(max_steps):
        # Choose an action based on epsilon greedy algorithm
        p = np.random.rand()
        if p > epsilon or (not np.any(Q[s,:])):
            a = env.action_space.sample() #explore
        else:
            a = np.argmax(Q[s,:]) # exploit
        s_new, r, done, _ = env.step(a)
        # Update Q-table
        Q[s,a] = (1-alpha)*Q[s,a] + alpha*(r +
gamma*np.max(Q[s_new,:]))
        #print(Q[s,a],r)
        s = s_new
        if done:
            break
```

4. Let's now see how the learned agent works:

```
s = env.reset()
done = False
env.render()
```

```
# Test the learned Agent
for i in range(max_steps):
 a = np.argmax(Q[s,:])
 s, _, done, _ = env.step(a)
 env.render()
 if done:
 break
```

The following diagram shows the agent behavior in a particular example. The empty car is shown as a yellow box, and the car with the passenger is shown by a green box. You can see that, in the given case, the agent picks up and drops off the passenger in 11 steps, and the desired location is marked (**B**) and the destination is marked (**R**):

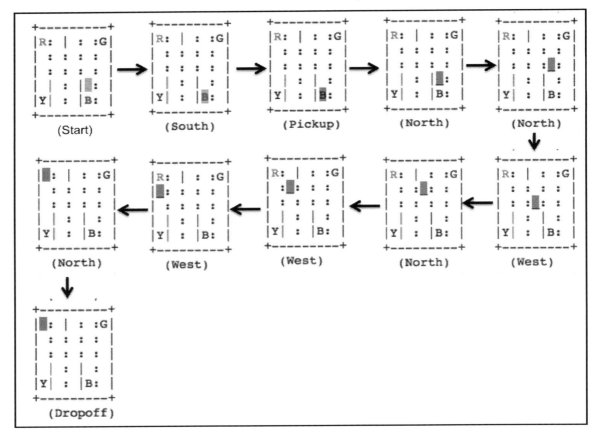

Agent picking up and dropping off a passenger using the learned Q-table

Cool, right? The complete code is available in the `Taxi_drop-off.ipynb` file available at GitHub.

Q-Network

The simple Q-learning algorithm involves maintaining a table of the size *m×n*, where *m* is the total number of states and *n* the total number of possible actions. This means we can't use it for large state space and action space. An alternative is to replace the table with a neural network acting as a function approximator, approximating the Q-function for each possible action. The weights of the neural network in this case store the Q-table information (they match a given state with the corresponding action and its Q-value). When the neural network that we use to approximate the Q-function is a deep neural network, we call it a **Deep Q-Network (DQN)**.

The neural network takes the state as its input and calculates the Q-value of all of the possible actions.

Taxi drop-off using Q-Network

If we consider the preceding *Taxi drop-off* example, our neural network will consist of *500* input neurons (the state represented by *1×500* one-hot vector) and *6* output neurons, each neuron representing the Q-value for the particular action for the given state. The neural network will here approximate the Q-value for each action. Hence, the network should be trained so that its approximated Q-value and the target Q-value are same. The target Q-value as obtained from the Bellman Equation is as follows:

$$Q_{target} = r + \gamma max_a Q(s_{t+1}, a_t)$$

We train the neural network so that the square error of the difference between the target Q and predicted Q is minimized—that is, the neural network minimizes the following loss function:

$$loss = E_\pi \left[Q_{target}(s,a) - Q_{pred}(s.W,a) \right]$$

The aim is to learn the unknown Q_{target} function. The weights of QNetwork are updated using backpropagation so that this loss is minimized. We make the neural network, QNetwork, to approximate the Q-value. It's a very simple single-layer neural network, with methods to provide action and their Q-values (get_action), train the network (learnQ), and get the predicted Q-value (Qnew):

```
class QNetwork:
    def __init__(self,m,n,alpha):
        self.s = tf.placeholder(shape=[1,m], dtype=tf.float32)
        W = tf.Variable(tf.random_normal([m,n], stddev=2))
        bias = tf.Variable(tf.random_normal([1, n]))
        self.Q = tf.matmul(self.s,W) + bias
        self.a = tf.argmax(self.Q,1)

        self.Q_hat = tf.placeholder(shape=[1,n],dtype=tf.float32)
        loss = tf.reduce_sum(tf.square(self.Q_hat-self.Q))
        optimizer = tf.train.GradientDescentOptimizer(learning_rate=alpha)
        self.train = optimizer.minimize(loss)
        init = tf.global_variables_initializer()

        self.sess = tf.Session()
        self.sess.run(init)

    def get_action(self,s):
        return self.sess.run([self.a,self.Q], feed_dict={self.s:s})

    def learnQ(self,s,Q_hat):
        self.sess.run(self.train, feed_dict= {self.s:s, self.Q_hat:Q_hat})

    def Qnew(self,s):
        return self.sess.run(self.Q, feed_dict={self.s:s})
```

We now incorporate this neural network in our earlier code where we trained an RL agent for the *Taxi drop-off* problem. We'll need to make some changes; first, the state returned by the OpenAI step and reset function in this case is just the numeric identification of state, so we need to convert it into a one-hot vector. Also, instead of a Q-table update, we'll now get the new Q-predicted from QNetwork, find the target Q, and train the network so as to minimize the loss. The code is as follows:

```
QNN = QNetwork(m,n, alpha)
rewards = []
for i in range(max_episode):
 # Start with new environment
 s = env.reset()
 S = np.identity(m)[s:s+1]
 done = False
 counter = 0
 rtot = 0
 for _ in range(max_steps):
 # Choose an action using epsilon greedy policy
 a, Q_hat = QNN.get_action(S)
 p = np.random.rand()
 if p > epsilon:
 a[0] = env.action_space.sample() #explore

 s_new, r, done, _ = env.step(a[0])
 rtot += r
 # Update Q-table
 S_new = np.identity(m)[s_new:s_new+1]
 Q_new = QNN.Qnew(S_new)
 maxQ = np.max(Q_new)
 Q_hat[0,a[0]] = r + gamma*maxQ
 QNN.learnQ(S,Q_hat)
 S = S_new
 #print(Q_hat[0,a[0]],r)
 if done:
 break
 rewards.append(rtot)
print ("Total reward per episode is: " + str(sum(rewards)/max_episode))
```

This should have done a good job but, as you can see, even after training for *1,000* episodes, the network has a high negative reward, and if you check the performance of the network, it appears to just take random steps. Yes, our network hasn't learned anything; the performance is worse than Q-table. This can also be verified from the reward plot while training—ideally, the rewards should increase as the agent learns, but nothing of the sort happens here; the rewards increase and decrease like a random walk around the mean (the complete code for this program is in the `Taxi_drop-off_NN.ipynb` file available at GitHub):

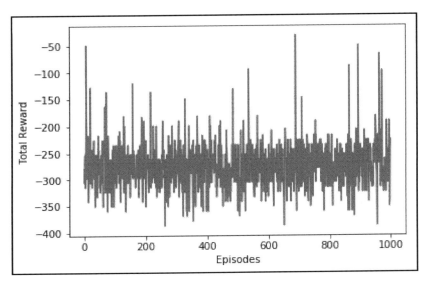

Total reward per episode obtained by the agent as it learns

What happened? Why is the neural network failing to learn, and can we make it better?

Consider the scenario when the taxi should go west to pick up and, randomly, the agent chose west; the agent gets a reward and the network will learn that, in the present state (represented by a one-hot vector), going west is favorable. Next, consider another state similar to this one (correlated state space): the agent again makes the west move, but this time it results in a negative reward, so now the agent will unlearn what it had learned earlier. Hence, similar state-actions but divergent targets confuse the learning process. This is called **catastrophic forgetting**. The problem arises here because consecutive states are highly correlated and so, if the agent learns in sequence (as it does here), this extremely correlated input state space won't let the agent learn.

Can we break the correlation between the input presented to the network? Yes, we can: we can construct a **replay buffer**, where we first store each state, its corresponding action, and the consecutive reward and resultant state (state, action, reward, new state). The actions, in this case, are chosen completely randomly, thereby ensuring a wide range of actions and resultant states. The replay buffer will finally consist of a large list of these tuples (S, A, R, S'). Next, we present the network with these tuples randomly (instead of sequentially); this randomness will break the correlation between consecutive input states. This is called **experience replay**. It not only resolves the issues with correlation in input state space but also allows us to learn from the same tuples more than once, recall rare occurrences, and in general, make better use of the experience. In one way, you can say that, by using a replay buffer, we've reduced the problem of the supervised learning (with the replay buffer as an input-output dataset), where the random sampling of input ensures that the network is able to generalize.

Another problem with our approach is that we're updating the target Q immediately. This too can cause harmful correlations. Remember that, in Q-learning, we're trying to minimize the difference between the Q_{target} and the currently predicted Q. This difference is called a **temporal difference** (TD) error (and hence Q-learning is a type of **TD learning**). At present, we update our Q_{target} immediately, hence there exists a correlation between the target and the parameters we're changing (weights through Q_{pred}). This is almost like chasing a moving target and hence won't give a generalized direction. We can resolve the issue by using **fixed Q-targets**—that is, use two networks, one for predicting Q and another for target Q. Both are exactly the same in terms of architecture, with the predicting Q-Network changing weights at each step, but the weight of the target Q-Network is updated after some fixed learning steps. This provides a more stable learning environment.

Finally, we make one more small change: right now our epsilon has had a fixed value throughout learning. But, in real life, this isn't so. Initially, when we know nothing, we explore a lot but, as we become familiar, we tend to take the learned path. The same can be done in our epsilon-greedy algorithm, by changing the value of epsilon as the network learns through each episode, so that epsilon decreases with time.

Equipped with these tricks, let's now build a DQN to play an Atari game.

DQN to play an Atari game

The DQN we'll learn here is based on a DeepMind paper (https://web.stanford.edu/class/psych209/Readings/MnihEtAlHassibis15NatureControlDeepRL.pdf). At the heart of DQN is a deep convolutional neural network that takes as input the raw pixels of the game environment (just like any human player would see), captured one screen at a time, and as output, returns the value for each possible action. The action with the maximum value is the chosen action:

1. The first step is to get all of the modules we'll need:

```
import gym
import sys
import random
import numpy as np
import tensorflow as tf
import matplotlib.pyplot as plt
from datetime import datetime
from scipy.misc import imresize
```

2. We chose the Breakout game from the list of OpenAI Atari games—you can try the code for other Atari games; the only change you may need to do would be in the preprocessing step. The input space of Breakout—our input space—consists of 210×160 pixels, with 128 possible colors for each pixel. It's an enormously large input space. To reduce the complexity, we'll choose a region of interest in the image, convert it into grayscale, and resize it to an image of the size *80×80*. We do this using the preprocess function:

```
def preprocess(img):
    img_temp = img[31:195] # Choose the important area of the image
    img_temp = img_temp.mean(axis=2) # Convert to Grayscale#
    # Downsample image using nearest neighbour interpolation
    img_temp = imresize(img_temp, size=(IM_SIZE, IM_SIZE),
interp='nearest')
    return img_temp
```

The following screenshot shows the environment before and after the preprocessing:

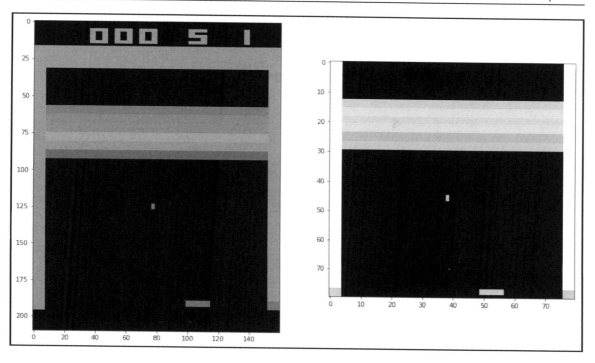

The original environment, size 210× 160 (colored image) and the processed environment, size 80×80 (grayscale)

3. As you can see from the preceding diagram, it isn't possible to tell whether the ball is coming down or going up. To deal with this problem, we combine four consecutive states (due to four unique actions) as one input. We define a function, update_state, that appends the current environment observation to the previous state array:

```
def update_state(state, obs):
    obs_small = preprocess(obs)
    return np.append(state[1:], np.expand_dims(obs_small, 0),
axis=0)
```

The function appends the processed new state in the sliced state, ensuring that the final input to the network consists of four frames. In the following screenshot, you can see the four consecutive frames. This is the input to our DQN:

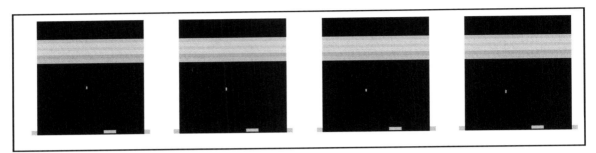

The input to DQN four consecutive game-states (frames)

4. We create a DQN that we define in the class DQN; it consists of three convolutional layers, the output of the last convolutional layer is flattened, and it's then followed by two fully connected layers. The network, as in the previous case, tries to minimize the difference between Q_{target} and $Q_{predicted}$. In the code, we're using the RMSProp optimizer, but you can play around with other optimizers:

```
def __init__(self, K, scope, save_path= 'models/atari.ckpt'):
    self.K = K
    self.scope = scope
    self.save_path = save_path
    with tf.variable_scope(scope):
        # inputs and targets
        self.X = tf.placeholder(tf.float32, shape=(None, 4,
IM_SIZE, IM_SIZE), name='X')
        # tensorflow convolution needs the order to be:
        # (num_samples, height, width, "color")
        # so we need to tranpose later
        self.Q_target = tf.placeholder(tf.float32, shape=(None,),
name='G')
        self.actions = tf.placeholder(tf.int32, shape=(None,),
name='actions')
        # calculate output and cost
        # convolutional layers
        Z = self.X / 255.0
        Z = tf.transpose(Z, [0, 2, 3, 1])
        cnn1 = tf.contrib.layers.conv2d(Z, 32, 8, 4,
activation_fn=tf.nn.relu)
        cnn2 = tf.contrib.layers.conv2d(cnn1, 64, 4, 2,
activation_fn=tf.nn.relu)
        cnn3 = tf.contrib.layers.conv2d(cnn2, 64, 3, 1,
```

```
activation_fn=tf.nn.relu)
        # fully connected layers
        fc0 = tf.contrib.layers.flatten(cnn3)
        fc1 = tf.contrib.layers.fully_connected(fc0, 512)
        # final output layer
        self.predict_op = tf.contrib.layers.fully_connected(fc1, K)
        Qpredicted = tf.reduce_sum(self.predict_op *
tf.one_hot(self.actions, K),
    reduction_indices=[1])
        self.cost = tf.reduce_mean(tf.square(self.Q_target -
Qpredicted))
        self.train_op = tf.train.RMSPropOptimizer(0.00025, 0.99,
0.0, 1e-6).minimize(self.cost)
```

The necessary methods that we require for this class are discussed in the following steps:

5. We add a method to return the predicted Q-values:

```
def predict(self, states):
    return self.session.run(self.predict_op, feed_dict={self.X:
states})
```

6. We need a method to determine the action with maximum value. In this method, we also implemented the epsilon-greedy policy, and the value of epsilon is changed in the main code:

```
def sample_action(self, x, eps):
    """Implements epsilon greedy algorithm"""
    if np.random.random() < eps:
        return np.random.choice(self.K)
    else:
        return np.argmax(self.predict([x])[0])
```

7. We need a method to update the weights of the network so as to minimize the loss. The function can be defined as follows:

```
def update(self, states, actions, targets):
    c, _ = self.session.run(
        [self.cost, self.train_op],
        feed_dict={
        self.X: states,
        self.Q_target: targets,
        self.actions: actions
        })
    return c
```

8. Copy the model weights to the fixed Q-Network:

```
def copy_from(self, other):
    mine = [t for t in tf.trainable_variables() if
t.name.startswith(self.scope)]
    mine = sorted(mine, key=lambda v: v.name)
    theirs = [t for t in tf.trainable_variables() if
t.name.startswith(other.scope)]
    theirs = sorted(theirs, key=lambda v: v.name)
    ops = []
    for p, q in zip(mine, theirs):
        actual = self.session.run(q)
        op = p.assign(actual)
        ops.append(op)
    self.session.run(ops)
```

9. Besides these methods, we need some helper functions to save the learned network, load the saved network, and set the TensorFlow session:

```
def load(self):
    self.saver = tf.train.Saver(tf.global_variables())
    load_was_success = True
    try:
        save_dir = '/'.join(self.save_path.split('/')[:-1])
        ckpt = tf.train.get_checkpoint_state(save_dir)
        load_path = ckpt.model_checkpoint_path
        self.saver.restore(self.session, load_path)
    except:
        print("no saved model to load. starting new session")
        load_was_success = False
    else:
        print("loaded model: {}".format(load_path))
        saver = tf.train.Saver(tf.global_variables())
        episode_number = int(load_path.split('-')[-1])

def save(self, n):
    self.saver.save(self.session, self.save_path, global_step=n)
    print("SAVED MODEL #{}".format(n))

def set_session(self, session):
    self.session = session
    self.session.run(tf.global_variables_initializer())
    self.saver = tf.train.Saver()
```

10. To implement the DQN algorithm, we use a `learn` function; it picks a random sample from the experience replay buffer and updates the Q-Network, using target Q from the target Q-Network:

```
def learn(model, target_model, experience_replay_buffer, gamma,
batch_size):
    # Sample experiences
    samples = random.sample(experience_replay_buffer, batch_size)
    states, actions, rewards, next_states, dones = map(np.array,
zip(*samples))
    # Calculate targets
     next_Qs = target_model.predict(next_states)
     next_Q = np.amax(next_Qs, axis=1)
     targets = rewards +      np.invert(dones).astype(np.float32) *
gamma * next_Q
    # Update model
     loss = model.update(states, actions, targets)
     return loss
```

11. Well, all of the ingredients are ready, so let's now decide the hyperparameters for our DQN and create our environment:

```
# Some Global parameters
MAX_EXPERIENCES = 500000
MIN_EXPERIENCES = 50000
TARGET_UPDATE_PERIOD = 10000
IM_SIZE = 80
K = 4 # env.action_space.n

# hyperparameters etc
gamma = 0.97
batch_sz = 64
num_episodes = 2700
total_t = 0
experience_replay_buffer = []
episode_rewards = np.zeros(num_episodes)
last_100_avgs = []
# epsilon for Epsilon Greedy Algorithm
epsilon = 1.0
epsilon_min = 0.1
epsilon_change = (epsilon - epsilon_min) / 700000

# Create Atari Environment
env = gym.envs.make("Breakout-v0")

# Create original and target Networks
model = DQN(K=K, scope="model")
target_model = DQN(K=K, scope="target_model")
```

12. And finally, the following is the code that calls then fills the experience replay buffer, plays the game step by step, and trains the model network at every step and `target_model` after every four steps:

```
with tf.Session() as sess:
    model.set_session(sess)
    target_model.set_session(sess)
    sess.run(tf.global_variables_initializer())
    model.load()
    print("Filling experience replay buffer...")
    obs = env.reset()
    obs_small = preprocess(obs)
    state = np.stack([obs_small] * 4, axis=0)
    # Fill experience replay buffer
    for i in range(MIN_EXPERIENCES):
        action = np.random.randint(0,K)
        obs, reward, done, _ = env.step(action)
        next_state = update_state(state, obs)
        experience_replay_buffer.append((state, action, reward,
next_state, done))
        if done:
            obs = env.reset()
            obs_small = preprocess(obs)
            state = np.stack([obs_small] * 4, axis=0)
        else:
            state = next_state
    # Play a number of episodes and learn
    for i in range(num_episodes):
        t0 = datetime.now()
        # Reset the environment
        obs = env.reset()
        obs_small = preprocess(obs)
        state = np.stack([obs_small] * 4, axis=0)
        assert (state.shape == (4, 80, 80))
        loss = None
        total_time_training = 0
        num_steps_in_episode = 0
        episode_reward = 0
        done = False
        while not done:
            # Update target network
            if total_t % TARGET_UPDATE_PERIOD == 0:
                target_model.copy_from(model)
                print("Copied model parameters to target
network. total_t = %s, period = %s" % (total_t,
TARGET_UPDATE_PERIOD))
            # Take action
            action = model.sample_action(state, epsilon)
```

```
                obs, reward, done, _ = env.step(action)
                obs_small = preprocess(obs)
                next_state = np.append(state[1:],
np.expand_dims(obs_small, 0), axis=0)
                episode_reward += reward
                # Remove oldest experience if replay buffer is full
                if len(experience_replay_buffer) ==
MAX_EXPERIENCES:
                    experience_replay_buffer.pop(0)
                    # Save the recent experience
                    experience_replay_buffer.append((state, action,
reward, next_state, done))

                # Train the model and keep measure of time
                t0_2 = datetime.now()
                loss = learn(model, target_model,
experience_replay_buffer, gamma, batch_sz)
                dt = datetime.now() - t0_2
                total_time_training += dt.total_seconds()
                num_steps_in_episode += 1
                state = next_state
                total_t += 1
                epsilon = max(epsilon - epsilon_change,
epsilon_min)

                duration = datetime.now() - t0
                episode_rewards[i] = episode_reward
                time_per_step = total_time_training /
num_steps_in_episode
                last_100_avg = episode_rewards[max(0, i - 100):i +
1].mean()
                last_100_avgs.append(last_100_avg)
                print("Episode:", i,"Duration:", duration, "Num
steps:", num_steps_in_episode, "Reward:", episode_reward, "Training
time per step:", "%.3f" % time_per_step, "Avg Reward (Last 100):",
"%.3f" % last_100_avg,"Epsilon:", "%.3f" % epsilon)
                if i % 50 == 0:
                    model.save(i)
                sys.stdout.flush()

#Plots
plt.plot(last_100_avgs)
plt.xlabel('episodes')
plt.ylabel('Average Rewards')
plt.show()
env.close()
```

We can see that now the reward is increasing with episodes, with an average reward of **20** by the end, though it can be higher, then we had only learned few thousand episodes and even our replay buffer with a size between (50,00 to 5,000,000):

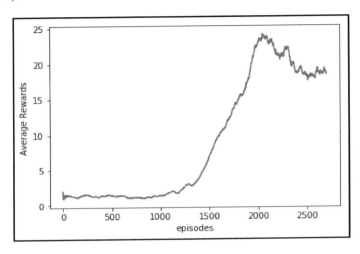

Average rewards as the agent learn

13. Let's see how our agent plays, after learning for about 2,700 episodes:

```
env = gym.envs.make("Breakout-v0")
frames = []
with tf.Session() as sess:
    model.set_session(sess)
    target_model.set_session(sess)
    sess.run(tf.global_variables_initializer())
    model.load()
    obs = env.reset()
    obs_small = preprocess(obs)
    state = np.stack([obs_small] * 4, axis=0)
    done = False
    while not done:
        action = model.sample_action(state, epsilon)
        obs, reward, done, _ = env.step(action)
        frames.append(env.render(mode='rgb_array'))
        next_state = update_state(state, obs)
        state = next_state
```

You can see the video of the learned agent here: `https://www.youtube.com/watch?v=rPy-3NodgCE`.

Cool, right? Without telling it anything, it learned to play a decent game after only 2,700 episodes.

There are some things that can help you to train the agent better:

- Since training takes a lot of time, unless you have a strong computational resource, it's better to save the model and restart the saved model.
- In the code, we used `Breakout-v0` and OpenAI gym, in this case, repeats the same step in the environment for consecutive (randomly chosen 1, 2, 3 or 4) frames. You can instead choose `BreakoutDeterministic-v4`, the one used by the DeepMind team; here, the steps are repeated for exactly four consecutive frames. The agent hence sees and selects the action after every fourth frame.

Double DQN

Now, recall that, we're using a max operator to both select an action and to evaluate an action. This can result in overestimated values for an action that may not be an ideal one. We can take care of this problem by decoupling the selection from evaluation. With Double DQN, we have two Q-Networks with different weights; both learn by random experience, but one is used to determine the action using the epsilon-greedy policy and the other to determine its value (hence, calculating the target Q).

To make it clearer, let's first see the case of the DQN. The action with maximum Q-value is selected; let W be the weight of the DQN, then what we're doing is as follows:

$$Q_{target} = r + \gamma max_a Q^W(s_{t+1}, argmax_a Q^W(s_t))$$

The superscript W tells the weights used to approximate the Q-value. In Double DQN, the equation changes to the following:

$$Q_{target} = r + \gamma max_a Q^{W'}(s_{t+1}, argmax_a Q^W(s_t))$$

Note the change: now the action is chosen using the Q-Network with the weights *W*, and max Q-value is predicted using a Q-Network with weights *W'*. This reduces the overestimation and helps us to train the agent quickly and more reliably. You can access the *Deep Reinforcement Learning with Double Q-Learning* paper here: https://www.aaai.org/ocs/index.php/AAAI/AAAI16/paper/download/12389/11847.

Dueling DQN

Dueling DQN decouples the Q-function into the value function and advantage function. The value function is the same as discussed earlier ; it represents the value of the state independent of action. The advantage function, on the other hand, provides a relative measure of the utility (advantage/goodness) of action *a* in the state *s*:

$$Q(s,a) = V^{\pi}(s) + A(s,a)$$

In Dueling DQN, the same convolutional is used to extract features but, in later stages, it's separated into two separate networks, one providing the value and another providing the advantage. Later, the two stages are recombined using an aggregating layer to estimate the Q-value. This ensures that the network produces separate estimates for the value function and the advantage function. The intuition behind this decoupling of value and advantage is that, for many states, it's unnecessary to estimate the value of each action choice. For example, in the car race, if there's no car in front, then the action turn left or turn right is not required and so there's no need to estimate the value of these actions on the given state. This allows it to learn which states are valuable, without having to determine the effect of each action for each state.

At the aggregate layer, the value and advantage are combined such that it's possible to recover both *V* and *A* uniquely from a given *Q*. This is achieved by enforcing that the advantage function estimator has zero advantage at the chosen action:

$$Q(s,a;\theta,\alpha,\beta) = V(s;\theta,\beta) + A(s,a;\theta,\alpha) - max_{a' \in |A|} A(s,a';\theta,\alpha)$$

Here, θ is the parameter of the common convolutional feature extractor, and α and β are the parameters for the advantage and value estimator network. The Dueling DQN too was proposed by Google's DeepMind team. You can read the complete paper at *arXiv*: https://arxiv.org/abs/1511.06581. The authors found that changing the preceding `max` operator with an average operator increases the stability of the network. The advantage, in this case, changes only as fast as the mean. Hence, in their results, they used the aggregate layer given by the following:

$$Q(s, a; \theta, \alpha, \beta) = V(s; \theta, \beta) + A(s, a; \theta, \alpha) - \frac{1}{|A|} \sum_{a'} A(s, a'; \theta, \alpha)$$

The following screenshot shows the basic architecture of a Dueling DQN:

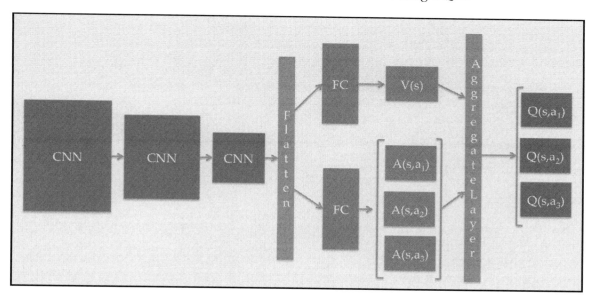

The basic architecture of Dueling DQN

Policy gradients

In the Q-learning-based methods, we generated a policy after estimating a value/Q-function. In policy-based methods, such as the policy gradient, we approximate the policy directly.

Continuing as earlier, here, we use a neural network to approximate the policy. In the simplest form, the neural network learns a policy for selecting the actions that maximize the rewards by adjusting its weights using steepest gradient ascent, hence the name policy gradients.

In policy gradients, the policy is represented by a neural network whose input is a representation of states and whose output is action selection probabilities. The weights of this network are the policy parameters that we need to learn. The natural question arises: how should we update the weights of this network? Since our goal is to maximize rewards, it makes sense that our network tries to maximize the expected rewards per episode:

$$J(\theta) = E\left[R|\pi(a|s,\theta)\right]$$

Here, we've taken a parametrized stochastic policy π—that is, the policy determines the probability of choosing an action a given state s, and the neural network parameters are θ. R represents the sum of all of the rewards in an episode. The network parameters are then updated using gradient ascent:

$$\theta_{t+1} = \theta_t + \eta \nabla_\theta J_\theta|_{\theta=\theta_t}$$

Here, η is the learning rate. Using the policy gradient theorem, we get the following:

$$\nabla_\theta J(\theta) \approx E\left[\sum_{t=0}^{T-1} r_t \sum_{t=0}^{T-1} \nabla_\theta log\pi(a_t|s_t,\theta)\right]$$

Hence, instead of maximizing the expected return, we can use loss function as log-loss (expected action and predicted action as labels and logits respectively) and the discounted reward as the weight to train the network. For more stability, it has been found that adding a baseline helps in variance reduction. The most common form of the baseline is the sum of the discounted rewards, resulting in the following:

$$\nabla_\theta J(\theta) \approx E\left[\sum_{t=0}^{T-1} \nabla_\theta log\pi(a_t|s_t,\theta) \left(\sum_{t'=t}^{T-1} \gamma^{t'-t} r^{t'} - b(s_t)\right)\right]$$

The baseline $b(s_t)$ is as follows:

$$b(s_t) \approx E\left[r_t + \gamma r_{t+1} + \gamma^2 r_{t+2} + \ldots + \gamma^{T-1-t} r_{T-1}\right]$$

Here, γ is the discount factor.

Why policy gradients?

Well, first of all, policy gradients, like other policy-based methods, directly estimate the optimal policy, without any need to store additional data (experience replay buffer). Hence, it's simple to implement. Secondly, we can train it to learn true stochastic policies. And finally, it's well suited for continuous action-space.

Pong using policy gradients

Let's try to use policy gradients to play a game of Pong. The Andrej Karpathy blog post, at http://karpathy.github.io/2016/05/31/rl/ inspires the implementation here. Recall that, in *Breakout*, we used four-game frames stacked together as input so that the game dynamics are known to the agent; here, we use the difference between two consecutive game frames as the input to the network. Hence, our agent has information about the present state and the previous state with it:

1. The first step, as always, is importing the modules necessary. We import TensorFlow, Numpy, Matplotlib, and gym for the environment:

```
import numpy as np
import gym
import matplotlib.pyplot as plt
import tensorflow as tf
from gym import wrappers
%matplotlib inline
```

2. We build our neural network, the `PolicyNetwork`; it takes as input the state of the game, and outputs the action selection probabilities. Here, we build a simple two-layered perceptron, with no biases. `weights` are initialized randomly using the `Xavier` initialization. The hidden layer uses the `ReLU` activation function, and the output layer uses the `softmax` activation function. We use the `tf_discount_rewards` method defined later to calculate the baseline. And finally, we've used TensorFlow `tf.losses.log_loss` with calculated action probabilities as predictions, and chosen one-hot action vector as labels and discounted reward corrected by variance as weight:

```
class PolicyNetwork(object):
    def __init__(self, N_SIZE, h=200, gamma=0.99, eta=1e-3,
decay=0.99, save_path = 'models1/pong.ckpt' ):
        self.gamma = gamma
        self.save_path = save_path
        # Placeholders for passing state....
        self.tf_x = tf.placeholder(dtype=tf.float32, shape=[None,
N_SIZE * N_SIZE], name="tf_x")
        self.tf_y = tf.placeholder(dtype=tf.float32, shape=[None,
n_actions], name="tf_y")
        self.tf_epr = tf.placeholder(dtype=tf.float32, shape=[None,
1], name="tf_epr")

        # Weights
        xavier_l1 = tf.truncated_normal_initializer(mean=0,
stddev=1. / N_SIZE, dtype=tf.float32)
        self.W1 = tf.get_variable("W1", [N_SIZE * N_SIZE, h],
initializer=xavier_l1)
        xavier_l2 = tf.truncated_normal_initializer(mean=0,
stddev=1. / np.sqrt(h), dtype=tf.float32)
        self.W2 = tf.get_variable("W2", [h, n_actions],
initializer=xavier_l2)

        #Build Computation
        # tf reward processing (need tf_discounted_epr for policy
gradient wizardry)
        tf_discounted_epr = self.tf_discount_rewards(self.tf_epr)
        tf_mean, tf_variance = tf.nn.moments(tf_discounted_epr,
[0], shift=None, name="reward_moments")
        tf_discounted_epr -= tf_mean
        tf_discounted_epr /= tf.sqrt(tf_variance + 1e-6)

        #Define Optimizer, compute and apply gradients
        self.tf_aprob = self.tf_policy_forward(self.tf_x)
        loss = tf.losses.log_loss(labels = self.tf_y,
        predictions = self.tf_aprob,
```

```
        weights = tf_discounted_epr)
        optimizer = tf.train.AdamOptimizer()
        self.train_op = optimizer.minimize(loss)
```

3. The class has methods to calculate the action probabilities (`tf_policy_forward` and `predict_UP`), calculate the baseline using `tf_discount_rewards`, update the weights of the network (`update`), and finally set the session (`set_session`), then load and save the model:

```
def set_session(self, session):
    self.session = session
    self.session.run(tf.global_variables_initializer())
    self.saver = tf.train.Saver()

def tf_discount_rewards(self, tf_r): # tf_r ~ [game_steps,1]
    discount_f = lambda a, v: a * self.gamma + v;
    tf_r_reverse = tf.scan(discount_f, tf.reverse(tf_r, [0]))
    tf_discounted_r = tf.reverse(tf_r_reverse, [0])
    return tf_discounted_r

def tf_policy_forward(self, x): #x ~ [1,D]
    h = tf.matmul(x, self.W1)
    h = tf.nn.relu(h)
    logp = tf.matmul(h, self.W2)
    p = tf.nn.softmax(logp)
    return p

def update(self, feed):
    return self.session.run(self.train_op, feed)

def load(self):
    self.saver = tf.train.Saver(tf.global_variables())
    load_was_success = True
    try:
        save_dir = '/'.join(self.save_path.split('/')[:-1])
        ckpt = tf.train.get_checkpoint_state(save_dir)
        load_path = ckpt.model_checkpoint_path
        print(load_path)
        self.saver.restore(self.session, load_path)
    except:
        print("no saved model to load. starting new session")
        load_was_success = False
    else:
        print("loaded model: {}".format(load_path))
```

```
        saver = tf.train.Saver(tf.global_variables())
        episode_number = int(load_path.split('-')[-1])


    def save(self):
        self.saver.save(self.session, self.save_path, global_step=n)
        print("SAVED MODEL #{}".format(n))

    def predict_UP(self,x):
        feed = {self.tf_x: np.reshape(x, (1, -1))}
        aprob = self.session.run(self.tf_aprob, feed);
        return aprob
```

4. Now that `PolicyNetwork` is made, we make a `preprocess` function to the game state; we won't process the complete 210×160 state space—instead, we'll reduce it to an 80×80 state space, in binary, and finally flatten it:

```
# downsampling
def preprocess(I):
    """
    prepro 210x160x3 uint8 frame into 6400 (80x80) 1D float vector
    """
    I = I[35:195] # crop
    I = I[::2,::2,0] # downsample by factor of 2
    I[I == 144] = 0 # erase background (background type 1)
    I[I == 109] = 0 # erase background (background type 2)
    I[I != 0] = 1 # everything else (paddles, ball) just set to 1
    return I.astype(np.float).ravel()
```

5. Let's define some variables that we'll require to hold state, labels, rewards, and action space size. We initialize the game state and instantiate the policy network:

```
# Create Game Environment
env_name = "Pong-v0"
env = gym.make(env_name)
env = wrappers.Monitor(env, '/tmp/pong', force=True)
n_actions = env.action_space.n # Number of possible actions
# Initializing Game and State(t-1), action, reward, state(t)
states, rewards, labels = [], [], []
obs = env.reset()
prev_state = None

running_reward = None
running_rewards = []
reward_sum = 0
n = 0
done = False
n_size = 80
```

```
num_episodes = 2500

#Create Agent
agent = PolicyNetwork(n_size)
```

6. Now we start the policy gradient algorithm. For each episode, the agent first plays the game, storing the states, rewards, and actions chosen. Once a game is over, it uses all of the stored data to train itself (just like in supervised learning). And it repeats this process for as many episodes as you want:

```
with tf.Session() as sess:
    agent.set_session(sess)
    sess.run(tf.global_variables_initializer())
    agent.load()
    # training loop
    done = False
    while not done and n< num_episodes:
        # Preprocess the observation
        cur_state = preprocess(obs)
        diff_state = cur_state - prev_state if prev_state isn't
None else np.zeros(n_size*n_size)
        prev_state = cur_state

        #Predict the action
        aprob = agent.predict_UP(diff_state) ; aprob = aprob[0,:]
        action = np.random.choice(n_actions, p=aprob)
        #print(action)
        label = np.zeros_like(aprob) ; label[action] = 1

        # Step the environment and get new measurements
        obs, reward, done, info = env.step(action)
        env.render()
        reward_sum += reward

        # record game history
        states.append(diff_state) ; labels.append(label) ;
rewards.append(reward)

        if done:
            # update running reward
            running_reward = reward_sum if running_reward is None
else    running_reward * 0.99 + reward_sum * 0.01
            running_rewards.append(running_reward)
            #print(np.vstack(rs).shape)
            feed = {agent.tf_x: np.vstack(states), agent.tf_epr:
np.vstack(rewards), agent.tf_y: np.vstack(labels)}
            agent.update(feed)
            # print progress console
```

```
            if n % 10 == 0:
                print ('ep {}: reward: {}, mean reward:
{:3f}'.format(n, reward_sum, running_reward))
            else:
                print ('\tep {}: reward: {}'.format(n, reward_sum))

            # Start next episode and save model
            states, rewards, labels = [], [], []
            obs = env.reset()
            n += 1 # the Next Episode

            reward_sum = 0
            if n % 50 == 0:
                agent.save()
            done = False

plt.plot(running_rewards)
plt.xlabel('episodes')
plt.ylabel('Running Averge')
plt.show()
env.close()
```

7. After training for 7,500 episodes, it started winning some games. After 1,200 episodes the winning rate improved, and it was winning 50% of the time. After 20,000 episodes, the agent was winning most games. The complete code is available at GitHub in the `Policy gradients.ipynb` file. And you can see the game played by the agent after learning for 20,000 episodes here: `https://youtu.be/hZo7kAco8is`. Note that, this agent learned to oscillate around its position; it also learned to pass the force created by its movement to the ball and has learned that the other player can be beaten only by attacking shots.

The actor-critic algorithm

In the policy gradient method, we introduced the baseline to reduce variance, but still, both action and baseline (look closely: the variance is the expected sum of rewards, or in other words, the goodness of the state or its value function) were changing simultaneously. Wouldn't it be better to separate the policy evaluation from the value evaluation? That's the idea behind the actor-critic method. It consists of two neural networks, one approximating the policy, called the **actor-network**, and the other approximating the value, called the **critic-network**. We alternate between a policy evaluation and a policy improvement step, resulting in more stable learning. The critic uses the state and action values to estimate a value function, which is then used to update the actor's policy network parameters so that the overall performance improves. The following diagram shows the basic architecture of the actor-critic network:

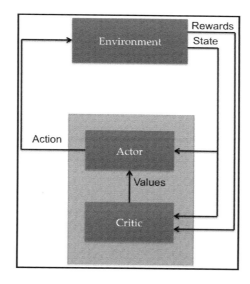

Actor-critic architecture

Summary

In this chapter, we learned about RL and how it's different from supervised and unsupervised learning. The emphasis of this chapter was on DRL, where deep neural networks are used to approximate the policy function or the value function or even both. This chapter introduced OpenAI gym, a library that provides a large number of environments to train RL agents. We learned about the value-based methods such as Q-learning and used it to train an agent to pick up and drop passengers off in a taxi. We also used a DQN to train an agent to play a Atari game . This chapter then moved on to policy-based methods, specifically policy gradients. We covered the intuition behind policy gradients and used the algorithm to train an RL agent to play Pong.

In the next chapter, we'll explore generative models and learn the secrets behind generative adversarial networks.

Generative Models for IoT
7

Machine learning (ML) and **Artificial Intelligence (AI)** have touched almost all fields related to man. Agriculture, music, health, defense—you won't find a single field where AI hasn't left its mark. The enormous success of AI/ML, besides the presence of computational powers, also depends on the generation of a significant amount of data. The majority of the data generated is unlabeled, and hence understanding the inherent distribution of the data is an important ML task. It's here that generative models come into the picture.

In the past few years, deep generative models have shown great success in understanding data distribution and have been used in a variety of applications. Two of the most popular generative models are **Variational Autoencoders (VAEs)** and **Generative Adversarial Networks (GANs)**.

In this chapter, we'll learn about both VAEs and GANs and use them to generate images. After reading this chapter, you'll have covered the following:

- Knowing the difference between generative networks and discriminative networks
- Learning about VAEs
- Understanding the intuitive functioning of GANs
- Implementing a vanilla GAN and using it to generate handwritten digits
- Knowing the most popular variation of GAN, the Deep Convolutional GAN
- Implementing the Deep Convolutional GAN in TensorFlow and using it to generate faces
- Knowing further modifications and applications of GANs

Introduction

Generative models are an exciting new branch of deep learning models that learn through unsupervised learning. The main idea is to generate new samples having the same distribution as the given training data; for example, a network trained on handwritten digits can create new digits that aren't in the dataset but are similar to them. Formally, we can say that if the training data follows the distribution $P_{data}(x)$, then the goal of generative models is to estimate the probability density function $P_{model}(x)$, which is similar to $P_{data}(x)$.

Generative models can be classified into two types:

- **Explicit generative models**: Here, the probability density function $P_{model}(x)$ is explicitly defined and solved. The density function may be tractable as in the case of PixelRNN/CNN, or an approximation of the density function as in the case of VAE.
- **Implicit generative models**: In these, the network learns to generate a sample from $P_{model}(x)$ without explicitly defining it. GANs are an example of this type of generative model.

In this chapter, we'll explore VAE, an explicit generative model, and GAN, an implicit generative model. Generative models can be instrumental in generating realistic samples, and they can be used to perform super-resolution, colorization, and so on. With time series data, we can even use them for simulation and planning. And last but not least, they can also help us in understanding the latent representation of data.

Generating images using VAEs

From `Chapter 4`, *Deep Learning for IOT*, you should be familiar with autoencoders and their functions. VAEs are a type of autoencoder; here, we retain the (trained) **Decoder** part, which can be used by feeding random latent features **z** to generate data similar to the training data. Now, if you remember, in autoencoders, the **Encoder** results in the generation of low-dimensional features, **z**:

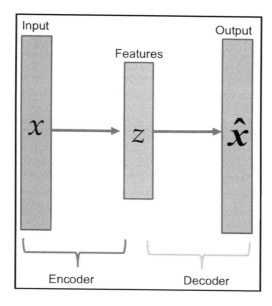

The architecture of autoencoders

The VAEs are concerned with finding the likelihood function $p(x)$ from the latent features z:

$$p_\theta(x) = \int p_\theta(z)p_\theta(x|z)dz$$

This is an intractable density function, and it isn't possible to directly optimize it; instead, we obtain a lower bound by using a simple Gaussian prior $p(z)$ and making both **Encoder** and **Decoder** networks probabilistic:

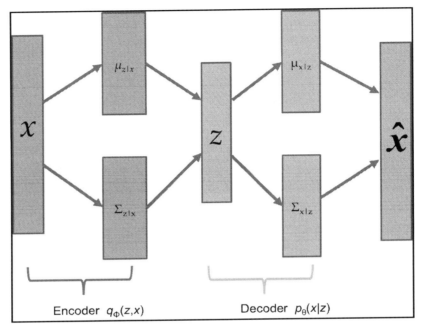

Architecture of a VAE

This allows us to define a tractable lower bound on the log likelihood, given by the following:

$$logp_\theta(x^{(i)}) \geq \mathcal{L}(x^{(i)}, \theta, \phi) = E_z[logp_\theta(x^{(i)}|z)] - D_{KL}(q_\phi(z|x^{(i)})||p_\theta(z|x^{(i)}))$$

In the preceding, θ represents the decoder network parameters and φ the encoder network parameters. The network is trained by maximizing this lower bound:

$$\theta^*, \phi^* = argmax_{\theta,\phi} \sum_{i=1}^{N} \mathcal{L}(x^{(i)}, \theta, \phi)$$

The first term in the lower bound is responsible for the reconstruction of the input data, and the second term for making the approximate posterior distribution close to prior. Once trained, the encoder network works as a recognition or inference network, and the decoder network acts as the generator.

 You can refer to the detailed derivation in the paper titled *Auto-Encoding Variational Bayes* by Diederik P Kingma and Max Welling, presented at ICLR 2014 (https://arxiv.org/abs/1312.6114).

VAEs in TensorFlow

Let's now see VAE in action. In this example code, we'll be using the standard MNIST dataset and train a VAE to generate handwritten digits. Since the MNIST dataset is simple, the encoder and decoder network will consist of only fully connected layers; this will allow us to concentrate on the VAE architecture. If you plan to generate complex images (such as CIFAR-10), you'll need to modify the encoder and decoder network to convolution and deconvolution networks:

1. The first step as in all previous cases is to import all of the necessary modules. Here, we'll use the TensorFlow higher API, tf.contrib, to make the fully connected layers. Note that this saves us from the hassle of declaring weights and biases for each layer independently:

```
import numpy as np
import tensorflow as tf

import matplotlib.pyplot as plt
%matplotlib inline

from tensorflow.contrib.layers import fully_connected
```

2. We read the data. The MNIST dataset is available in TensorFlow tutorials, so we'll take it directly from there:

```
# Load MNIST data in a format suited for tensorflow.
from tensorflow.examples.tutorials.mnist import input_data
mnist = input_data.read_data_sets('MNIST_data', one_hot=True)
n_samples = mnist.train.num_examples
n_input = mnist.train.images[0].shape[0]
```

3. We define the `VariationalAutoencoder` class; this class is the core code. It contains methods for defining the encoder and decoder network. The encoder generates the mean and variance of the latent feature z as `z_mu` and `z_sigma` respectively. Using these, a sample z is taken. The latent feature z is then passed to the decoder network to generate `x_hat`. The network minimizes the sum of the reconstruction loss and latent loss using the Adam optimizer. The class also defines methods for reconstruction, generation, transformation (to latent space), and training a single step:

```python
class VariationalAutoencoder(object):
    def __init__(self,n_input, n_z,
        learning_rate=0.001, batch_size=100):
        self.batch_size = batch_size
        self.n_input = n_input
        self.n_z = n_z

        # Place holder for the input
        self.x = tf.placeholder(tf.float32, shape = [None,
n_input])


        # Use Encoder Network to determine mean and
        # (log) variance of Gaussian distribution in the latent
space
        self.z_mean, self.z_log_sigma_sq = self._encoder_network()
        # Draw a sample z from Gaussian distribution
        eps = tf.random_normal((self.batch_size, n_z), 0, 1,
dtype=tf.float32)
        # z = mu + sigma*epsilon
        self.z =
tf.add(self.z_mean,tf.multiply(tf.sqrt(tf.exp(self.z_log_sigma_sq))
, eps))
        # Use Decoder network to determine mean of
        # Bernoulli distribution of reconstructed input
        self.x_hat = self._decoder_network()


        # Define loss function based variational upper-bound and
        # corresponding optimizer
        # define generation loss
        reconstruction_loss = \
            -tf.reduce_sum(self.x * tf.log(1e-10 + self.x_hat)
            + (1-self.x) * tf.log(1e-10 + 1 - self.x_hat), 1)
        self.reconstruction_loss =
tf.reduce_mean(reconstruction_loss)

        latent_loss = -0.5 * tf.reduce_sum(1 + self.z_log_sigma_sq
```

```
                    - tf.square(self.z_mean)- tf.exp(self.z_log_sigma_sq),
1)
        self.latent_loss = tf.reduce_mean(latent_loss)
        self.cost = tf.reduce_mean(reconstruction_loss +
latent_loss)
        # average over batch
        # Define the optimizer
        self.optimizer =
tf.train.AdamOptimizer(learning_rate).minimize(self.cost)


        # Initializing the tensor flow variables
        init = tf.global_variables_initializer()
        # Launch the session
        self.sess = tf.InteractiveSession()
        self.sess.run(init)



    # Create encoder network
    def _encoder_network(self):
        # Generate probabilistic encoder (inference network), which
        # maps inputs onto a normal distribution in latent space.
        layer_1 =
fully_connected(self.x,500,activation_fn=tf.nn.softplus)
        layer_2 = fully_connected(layer_1, 500,
activation_fn=tf.nn.softplus)
        z_mean = fully_connected(layer_2,self.n_z,
activation_fn=None)
        z_log_sigma_sq = fully_connected(layer_2, self.n_z,
activation_fn=None)
        return (z_mean, z_log_sigma_sq)

    # Create decoder network
    def _decoder_network(self):
        # Generate probabilistic decoder (generator network), which
        # maps points in the latent space onto a Bernoulli
distribution in the data space.
        layer_1 =
fully_connected(self.z,500,activation_fn=tf.nn.softplus)
        layer_2 = fully_connected(layer_1, 500,
activation_fn=tf.nn.softplus)
        x_hat = fully_connected(layer_2, self.n_input,
activation_fn=tf.nn.sigmoid)

        return x_hat
```

```
    def single_step_train(self, X):
        _,cost,recon_loss,latent_loss =
self.sess.run([self.optimizer,
self.cost,self.reconstruction_loss,self.latent_loss],feed_dict={sel
f.x: X})
        return cost, recon_loss, latent_loss

    def transform(self, X):
        """Transform data by mapping it into the latent space."""
        # Note: This maps to mean of distribution, we could
alternatively
        # sample from Gaussian distribution
        return self.sess.run(self.z_mean, feed_dict={self.x: X})

    def generate(self, z_mu=None):
        """ Generate data by sampling from latent space.

        If z_mu isn't None, data for this point in latent space is
        generated. Otherwise, z_mu is drawn from prior in latent
        space.
        """
        if z_mu is None:
            z_mu = np.random.normal(size=n_z)
            # Note: This maps to mean of distribution, we could
alternatively
            # sample from Gaussian distribution
        return self.sess.run(self.x_hat,feed_dict={self.z: z_mu})

    def reconstruct(self, X):
        """ Use VAE to reconstruct given data. """
        return self.sess.run(self.x_hat, feed_dict={self.x: X})
```

4. With all ingredients in place, let's train our VAE. We do this with the help of the `train` function:

```
def train(n_input,n_z, learning_rate=0.001,
    batch_size=100, training_epochs=10, display_step=5):
    vae = VariationalAutoencoder(n_input,n_z,
        learning_rate=learning_rate,
        batch_size=batch_size)
    # Training cycle
    for epoch in range(training_epochs):
        avg_cost, avg_r_loss, avg_l_loss = 0., 0., 0.
        total_batch = int(n_samples / batch_size)
        # Loop over all batches
        for i in range(total_batch):
            batch_xs, _ = mnist.train.next_batch(batch_size)
            # Fit training using batch data
```

```
cost,r_loss, l_loss = vae.single_step_train(batch_xs)
# Compute average loss
avg_cost += cost / n_samples * batch_size
avg_r_loss += r_loss / n_samples * batch_size
avg_l_loss += l_loss / n_samples * batch_size
# Display logs per epoch step
if epoch % display_step == 0:
    print("Epoch: {:4d} cost={:.4f} Reconstruction loss =
{:.4f} Latent Loss =
{:.4f}".format(epoch,avg_cost,avg_r_loss,avg_l_loss))
    return vae
```

5. In the following screenshot, you can see the reconstructed digits (left) and generated handwritten digits (right) for a VAE with the latent space of size 10:

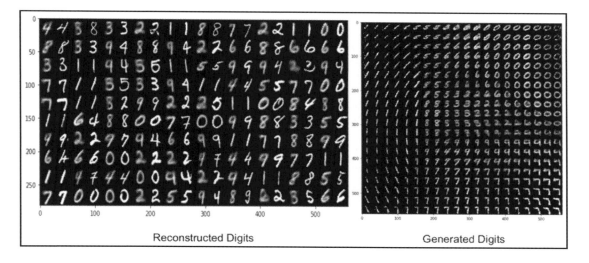

Reconstructed Digits   Generated Digits

6. As discussed earlier, the encoder network reduces the dimensions of the input space. To make it clearer, we reduce the dimension of latent space to 2. In the following, you can see that each label is separated in the two-dimensional z-space:

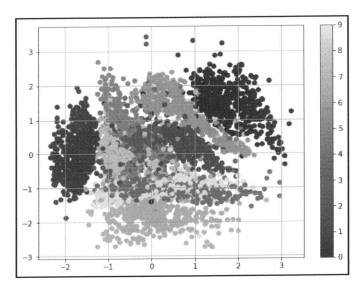

7. The reconstructed and generated digits from a VAE with a latent space of the dimension 2 are as follows:

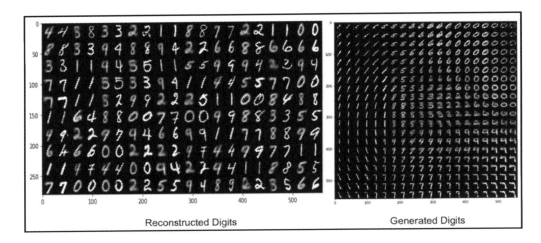

Reconstructed Digits   Generated Digits

The interesting thing to note from the preceding screenshot (right) is how changing the values of the two-dimensional z results in different strokes and different numbers. The complete code is on GitHub in Chapter 07, in the file named VariationalAutoEncoders_MNIST.ipynb:

```
tf.contrib.layers.fully_connected(
    inputs,
    num_outputs,
    activation_fn=tf.nn.relu,
    normalizer_fn=None,
    normalizer_params=None,
    weights_initializer=intializers.xavier_intializer(),
    weights_regularizer= None,
    biases_initializer=tf.zeros_intializer(),
    biases_regularizer=None,
    reuse=None,
    variables_collections=None,
    outputs_collections=None,
    trainable=True,
    scope=None
)
```

> The layers (contrib) is a higher level package included in TensorFlow. It provides operations for building neural network layers, regularizers, summaries, and so on. In the preceding code, we used the tf.contrib.layers.fully_connected() operation, defined in tensorflow/contrib/layers/python/layers/layers.py, which adds a fully connected layer. By default, it creates weights representing a fully connected interconnection matrix, initialized by default using the Xavier initialization. It also creates biases initialized to zero. It provides an option for choosing normalization and activation function as well.

GANs

GANs are implicit generative networks. During a session at Quora, Yann LeCun, Director of AI Research at Facebook and Professor at NYU, described GANs as *the most interesting idea in the last 10 years in ML*. At present, lots of research is happening in GANs. Major AI/ML conferences conducted in the last few years have reported a majority of papers related to GANs.

GANs were proposed by Ian J. Goodfellow and Yoshua Bengio in the paper *Generative Adversarial Networks* in the year 2014 (`https://arxiv.org/abs/1406.2661`). They're inspired by the two-player game scenario. Like the two players of the game, in GANs, two networks—one called the **discriminative network** and the other the **generative network**—compete with each other. The generative network tries to generate data similar to the input data, and the discriminator network has to identify whether the data it's seeing is real or fake (that is, generated by a generator). Every time the discriminator finds a difference between the distribution of true input and fake data, the generator adjusts its weights to reduce the difference. To summarize, the discriminative network tries to learn the boundary between counterfeit and real data, and the generative network tries to learn the distribution of training data. As the training ends, the generator learns to produce images exactly like the input data distribution, and the discriminator can no longer differentiate the two. The general architecture of a GAN is as follows:

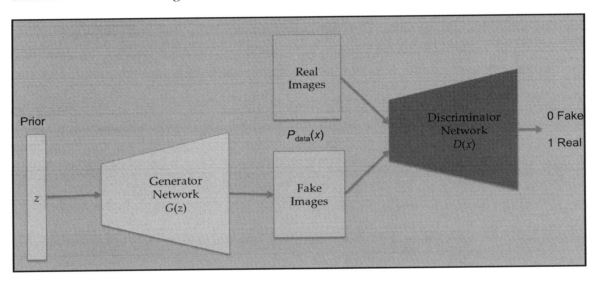

Architecture of GANs

Let's now delve deep into how GANs learn. Both the discriminator and generator take turns to learn. The learning can be divided into two steps:

1. Here the **Discriminator**, $D(x)$, learns. The **Generator**, $G(z)$, is used to generate **Fake Images** from random noise **z** (which follows some **Prior** distribution $P(z)$). The **Fake Images** from the **Generator** and the **Real Images** from the training dataset are both fed to the **Discriminator** and it performs supervised learning trying to separate fake from real. If $P_{data}(x)$ is the training dataset distribution, then the **Discriminator Network** tries to maximize its objective so that $D(x)$ is close to 1 when the input data is real, and close to 0 when the input data is fake. This can be achieved by performing the gradient ascent on the following objective function:

$$\theta_d^{max} \left[E_{x \sim P_{data}} log D_{\theta_d}(x) + E_{z \sim P(z)} log(1 - D_{\theta_d}(G_{\theta_g}(z))) \right]$$

2. In the next step, the **Generator Network** learns. Its goal is to fool the **Discriminator Network** into thinking that generated $G(z)$ is real, that is, force $D(G(z))$ close to 1. To achieve this, the **Generator Network** minimizes the objective:

$$\theta_d^{min} \left[E_{z \sim P(z)} log(1 - D_{\theta_d}(G_{\theta_g}(z))) \right]$$

The two steps are repeated sequentially. Once the training ends, the discriminator is no longer able to discriminate between real and fake data and the generator becomes a pro at creating data very similar to the training data. Well, it's easier said than done: as you experiment with GANs, you'll find that the training isn't very stable. It's an open research issue, and many variants of GAN have been proposed to rectify the problem.

Implementing a vanilla GAN in TensorFlow

In this section, we'll write a TensorFlow code to implement a GAN, as we learned in the previous section. We'll use simple MLP networks for both the discriminator and generator. And for simplicity, we'll use the MNIST dataset:

1. As always, the first step is to add all of the necessary modules. Since we'll need to access and train the generator and discriminator parameters alternatively, we'll define our weights and biases in the present code for clarity. It's always better to initialize weights using the Xavier initialization and biases to all zeros. So, we also import from TensorFlow a method to perform Xavier initialization, from `tensorflow.contrib.layers import xavier_initializer`:

```
# import the necessaey modules
import tensorflow as tf
import numpy as np
import matplotlib.pyplot as plt
import matplotlib.gridspec as gridspec
import os
from tensorflow.contrib.layers import xavier_initializer
%matplotlib inline
```

2. Let's read the data and define hyperparameters:

```
# Load data
from tensorflow.examples.tutorials.mnist import input_data
data = input_data.read_data_sets('MNIST_data', one_hot=True)

# define hyperparameters
batch_size = 128
Z_dim = 100
im_size = 28
h_size=128
learning_rate_D = .0005
learning_rate_G = .0006
```

3. We define the training parameters for both generator and discriminator. We also define the placeholders for input X and latent Z:

```
#Create Placeholder for input X and random noise Z
X = tf.placeholder(tf.float32, shape=[None, im_size*im_size])
Z = tf.placeholder(tf.float32, shape=[None, Z_dim])
initializer=xavier_initializer()

# Define Discriminator and Generator training variables
#Discriminiator
```

```
D_W1 = tf.Variable(initializer([im_size*im_size, h_size]))
D_b1 = tf.Variable(tf.zeros(shape=[h_size]))

D_W2 = tf.Variable(initializer([h_size, 1]))
D_b2 = tf.Variable(tf.zeros(shape=[1]))

theta_D = [D_W1, D_W2, D_b1, D_b2]

#Generator
G_W1 = tf.Variable(initializer([Z_dim, h_size]))
G_b1 = tf.Variable(tf.zeros(shape=[h_size]))

G_W2 = tf.Variable(initializer([h_size, im_size*im_size]))
G_b2 = tf.Variable(tf.zeros(shape=[im_size*im_size]))

theta_G = [G_W1, G_W2, G_b1, G_b2]
```

4. Now that we have the placeholders and weights in place, we define functions for generating random noise from z. Here, we're using a uniform distribution to generate noise; people have also experimented with using Gaussian noise—to do so, you just change the random function from uniform to normal:

```
def sample_Z(m, n):
    return np.random.uniform(-1., 1., size=[m, n])
```

5. We construct the discriminator and generator networks:

```
def generator(z):
    """ Two layer Generator Network Z=>128=>784 """
    G_h1 = tf.nn.relu(tf.matmul(z, G_W1) + G_b1)
    G_log_prob = tf.matmul(G_h1, G_W2) + G_b2
    G_prob = tf.nn.sigmoid(G_log_prob)
    return G_prob


def discriminator(x):
    """ Two layer Discriminator Network X=>128=>1 """
    D_h1 = tf.nn.relu(tf.matmul(x, D_W1) + D_b1)
    D_logit = tf.matmul(D_h1, D_W2) + D_b2
    D_prob = tf.nn.sigmoid(D_logit)
    return D_prob, D_logit
```

6. We'll also need a helper function to plot the handwritten digits generated. The following function plots 25 samples generated in a grid of 5×5:

```
def plot(samples):
    """function to plot generated samples"""
    fig = plt.figure(figsize=(10, 10))
    gs = gridspec.GridSpec(5, 5)
    gs.update(wspace=0.05, hspace=0.05)
    for i, sample in enumerate(samples):
        ax = plt.subplot(gs[i])
        plt.axis('off')
        ax.set_xticklabels([])
        ax.set_yticklabels([])
        ax.set_aspect('equal')
        plt.imshow(sample.reshape(28, 28), cmap='gray')
    return fig
```

7. Now, we define the TensorFlow operations to generate a sample from the generator and a prediction from the discriminator for both fake and real input data:

```
G_sample = generator(Z)
D_real, D_logit_real = discriminator(X)
D_fake, D_logit_fake = discriminator(G_sample)
```

8. Next, we define cross-entropy losses for the generator and discriminator network, and alternatively, minimize them, keeping the other weight parameters frozen:

```
D_loss_real =
tf.reduce_mean(tf.nn.sigmoid_cross_entropy_with_logits(logits=D_log
it_real, labels=tf.ones_like(D_logit_real)))
D_loss_fake =
tf.reduce_mean(tf.nn.sigmoid_cross_entropy_with_logits(logits=D_log
it_fake, labels=tf.zeros_like(D_logit_fake)))
D_loss = D_loss_real + D_loss_fake
G_loss =
tf.reduce_mean(tf.nn.sigmoid_cross_entropy_with_logits(logits=D_log
it_fake, labels=tf.ones_like(D_logit_fake)))

D_solver =
tf.train.AdamOptimizer(learning_rate=learning_rate_D).minimize(D_lo
ss, var_list=theta_D)
G_solver =
tf.train.AdamOptimizer(learning_rate=learning_rate_G).minimize(G_lo
ss, var_list=theta_G)
```

9. Finally, let's perform the training within a TensorFlow session:

```
sess = tf.Session()
sess.run(tf.global_variables_initializer())
GLoss = []
DLoss = []
if not os.path.exists('out/'):
    os.makedirs('out/')

for it in range(100000):
    if it % 100 == 0:
        samples = sess.run(G_sample, feed_dict={Z: sample_Z(25,
Z_dim)})
        fig = plot(samples)
        plt.savefig('out/{}.png'.format(str(it).zfill(3)),
bbox_inches='tight')
        plt.close(fig)
    X_mb, _ = data.train.next_batch(batch_size)
    _, D_loss_curr = sess.run([D_solver, D_loss], feed_dict={X:
X_mb, Z: sample_Z(batch_size, Z_dim)})
    _, G_loss_curr = sess.run([G_solver, G_loss], feed_dict={Z:
sample_Z(batch_size, Z_dim)})
    GLoss.append(G_loss_curr)
    DLoss.append(D_loss_curr)
    if it % 100 == 0:
        print('Iter: {} D loss: {:.4} G_loss:
{:.4}'.format(it,D_loss_curr, G_loss_curr))

print('Done')
```

10. In the following screenshot, you can see how the loss for both the generative and discriminatives network varies:

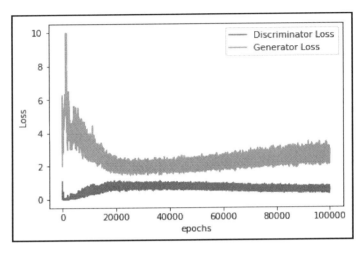

Loss for both generative and discriminatives network

11. Let's also see the handwritten digits generated at different epochs:

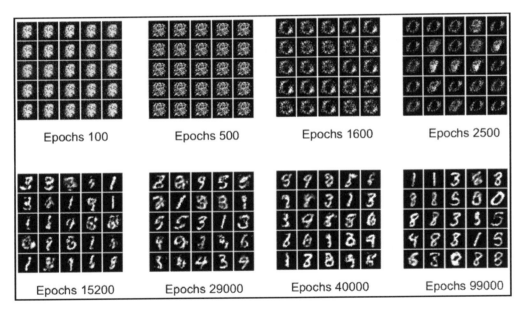

Handwritten digits

While the handwritten digits are good enough, we can see that a lot of improvements can be made. Some approaches used by researchers to stabilize the performance are as follows:

- Normalize the input images from (0,1) to (-1,1). And, instead of the sigmoid as the activation function for the final output of the generator, use the tangent hyperbolic activation function.
- Instead of minimizing the generator loss minimum `log 1-D`, we can maximize the loss maximum `log D`; this can be achieved in TensorFlow by simply flipping the labels while training the generator, for example (convert real into fake and fake into real).
- Another approach is to store previously generated images and train the discriminator by choosing randomly from them. (Yes, you guessed right—it's similar to the experience replay buffer we learned in `Chapter 6`, *Reinforcement Learning for IoT*.)
- People have also experimented with updating the generator or discriminator only if their loss is above a certain threshold.
- Instead of the ReLU activation function for the hidden layers of the discriminator and generator, use Leaky ReLU.

Deep Convolutional GANs

In 2016, Alec Radford *et al.* proposed a variation of the GAN called the **Deep Convolutional GAN (DCGAN)**. (The link to the full paper is: `https://arxiv.org/abs/1511.06434`.) They replaced the MLP layers with convolutional layers. They also added batch normalization in both the generator and discriminator networks. We'll implement DCGAN here on a celebrity images dataset. You can download the ZIP file, `img_align_celeba.zip`, from `http://mmlab.ie.cuhk.edu.hk/projects/CelebA.html`. We make use of the `loader_celebA.py` file we made in `Chapter 2`, *Data Access and Distributed Processing for IoT*, to unzip and read the images:

1. We'll import statements for all of the modules we'll be requiring:

```
import loader
import os
from glob import glob
import numpy as np
from matplotlib import pyplot
import tensorflow as tf
%matplotlib inline
```

2. We use `loader_celebA.py` to unzip `img_align_celeba.zip`. Since the number of images is very high, we use the `get_batches` function defined in this file to generate batches for training the network:

```
loader.download_celeb_a()

# Let's explore the images
data_dir = os.getcwd()
test_images = loader.get_batch(glob(os.path.join(data_dir,
'celebA/*.jpg'))[:10], 56, 56)
pyplot.imshow(loader.plot_images(test_images))
```

In the following, you can see the dataset images:

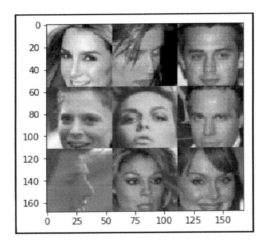

3. We define the discriminator network. It consists of three convolutional layers with 64, 128, and 256 filters respectively, each of size 5×5. The first two layers use a stride of 2 and the third convolutional layer uses a stride of 1. All three convolutional layers use `leakyReLU` as the activation function. Each convolutional layer is also followed by a batch normalization layer. The result of the third convolutional layer is flattened and passed to the last fully connected (dense) layer with the sigmoid activation function:

```
def discriminator(images, reuse=False):
    """
    Create the discriminator network
    """
    alpha = 0.2

    with tf.variable_scope('discriminator', reuse=reuse):
```

```
# using 4 layer network as in DCGAN Paper

# First convolution layer
conv1 = tf.layers.conv2d(images, 64, 5, 2, 'SAME')
lrelu1 = tf.maximum(alpha * conv1, conv1)

# Second convolution layer
conv2 = tf.layers.conv2d(lrelu1, 128, 5, 2, 'SAME')
batch_norm2 = tf.layers.batch_normalization(conv2,
training=True)
lrelu2 = tf.maximum(alpha * batch_norm2, batch_norm2)
# Third convolution layer
conv3 = tf.layers.conv2d(lrelu2, 256, 5, 1, 'SAME')
batch_norm3 = tf.layers.batch_normalization(conv3,
training=True)
lrelu3 = tf.maximum(alpha * batch_norm3, batch_norm3)
# Flatten layer
flat = tf.reshape(lrelu3, (-1, 4*4*256))
# Logits
logits = tf.layers.dense(flat, 1)
# Output
out = tf.sigmoid(logits)
return out, logits
```

4. The generator network is the reverse of the discriminator; the input to the generator is first fed to a dense layer with 2×2×512 units. The output of the dense layer is reshaped so that we can feed it to the convolution stack. We use the `tf.layers.conv2d_transpose()` method to get the transposed convolution output. The generator has three transposed convolutional layers. All of the layers except the last convolutional layer have `leakyReLU` as the activation function. The last transposed convolution layer uses the tangent hyperbolic activation function so that output lies in the range (−1 to 1):

```
def generator(z, out_channel_dim, is_train=True):
    """
    Create the generator network
    """
    alpha = 0.2
    with tf.variable_scope('generator', reuse=False if
is_train==True else True):
        # First fully connected layer
        x_1 = tf.layers.dense(z, 2*2*512)
        # Reshape it to start the convolutional stack
        deconv_2 = tf.reshape(x_1, (-1, 2, 2, 512))
        batch_norm2 = tf.layers.batch_normalization(deconv_2,
training=is_train)
        lrelu2 = tf.maximum(alpha * batch_norm2, batch_norm2)
```

```
            # Deconv 1
            deconv3 = tf.layers.conv2d_transpose(lrelu2, 256, 5, 2,
padding='VALID')
            batch_norm3 = tf.layers.batch_normalization(deconv3,
training=is_train)
            lrelu3 = tf.maximum(alpha * batch_norm3, batch_norm3)
            # Deconv 2
            deconv4 = tf.layers.conv2d_transpose(lrelu3, 128, 5, 2,
padding='SAME')
            batch_norm4 = tf.layers.batch_normalization(deconv4,
training=is_train)
            lrelu4 = tf.maximum(alpha * batch_norm4, batch_norm4)
            # Output layer
            logits = tf.layers.conv2d_transpose(lrelu4,
out_channel_dim, 5, 2, padding='SAME')
            out = tf.tanh(logits)
            return out
```

5. We define functions to calculate the model loss; it defines both the generator and discriminator loss and returns them:

```
def model_loss(input_real, input_z, out_channel_dim):
    """
    Get the loss for the discriminator and generator
    """
    label_smoothing = 0.9
    g_model = generator(input_z, out_channel_dim)
    d_model_real, d_logits_real = discriminator(input_real)
    d_model_fake, d_logits_fake = discriminator(g_model,
reuse=True)
    d_loss_real = tf.reduce_mean(
tf.nn.sigmoid_cross_entropy_with_logits(logits=d_logits_real,
labels=tf.ones_like(d_model_real) * label_smoothing))
    d_loss_fake = tf.reduce_mean(
tf.nn.sigmoid_cross_entropy_with_logits(logits=d_logits_fake,
labels=tf.zeros_like(d_model_fake)))
    d_loss = d_loss_real + d_loss_fake
    g_loss = tf.reduce_mean(
tf.nn.sigmoid_cross_entropy_with_logits(logits=d_logits_fake,
labels=tf.ones_like(d_model_fake) * label_smoothing))
    return d_loss, g_loss
```

6. We next need to define optimizers to make the discriminator and generator learn sequentially. To achieve this, we make use of `tf.trainable_variables()` to get a list of all training variables, and then first optimize only the discriminator training variables, and then the generator training variables:

```
def model_opt(d_loss, g_loss, learning_rate, beta1):
    """
    Get optimization operations
    """
    t_vars = tf.trainable_variables()
    d_vars = [var for var in t_vars if
var.name.startswith('discriminator')]
    g_vars = [var for var in t_vars if
var.name.startswith('generator')]

    # Optimize
    with
tf.control_dependencies(tf.get_collection(tf.GraphKeys.UPDATE_OPS))
:
        d_train_opt = tf.train.AdamOptimizer(learning_rate,
beta1=beta1).minimize(d_loss, var_list=d_vars)
        g_train_opt = tf.train.AdamOptimizer(learning_rate,
beta1=beta1).minimize(g_loss, var_list=g_vars)

    return d_train_opt, g_train_opt
```

7. Now, we have all of the necessary ingredients to train the DCGAN. It's always good to keep an eye how the generator has learned, so we define a helper function to display the images generated by the generator network as it learns:

```
def generator_output(sess, n_images, input_z, out_channel_dim):
    """
    Show example output for the generator
    """
    z_dim = input_z.get_shape().as_list()[-1]
    example_z = np.random.uniform(-1, 1, size=[n_images, z_dim])

    samples = sess.run(
        generator(input_z, out_channel_dim, False),
        feed_dict={input_z: example_z})

    pyplot.imshow(loader.plot_images(samples))
    pyplot.show()
```

8. Finally, comes the training part. Here, we use the `ops` defined previously to train the DCGAN, and the images are fed to the network in batches:

```
def train(epoch_count, batch_size, z_dim, learning_rate, beta1,
get_batches, data_shape, data_files):
    """
    Train the GAN
    """
    w, h, num_ch = data_shape[1], data_shape[2], data_shape[3]
    X = tf.placeholder(tf.float32, shape=(None, w, h, num_ch),
name='input_real')
    Z = tf.placeholder(tf.float32, (None, z_dim), name='input_z')
    #model_inputs(data_shape[1], data_shape[2], data_shape[3],
z_dim)
    D_loss, G_loss = model_loss(X, Z, data_shape[3])
    D_solve, G_solve = model_opt(D_loss, G_loss, learning_rate,
beta1)
    with tf.Session() as sess:
        sess.run(tf.global_variables_initializer())
        train_loss_d = []
        train_loss_g = []
        for epoch_i in range(epoch_count):
            num_batch = 0
            lossD, lossG = 0,0
            for batch_images in get_batches(batch_size, data_shape,
data_files):
                # values range from -0.5 to 0.5 so we scale to
range -1, 1
                batch_images = batch_images * 2
                num_batch += 1
                batch_z = np.random.uniform(-1, 1,
size=(batch_size, z_dim))
                _,d_loss = sess.run([D_solve,D_loss], feed_dict={X:
batch_images, Z: batch_z})
                _,g_loss = sess.run([G_solve,G_loss], feed_dict={X:
batch_images, Z: batch_z})
                lossD += (d_loss/batch_size)
                lossG += (g_loss/batch_size)
                if num_batch % 500 == 0:
                    # After every 500 batches
                    print("Epoch {}/{} For Batch {} Discriminator
Loss: {:.4f} Generator Loss: {:.4f}".
                          format(epoch_i+1, epochs, num_batch,
lossD/num_batch, lossG/num_batch))
                    generator_output(sess, 9, Z, data_shape[3])
            train_loss_d.append(lossD/num_batch)
            train_loss_g.append(lossG/num_batch)
    return train_loss_d, train_loss_g
```

9. Let's now define the parameters of our data and train it:

```
# Data Parameters
IMAGE_HEIGHT = 28
IMAGE_WIDTH = 28
data_files = glob(os.path.join(data_dir, 'celebA/*.jpg'))

#Hyper parameters
batch_size = 16
z_dim = 100
learning_rate = 0.0002
beta1 = 0.5
epochs = 2
shape = len(data_files), IMAGE_WIDTH, IMAGE_HEIGHT, 3
with tf.Graph().as_default():
    Loss_D, Loss_G = train(epochs, batch_size, z_dim,
learning_rate, beta1, loader.get_batches, shape, data_files)
```

After each batch, you can see that the generator output is improving:

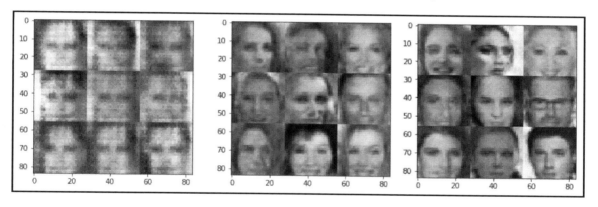

DCGAN generator output as learning progresses

Variants of GAN and its cool applications

In the last few years, a large number of variants of GANs have been proposed. You can access the complete list of different variants of GAN from the GAN Zoo GitHub: https://github.com/hindupuravinash/the-gan-zoo. In this section, we'll list some of the more popular and successful variants.

Cycle GAN

At the beginning of the 2018, the Berkeley AI research lab published a paper entitled *Unpaired Image-to-Image Translation using Cycle-Consistent Adversarial Networks* (arXiv link: `https://arxiv.org/pdf/1703.10593.pdf`). This paper is special not only because it proposed a new architecture, CycleGAN, with improved stability, but also because they demonstrated that such an architecture can be used for complex image transformations. The following diagram shows the architecture of a cycle GAN; the two sections highlight the **Generator** and **Discriminators** playing a role in calculating the two adversarial losses:

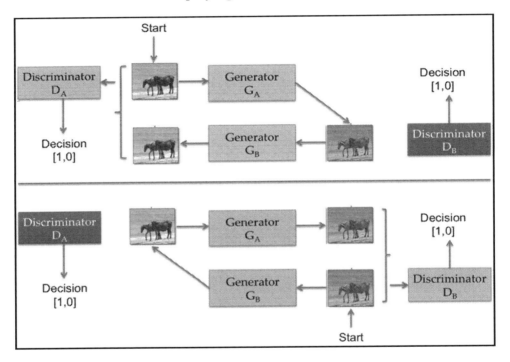

The architecture of CycleGAN

The CycleGAN consists of two GANs. They are trained on two different datasets, $x \sim P_{data}(x)$ and $y \sim P_{data}(y)$. The generator is trained to perform the mappings, namely, $G_A: x \rightarrow y$ and $G_B: y \rightarrow x$ respectively. Each discriminator is trained so that it can differentiate between the image x and transformed image $G_B(y)$, hence resulting in the adversary loss functions for the two transformations, defined as follows:

$$\mathcal{L}(G_A, D_B, x, y) = E_{y \sim P_{data}(y)} \left[log D_B(y) \right] + E_{x \sim P_{data}(x)} \left[log(1 - D_B(G_A(x))) \right]$$

And, the second is as follows:

$$\mathcal{L}(G_B, D_A, y, x) = E_{x \sim P_{data}(x)} \left[log D_A(x) \right] + E_{y \sim P_{data}(y)} \left[log(1 - D_A(G_B(y))) \right]$$

The generators of the two GANs are connected to each other in a cyclic fashion, so that if the output of one is fed to another and the corresponding output fed back to the first one, we get the same data. Let's make it clearer with an example; let's say the **Generator A (G_A)** is fed an image x, so the output is a transformation $G_A(x)$. This transformed image now is fed to **Generator B (G_B)** $G_B(G_A(x)) \approx x$ and the result should be the initial image x. Similarly, we shall have $G_A(G_B(y)) \approx y$. This is made possible by introducing a cyclic loss term:

$$\mathcal{L}_{cyc}(G_A, G_B) = E_{x \sim P_{data}(x)} \left[||G_B(G_A(x)) - x||_1 \right] + E_{y \sim P_{data}(y)} \left[||G_A(G_B(y)) - y||_1 \right]$$

Hence, the net objective function is as follows:

$$\mathcal{L}_{total} = \mathcal{L}(G_B, D_A, y, x) + \mathcal{L}(G_A, D_B, x, y) + \lambda \mathcal{L}_{cyc}(G_A, G_B)$$

Here, λ controls the relative importance of the two objectives. They also retained previous images in an experience buffer to train the discriminator. In the following screenshot, you can see some of the results obtained from the CycleGANs as reported in the paper:

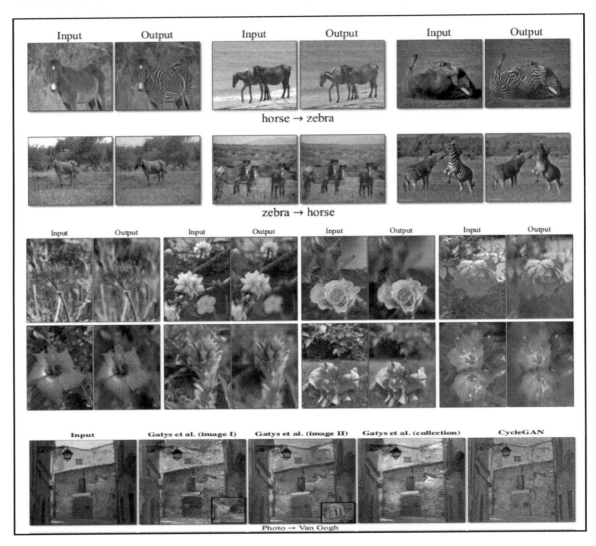

Results of CycleGAN (taken from the original paper)

The authors showed that CycleGANs can be used for the following:

- **Image transformation**: Such as changing horses to zebra and vice versa
- **Enhancing the resolution**: The CycleGAN, when trained by a dataset consisting of low-resolution and super-resolution images, could perform super-resolution when given with low-resolution images
- **Style transfer**: Given an image, it can be transformed into different painting styles

Applications of GANs

GANs are indeed interesting networks; besides the applications you've seen, GANs have been explored in many other exciting applications. In the following, we list a few:

- **Music generation**: MIDINet, a convolutional GAN, has been demonstrated to generate melodies. You can refer to the paper here: `https://arxiv.org/pdf/1703.10847.pdf`.

- **Medical anomaly detection**: AnoGAN is a DCGAN shown by Thomas Schlegl et al. to learn a manifold of normal anatomical variability. They were able to train the network to label anomalies on optical coherence tomography images of the retina. If the work interests you, you can see the related paper on arXiv at `https://arxiv.org/pdf/1703.05921.pdf`.

- **Vector arithmetic on faces using GANs**: In the joint research paper by Indico Research and Facebook, they demonstrated that it's possible to use GANs and perform image arithmetic. For example, *Man with glasses—Man without glasses + Woman without glasses = Woman with glasses*. It's an interesting paper and you can read more about it on Arxiv (`https://arxiv.org/pdf/1511.06434.pdf`).

- **Text to image synthesis**: GANs have been demonstrated to generate images of birds and flowers from human-written textual descriptions. The model uses DCGAN along with a hybrid character level convolutional recurrent network. The details of the work are given in the paper, *Generative Adversarial Text to Image Synthesis*. The link to the paper is `https://arxiv.org/pdf/1605.05396.pdf`.

Summary

This was an interesting chapter, and I hope you enjoyed reading it as much as I enjoyed writing it. It's at present the hot topic of research. This chapter introduced generative models and their classification, namely implicit generative models and explicit generative models. The first generative model that was covered is VAEs; they're an explicit generative model and try to estimate the lower bound on the density function. The VAEs were implemented in TensorFlow and were used to generate handwritten digits.

This chapter then moved on to a more popular explicit generative model: GANs. The GAN architecture, especially how the discriminator network and generative network compete with each other, was explained. We implemented a GAN using TensorFlow for generating handwritten digits. This chapter then moved on to the more successful variation of GAN: the DCGAN. We implemented a DCGAN to generate celebrity images. This chapter also covered the architecture details of CycleGAN, a recently proposed GAN, and some of its cool applications.

With this chapter, we mark the end of part one of this book. Till now, we concentrated on different ML and DL models, which we'll require to understand our data and use it for prediction/classification, and other tasks. From the next chapter onward, we'll be talking more about the data itself and how we can process the data in the present IoT-driven environment.

In the next chapter, we'll move toward distributed processing, a necessity when dealing with a large amount of data, and explore two platforms that offer distributed processing.

Distributed AI for IoT

8

The advances in distributed computing environments and an easy availability of internet worldwide has resulted in the emergence of **Distributed Artificial Intelligence (DAI)**. In this chapter, we will learn about two frameworks, one by Apache the **machine learning library (MLlib)**, and another H2O.ai, both provide distributed and scalable **machine learning (ML)** for large, streaming data. The chapter will start with an introduction to Apache's Spark, the de facto distributed data processing system. This chapter will cover the following topics:

- Spark and its importance in distributed data processing
- Understanding the Spark architecture
- Learning about MLlib
- Using MLlib in your deep learning pipeline
- Delving deep into the H2O.ai platform

Introduction

IoT systems generate a lot of data; while in many cases it is possible to analyze the data at leisure, for certain tasks such as security, fraud detection, and so on, this latency is not acceptable. What we need in such a situation is a way to handle large data within a specified time—the solution—DAI, many machines in the cluster processing the big data (data parallelism) and/or training the deep learning models (model parallelism) in a distributed manner. There are many ways to perform DAI, and most of the approaches are built upon or around Apache Spark. Released in the year 2010 under the BSD licence, Apache Spark today is the largest open source project in big data. It helps the user to create a fast and general purpose cluster computing system.

Spark runs on a Java virtual machine, making it possible to run it on any machine with Java installed, be it a laptop or a cluster. It supports a variety of programming languages including Python, Scala, and R. A large number of deep learning frameworks and APIs are built around Spark and TensorFlow to make the task of DAI easier, for example, **TensorFlowOnSpark** (**TFoS**), Spark MLlib, SparkDl, and Hydrogen Sparkling (a combination of H2O.ai and Spark).

Spark components

Spark uses master-slave architecture, with one central coordinator (called the **Spark driver**) and many distributed workers (called **Spark executors**). The driver process creates a SparkContext object and divides the user application into smaller execution units (tasks). These tasks are executed by the workers. The resources among the workers are managed by a **Cluster Manager**. The following diagram shows the workings of Spark:

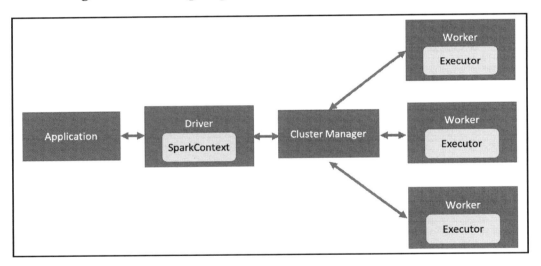

Working of Spark

Let's now go through the different components of Spark. The following diagram shows the basic components that constitute Spark:

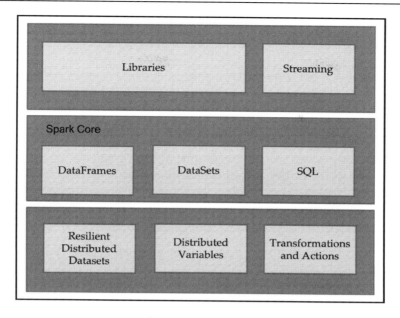

Components that constitute Spark

Let's see, in brief, some of the components that we will be using in this chapter, as follows:

- **Resilient Distributed Datasets**: **Resilient Distributed Datasets (RDDs)** are the primary API in Spark. They represent an immutable, partitioned collection of data that can be operated in parallel. The higher APIs DataFrames and DataSets are built on top of RDDs.
- **Distributed Variables**: Spark has two types of distributed variables: broadcast variables and accumulators. They are used by user-defined functions. Accumulators are used for aggregating the information from all the executors into a shared result. The broadcast variables, alternatively, are the variables that are shared throughout the cluster.
- **DataFrames**: It is a distributed collection of data, very much like the pandas DataFrame. They can read from various file formats and perform the operation on the entire DataFrame using a single command. They are distributed across the cluster.
- **Libraries**: Spark has built-in libraries for MLlib, and for working with graphs (GraphX). In this chapter, we will use MLlib and SparkDl that uses Spark framework. We will learn how to apply them to make ML predictions.

Spark is a big topic, and it is beyond the scope of this book to give further details on Spark. We recommend the interested reader refer to the Spark documentation: http://spark.apache.org/docs/latest/index.html.

Apache MLlib

Apache Spark MLlib provides a powerful computational environment for ML. It provides a distributed architecture on a large-scale basis, allowing one to run ML models more quickly and efficiently. That's not all; it is open source with a growing and active community continuously working to improve and provide the latest features. It provides a scalable implementation of the popular ML algorithms. It includes algorithms for the following:

- **Classification**: Logistic regression, linear support vector machine, Naive Bayes
- **Regression**: Generalized linear regression
- **Collaborative filtering**: Alternating least square
- **Clustering**: K-means
- **Decomposition**: Singular value decomposition and principal component analysis

It has proved to be faster than Hadoop MapReduce. We can write applications in Java, Scala, R, or Python. It can also be easily integrated with TensorFlow.

Regression in MLlib

Spark MLlib has built-in methods for regression. To be able to use the built-in methods of Spark, you will have to install pyspark on your cluster (standalone or distributed cluster). The installation can be done using the following:

```
pip install pyspark
```

The MLlib library has the following regression methods:

- **Linear regression**: We already learned about linear regression in earlier chapters; we can use this method using the LinearRegression class defined at pyspark.ml.regression. By default, it uses minimized squared error with regularization. It supports L1 and L2 regularization, and a combination of them.
- **Generalized linear regression**: The Spark MLlib has a subset of exponential family distributions like Gaussian, Poissons, and so on. The regression is instantiated using the class GeneralizedLinearRegression.

- **Decision tree regression**: The `DecisionTreeRegressor` class can be used to make a prediction using decision tree regression.
- **Random forest regression**: One of the popular ML methods, they are defined in the `RandomForestRegressor` class.
- **Gradient boosted tree regression**: We can use an ensemble of decision trees using the `GBTRegressor` class.

Besides, the MLlib also has support for survival regression and isotonic regression using the `AFTSurvivalRegression` and `IsotonicRegression` classes.

With the help of these classes, we can build a ML model for regression (or classification as you will see in next section) in as little as 10 lines of code. The basic steps are outlined as follows:

1. Build a Spark session
2. Implement the data-loading pipeline: load the data file, specify the format, and read it into Spark DataFrames
3. Identify the features to be used as input and as the target (optionally split dataset in train/test)
4. Instantiate the desired class object
5. Use the `fit()` method with training dataset as an argument
6. Depending upon the regressor chosen, you can see the learned parameters and evaluate the fitted model

Let's use linear regression for the Boston house price prediction dataset (https://www.cs.toronto.edu/~delve/data/boston/bostonDetail.html), where we have the dataset in csv format:

1. Import the necessary modules. We will be using `LinearRegressor` for defining the linear regression class, `RegressionEvaluator` to evaluate the model after training, `VectorAssembler` to combine features as one input vector, and `SparkSession` to start the Spark session:

```
from pyspark.ml.regression import LinearRegression as LR
from pyspark.ml.feature import VectorAssembler
from pyspark.ml.evaluation import RegressionEvaluator

from pyspark.sql import SparkSession
```

2. Next, start a Spark session using `SparkSession` class as follows:

```
spark = SparkSession.builder \
 .appName("Boston Price Prediction") \
 .config("spark.executor.memory", "70g") \
 .config("spark.driver.memory", "50g") \
 .config("spark.memory.offHeap.enabled",True) \
 .config("spark.memory.offHeap.size","16g") \
 .getOrCreate()
```

3. Let's now read the data; we first load the data from the given path, define the format we want to use, and finally, read it into Spark DataFrames, as follows:

```
house_df = spark.read.format("csv"). \
    options(header="true", inferschema="true"). \
    load("boston/train.csv")
```

4. You can see the DataFrame now loaded in the memory, and its structure, shown in the following screenshot:

```
In [3]: house_df.show(3)

+---+-------+----+-----+----+-----+-----+----+------+---+---+-------+------+-----+----+
| ID|   crim|  zn|indus|chas|  nox|   rm| age|   dis|rad|tax|ptratio| black|lstat|medv|
+---+-------+----+-----+----+-----+-----+----+------+---+---+-------+------+-----+----+
|  1|0.00632|18.0| 2.31|   0|0.538|6.575|65.2|  4.09|  1|296|   15.3| 396.9| 4.98|24.0|
|  2|0.02731| 0.0| 7.07|   0|0.469|6.421|78.9|4.9671|  2|242|   17.8| 396.9| 9.14|21.6|
|  4|0.03237| 0.0| 2.18|   0|0.458|6.998|45.8|6.0622|  3|222|   18.7|394.63| 2.94|33.4|
+---+-------+----+-----+----+-----+-----+----+------+---+---+-------+------+-----+----+
only showing top 3 rows

In [4]: # DataFrame Schema
        house_df.printSchema()

root
 |-- ID: integer (nullable = true)
 |-- crim: double (nullable = true)
 |-- zn: double (nullable = true)
 |-- indus: double (nullable = true)
 |-- chas: integer (nullable = true)
 |-- nox: double (nullable = true)
 |-- rm: double (nullable = true)
 |-- age: double (nullable = true)
 |-- dis: double (nullable = true)
 |-- rad: integer (nullable = true)
 |-- tax: integer (nullable = true)
 |-- ptratio: double (nullable = true)
 |-- black: double (nullable = true)
 |-- lstat: double (nullable = true)
 |-- medv: double (nullable = true)
```

5. Like pandas DataFrames, Spark DataFrames can also be processed with a single command. Let's gain a little more insight into our dataset as seen in the following screenshot:

```
In [5]: house_df.describe().toPandas().transpose()
```

Out[5]:

	0	1	2	3	4
summary	count	mean	stddev	min	max
ID	333	250.95195195195194	147.8594378018597	1	506
crim	333	3.3603414714714708	7.352271836781104	0.00632	73.5341
zn	333	10.68918918918919	22.674761796618217	0.0	100.0
indus	333	11.29348348348346	6.998123104477312	0.74	27.74
chas	333	0.06006006006006006	0.2379556428164483	0	1
nox	333	0.557144144144145	0.11495450830289312	0.385	0.871
rm	333	6.265618618618616	0.7039515757334471	3.561	8.725
age	333	68.22642642642641	28.13334360562338	6.0	100.0
dis	333	3.7099336336336335	1.9811230514407001	1.1296	10.7103
rad	333	9.633633633633634	8.742174349631064	1	24
tax	333	409.27927927927925	170.84198846058237	188	711
ptratio	333	18.448048048047994	2.1518213294390836	12.6	21.2
black	333	359.4660960960953	86.58456685718393	3.5	396.9
lstat	333	12.515435435435432	7.0677808035857845	1.73	37.97
medv	333	22.768768768768783	9.173468027315415	5.0	50.0

6. Next, we define the features we want to use for training; to do this, we make use of the VectorAssembler class. We define the columns from the house_df DataFrame to be combined together as an input feature vector and corresponding output prediction (similar to defining X_train, Y_train), and then perform the corresponding transformation, as follows:

```
vectors = VectorAssembler(inputCols = ['crim', 'zn','indus','chas',
    'nox','rm','age','dis', 'rad', 'tax',
    'ptratio','black', 'lstat'],
    outputCol = 'features')
vhouse_df = vectors.transform(house_df)
vhouse_df = vhouse_df.select(['features', 'medv'])
vhouse_df.show(5)
```

```
+--------------------+----+
|            features|medv|
+--------------------+----+
|[0.00632,18.0,2.3...|24.0|
|[0.02731,0.0,7.07...|21.6|
|[0.03237,0.0,2.18...|33.4|
|[0.06905,0.0,2.18...|36.2|
|[0.08829,12.5,7.8...|22.9|
+--------------------+----+
only showing top 5 rows
```

7. The dataset is then split into train/test datasets, shown in the following code:

```
train_df, test_df = vhouse_df.randomSplit([0.7,0.3])
```

8. Now that we have our dataset ready, we instantiate the LinearRegression class and fit it for the training dataset, as follows:

```
regressor = LR(featuresCol = 'features', labelCol='medv',\
    maxIter=20, regParam=0.3, elasticNetParam=0.8)
model = regressor.fit(train_df)
```

9. We can obtain the result coefficients of linear regression, as follows:

```
print("Coefficients:", model.coefficients)
print("Intercept:", model.intercept)
```

```
Coefficients: [-0.010279413081980417,0.034113414577108085,0.0,5.6415385374198,-7.783264348644399,3.085680504353533,0.0,-0.8290283633263736,0.016467345168122184,0.0,-0.5849152858717687,0.009195354138663316,-0.5627105522578837]
Intercept: 24.28872820161242
```

10. The model provides an RMSE value of 4.73 and an $r2$ value of 0.71 on the training dataset in 21 iterations:

```
modelSummary = model.summary
print("RMSE is {} and r2 is {}"\
    .format(modelSummary.rootMeanSquaredError,\
    modelSummary.r2))
print("Number of Iterations is ",modelSummary.totalIterations)
```

11. Next, we evaluate our model on the test dataset; we obtain an RMSE of 5.55 and R2 value of 0.68:

```
model_evaluator = RegressionEvaluator(predictionCol="prediction",\
    labelCol="medv", metricName="r2")
print("R2 value on test dataset is: ",\
    model_evaluator.evaluate(model_predictions))
print("RMSE value is",
model.evaluate(test_df).rootMeanSquaredError)
```

Once the work is done, you should stop the Spark session using the `stop()` method. The complete code is available in `Chapter08/Boston_Price_MLlib.ipynb`. The reason for a low $r2$ value and high RMSE is that we have considered all the features in the training dataset as an input feature vector, and many of them play no significant role in determining the house price. Try reducing the features, keeping the ones that have a high correlation with the price.

Classification in MLlib

MLlib also offers a wide range of classifiers; it provides both binomial and multinomial logistic regressor. The decision tree classifier, random forest classifier, gradient-boosted tree classifier, multilayered perceptron classifier, linear support vector machine classifier, and Naive Bayes classifier are supported. Each of them is defined in its class; for details, refer to `https://spark.apache.org/docs/2.2.0/ml-classification-regression.html`. The basic steps remain the same as we learned in the case of regression; the only difference is now, instead of RMSE or r2 metrics, the models are evaluated on accuracy.

This section will treat you to the wine quality classification problem implemented using Spark MLlib logistic regression classifier:

1. For this classification problem, we will use logistic regression available through the `LogisticRegressor` class. The `VectorAssembler`, like in the previous example, will be used to combine the input features as one vector. In the wine quality dataset we have seen (Chapter 1, *Principles and Foundations of IoT and AI*), the quality was an integer number given between 0–10, and we needed to process it. Here, we will process using `StringIndexer`.

    One of the great features of Spark is that we can define all the preprocessing steps as a pipeline. This becomes very useful when there are a large number of preprocessing steps. Here, we have only two preprocessing steps, but just to showcase how pipelines are formed, we will make use of the `Pipeline` class. We import all these modules as our first step and create a Spark session, shown in the following code:

    ```
    from pyspark.ml.classification import LogisticRegression as LR
    from pyspark.ml.feature import VectorAssembler
    from pyspark.ml.feature import StringIndexer
    from pyspark.ml import Pipeline

    from pyspark.sql import SparkSession

    spark = SparkSession.builder \
        .appName("Wine Quality Classifier") \
        .config("spark.executor.memory", "70g") \
        .config("spark.driver.memory", "50g") \
        .config("spark.memory.offHeap.enabled",True) \
        .config("spark.memory.offHeap.size","16g") \
        .getOrCreate()
    ```

2. We will load and read the `winequality-red.csv` data file, as follows:

    ```
    wine_df = spark.read.format("csv"). \
        options(header="true",\
        inferschema="true",sep=';'). \
        load("winequality-red.csv")
    ```

3. We process the `quality` label in the given dataset, and split it into three different classes, and add it to the existing Spark DataFrame as a new `quality_new` column, shown in the following code:

```
from pyspark.sql.functions import when
wine_df = wine_df.withColumn('quality_new',\
    when(wine_df['quality']< 5, 0 ).\
    otherwise(when(wine_df['quality']<8,1)\
    .otherwise(2)))
```

4. Though the modified quality, `quality_new` is an integer already, and we can use it directly as our label. In this example, we have added `StringIndexer` to convert it into numeric indices for the purpose of illustration. One can use `StringIndexer` to convert string labels to numeric indices. We also use `VectorAssembler` to combine the columns into one feature vector. The two stages are combined together using `Pipeline`, as follows:

```
string_index = StringIndexer(inputCol='quality_new',\
    outputCol='quality'+'Index')
vectors = VectorAssembler(inputCols = \
    ['fixed acidity','volatile acidity',\
    'citric acid','residual sugar','chlorides',\
    'free sulfur dioxide', 'total sulfur dioxide', \
    'density','pH','sulphates', 'alcohol'],\
    outputCol = 'features')

stages = [vectors, string_index]

pipeline = Pipeline().setStages(stages)
pipelineModel = pipeline.fit(wine_df)
pl_data_df = pipelineModel.transform(wine_df)
```

5. The data obtained after the pipeline is then split into training and testing datasets, shown in the following code:

```
train_df, test_df = pl_data_df.randomSplit([0.7,0.3])
```

6. Next, we instantiate the `LogisticRegressor` class and train it on the training dataset using the `fit` method, as follows:

```
classifier= LR(featuresCol = 'features', \
    labelCol='qualityIndex',\
    maxIter=50)
model = classifier.fit(train_df)
```

7. In the following screenshot, we can see the model parameters learned:

```
In [12]:  print("Beta Coefficients:", model.coefficientMatrix)
          print("Interceptors: ", model.interceptVector)

          Beta Coefficients: DenseMatrix([[-3.53097049e-02, -1.25709923e+00, -1.270
          86275e+00,
                        -8.55944290e-02, -4.85804489e-01,  1.46697237e-02,
                         3.27206803e-03,  8.87358597e+00, -6.98378596e-01,
                        -4.19883998e-01, -4.15213016e-01],
                       [-1.84038640e-03,  2.97769739e+00, -3.08531351e-01,
                         8.04546607e-02,  5.70434666e+00, -1.80503443e-02,
                        -3.20013995e-03, -4.47205103e+00,  2.46506380e+00,
                        -1.47617653e+00, -4.08041588e-01],
                       [ 3.71500913e-02, -1.72059816e+00,  1.57939410e+00,
                         5.13976829e-03, -5.21854217e+00,  3.38062055e-03,
                        -7.19280761e-05, -4.40153494e+00, -1.76668521e+00,
                         1.89606053e+00,  8.23254604e-01]])
          Interceptors:  [2.5177699762432026,-0.5458267035288586,-1.971943272714343
          8]
```

8. The accuracy of the model is 94.75%. We can also see other evaluation metrics like `precision` and `recall`, F measure, true positive rate, and false positive rate in the following code:

```
modelSummary = model.summary

accuracy = modelSummary.accuracy
fPR = modelSummary.weightedFalsePositiveRate
tPR = modelSummary.weightedTruePositiveRate
fMeasure = modelSummary.weightedFMeasure()
precision = modelSummary.weightedPrecision
recall = modelSummary.weightedRecall
print("Accuracy: {} False Positive Rate {} \
    True Positive Rate {} F {} Precision {} Recall {}"\
    .format(accuracy, fPR, tPR, fMeasure, precision, recall))
```

We can see that the performance of the wine quality classifier using MLlib is comparable to our earlier approaches. The complete code is available in the GitHub repository under `Chapter08/Wine_Classification_MLlib.pynb`.

Transfer learning using SparkDL

The previous sections elaborated how you can use the Spark framework with its MLlib for ML problems. In most complex tasks, however, deep learning models provide better performance. Spark supports SparkDL, a higher-level API working over MLlib. It uses TensorFlow at its backend, and it also requires TensorFrames, Keras, and TFoS modules.

In this section, we will make use of SparkDL for classifying images. This will allow you to get acquainted with the Spark support for the images. For images, as we learned in `Chapter 4`, *Deep Learning for IoT*, **Convolutional Neural Networks** (**CNNs**) are the de facto choice. In `Chapter 4`, *Deep Learning for IoT*, we built CNNs from scratch, and also learned about some popular CNN architectures. A very interesting property of CNNs is that each convolutional layer learns to identify different features from the image, which is they act as feature extractors. The lower convolutional layers filter out basic shapes like lines and circles, while higher layers filter more abstract shapes. This property can be used to employ a CNN trained on one set of images to classify another set of similar domain images by just changing the top fully connected layers. This technique is called **transfer learning**. Depending upon the availability of new dataset images and similarity between the two domains, transfer learning can significantly help in reducing the training time and need for large datasets.

In the NIPS 2016 tutorial, Andrew Ng, one of the key figures in the AI field, said that *transfer learning will be the next driver for commercial success*. In the image domain, great success in transfer learning has been achieved using CNNs trained in ImageNet data for classifying images on other domains. A lot of research is being carried out in applying transfer learning to other data domains. You can get a primer on *Transfer Learning* from this blog post by Sebastian Ruder: `http://ruder.io/transfer-learning/`.

We will employ InceptionV3, a CNN architecture proposed by Google (`https://arxiv.org/pdf/1409.4842.pdf`), trained on the ImageNet dataset (`http://www.image-net.org`) to identify vehicles on roads (at present we restrict ourselves to only buses and cars).

Before we can start, ensure that the following modules are installed in your working environment:

- PySpark
- TensorFlow
- Keras
- TFoS
- TensorFrames
- Wrapt
- Pillow
- pandas
- Py4J
- SparkDL
- Kafka
- Jieba

These can be installed using the `pip install` command on your standalone machine or machines in the cluster.

Next you will learn how to use Spark and SparkDL for image classification. We have taken screenshots of two different flowers, daisies and tulips, using Google image search; there are 42 images of daisies and 65 images of tulips. In the following screenshot, you can see the sample screenshots of the daisies:

The following screenshot shows the sample images of tulips:

Our dataset is too small, and hence if we make a CNN from scratch, it will not be able to give any useful performance. In cases like these, we can make use of transfer learning. The SparkDL module provides an easy and convenient way to use pre-trained models with the help of the class `DeepImageFeaturizer`. It supports the following CNN models (pre-trained on the ImageNet dataset (`http://www.image-net.org`):

- InceptionV3
- Xception
- ResNet50
- VGG16
- VGG19

We will use Google's InceptionV3 as our base model. The complete code can be accessed from the GitHub repository under `Chapter08/Transfer_Learning_Sparkdl.ipynb`:

1. In the first step, we will need to specify the environment for the SparkDL library. It is an important step; without it, the kernel will not know from where the SparkDL packages are to be loaded:

```
import os
SUBMIT_ARGS = "--packages databricks:spark-deep-learning:1.3.0-
spark2.4-s_2.11 pyspark-shell"
os.environ["PYSPARK_SUBMIT_ARGS"] = SUBMIT_ARGS
```

Even when you install SparkDL using `pip` on some OSes, it is required that you specify the OS environment or SparkDL.

2. Next, let's initiate a `SparkSession`, shown in the following code:

```
from pyspark.sql import SparkSession
spark = SparkSession.builder \
    .appName("ImageClassification") \
    .config("spark.executor.memory", "70g") \
    .config("spark.driver.memory", "50g") \
    .config("spark.memory.offHeap.enabled",True) \
    .config("spark.memory.offHeap.size","16g") \
    .getOrCreate()
```

3. We import the necessary modules and read the data images. Along with reading the image paths, we also assign the labels to each image in the Spark DataFrame, as follows:

```
import pyspark.sql.functions as f
import sparkdl as dl
from pyspark.ml.image import ImageSchema
from sparkdl.image import imageIO
dftulips = ImageSchema.readImages('data/flower_photos/tulips').\
    withColumn('label', f.lit(0))
dfdaisy = ImageSchema.readImages('data/flower_photos/daisy').\
    withColumn('label', f.lit(1))
```

4. Next, you can see the top five rows of the two DataFrames. The first column contains the path of each image, and the column shows its label (whether it belongs to daisy (label 1) or it belongs to tulips (label 0)):

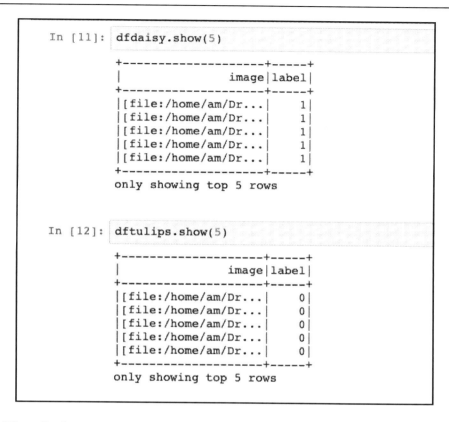

```
In [11]: dfdaisy.show(5)

         +--------------------+-----+
         |               image|label|
         +--------------------+-----+
         |[file:/home/am/Dr...|    1|
         |[file:/home/am/Dr...|    1|
         |[file:/home/am/Dr...|    1|
         |[file:/home/am/Dr...|    1|
         |[file:/home/am/Dr...|    1|
         +--------------------+-----+
         only showing top 5 rows


In [12]: dftulips.show(5)

         +--------------------+-----+
         |               image|label|
         +--------------------+-----+
         |[file:/home/am/Dr...|    0|
         |[file:/home/am/Dr...|    0|
         |[file:/home/am/Dr...|    0|
         |[file:/home/am/Dr...|    0|
         |[file:/home/am/Dr...|    0|
         +--------------------+-----+
         only showing top 5 rows
```

5. We split the two image dataset into training and testing set (it is always a good practice), using the randomSplit function. Conventionally, people choose a test-train split of 60%—40%, 70%—30%, or 80%—20%. We have chosen a 70%—30% split here. For the purpose of training, we then combine the training images of both flowers in the trainDF DataFrame and test dataset images in the testDF DataFrame, as follows:

```
trainDFdaisy, testDFdaisy = dfdaisy.randomSplit([0.70,0.30],\
        seed = 123)
trainDFtulips, testDFtulips = dftulips.randomSplit([0.70,0.30],\
        seed = 122)
trainDF = trainDFdaisy.unionAll(trainDFtulips)
testDF = testDFdaisy.unionAll(testDFtulips)
```

6. Next, we build the pipeline with `InceptionV3` as the feature extractor followed by a logistic regressor classifier. We use the `trainDF` DataFrame to train the model:

```
from pyspark.ml.classification import LogisticRegression
from pyspark.ml import Pipeline

vectorizer = dl.DeepImageFeaturizer(inputCol="image",\
        outputCol="features", modelName="InceptionV3")
logreg = LogisticRegression(maxIter=20, labelCol="label")
pipeline = Pipeline(stages=[vectorizer, logreg])
pipeline_model = pipeline.fit(trainDF)
```

7. Let's now evaluate our trained model on the test dataset. We can see that, on the test dataset, we get an accuracy of 90.32% using the following code:

```
predictDF = pipeline_model.transform(testDF) #predict on test
dataset

from pyspark.ml.evaluation import MulticlassClassificationEvaluator
as MCE
scoring = predictDF.select("prediction", "label")
accuracy_score = MCE(metricName="accuracy")
rate = accuracy_score.evaluate(scoring)*100
print("accuracy: {}%" .format(round(rate,2)))
```

8. Here is the confusion matrix for the two classes:

```
In [17]: predictDF.crosstab('prediction', 'label').show()

+----------------+---+---+
|prediction_label|  0|  1|
+----------------+---+---+
|             1.0|  0| 12|
|             0.0| 16|  3|
+----------------+---+---+
```

In fewer than 20 lines of code, we were able to train the model and obtain a good 90.32% accuracy. Remember, here the dataset used is raw; by increasing the dataset images, and filtering out low-quality images, you can improve the performance of your model. You can learn more about the deep learning library SparkDL from the official GitHub repository: https://github.com/databricks/spark-deep-learning.

Introducing H2O.ai

H2O is a fast, scalable ML and deep learning framework developed by H2O.ai, released under the open source Apache license. According to the company-provided details, more than 9,000 organizations and 80,000+ data scientists use H2O for their ML/deep learning needs. It uses in-memory compression, which allows it to handle a large amount of data in memory, even with a small cluster of machines. It has an interface for R, Python, Java, Scala, and JavaScript, and even has a built-in web interface. H2O can run in standalone mode, and on Hadoop or Spark cluster.

H2O includes a large number of ML algorithms like generalized linear modeling, Naive Bayes, random forest, gradient boosting, and deep learning algorithms. The best part of H2O is that one can build thousands of models, compare the results, and even do hyperparameter tuning with a few lines of codes. H2O also has better data preprocessing tools.

H2O requires Java, so, ensure that Java is installed on your system. You can install H2O to work in Python using `PyPi`, shown in the following code:

```
pip install h2o
```

H2O AutoML

One of the most exciting features of H2O is **AutoML**, the automatic ML. It is an attempt to develop a user-friendly ML interface that can be used by non-experts. H2O AutoML automates the process of training and tuning a large selection of candidate models. Its interface is designed so that users just need to specify their dataset, input and output features, and any constraints they want on the number of total models trained, or time constraint. The rest of the work is done by AutoML itself; in the specified time constraint, it identifies the best performing models, and provides a leaderboard. It has been observed that, usually, the Stacked Ensemble model, the ensemble of all the previously trained models, occupies the top position on the leaderboard. There is a large number of options that advanced users can use; details of these options and their various features are available at `http://docs.h2o.ai/h2o/latest-stable/h2o-docs/automl.html`.

To know more about H2O you can visit their website: `http://h2o.ai`.

Regression in H2O

We will first show how regression can be done in H2O. We will use the same dataset as we used earlier with MLlib, the Boston house prices, and predict the cost of the houses. The complete code can be found at GitHub: `Chapter08/boston_price_h2o.ipynb`:

1. The necessary modules for the task are as follows:

```
import h2o
import time
import seaborn
import itertools
import numpy as np
import pandas as pd
import seaborn as sns
import matplotlib.pyplot as plt
from h2o.estimators.glm import H2OGeneralizedLinearEstimator as GLM
from h2o.estimators.gbm import H2OGradientBoostingEstimator as GBM
from h2o.estimators.random_forest import H2ORandomForestEstimator as RF
%matplotlib inline
```

2. After importing the necessary modules, the first step is starting an h2o server. We do this using the `h2o.init()` command. It checks for any existing h20 instances first, and if none are available, it will start one. There is also the possibility of connecting to an existing cluster by specifying the IP address and the port number as arguments to the `init()` function. In the following screenshot, you can see the result of `init()` on the standalone system:

```
Checking whether there is an H2O instance running at http://localhost:54321..... not found.
Attempting to start a local H2O server...
  Java Version: java version "1.8.0_191"; Java(TM) SE Runtime Environment (build 1.8.0_191-b12
); Java HotSpot(TM) 64-Bit Server VM (build 25.191-b12, mixed mode)
  Starting server from /home/am/anaconda3/envs/h2o/lib/python3.5/site-packages/h2o/backend/bin
/h2o.jar
  Ice root: /tmp/tmp7hjshd9o
  JVM stdout: /tmp/tmp7hjshd9o/h2o_am_started_from_python.out
  JVM stderr: /tmp/tmp7hjshd9o/h2o_am_started_from_python.err
  Server is running at http://127.0.0.1:54321
Connecting to H2O server at http://127.0.0.1:54321... successful.
```

H2O cluster uptime:	01 secs
H2O cluster timezone:	Asia/Kolkata
H2O data parsing timezone:	UTC
H2O cluster version:	3.22.0.2
H2O cluster version age:	18 days
H2O cluster name:	H2O_from_python_am_3z4r3u
H2O cluster total nodes:	1
H2O cluster free memory:	6.957 Gb
H2O cluster total cores:	8
H2O cluster allowed cores:	8
H2O cluster status:	accepting new members, healthy
H2O connection url:	http://127.0.0.1:54321
H2O connection proxy:	None
H2O internal security:	False
H2O API Extensions:	XGBoost, Algos, AutoML, Core V3, Core V4
Python version:	3.5.6 final

3. Next, we read the data file using the h2o import_file function. It loads it into an H2O DataFrame, which can be processed just as easily as the panda's DataFrame. We can find the correlation among the different input features in the h2o DataFrame very easily using the cor() method:

```
boston_df = h2o.import_file("../Chapter08/boston/train.csv",
destination_frame="boston_df")

plt.figure(figsize=(20,20))
corr = boston_df.cor()
corr = corr.as_data_frame()
corr.index = boston_df.columns
#print(corr)
sns.heatmap(corr, annot=True, cmap='YlGnBu',vmin=-1, vmax=1)
plt.title("Correlation Heatmap")
```

The following is the output of correlation map among different features of the Boston house price dataset:

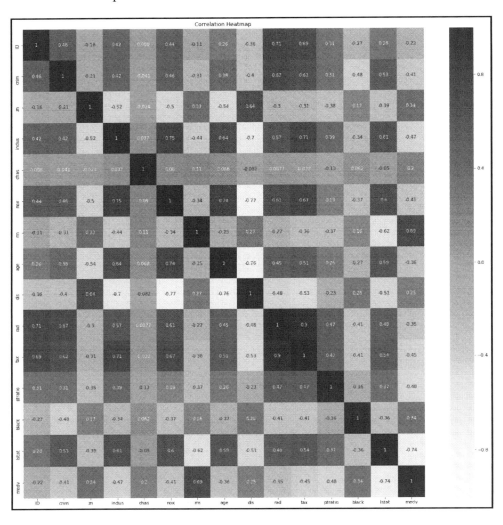

4. Now, as usual, we split the dataset into training, validation, and test datasets. Define the features to be used as input features (x):

```
train_df,valid_df,test_df = boston_df.split_frame(ratios=[0.6,
0.2],\
        seed=133)
features =  boston_df.columns[:-1]
```

5. Once this work is done, the process is very simple. We just instantiate the regression model class available from the H2O library, and use `train()` with the training and validation datasets as arguments. In the `train` function, we also specify what are the input features (x) and the output features (y). In the present case, we are taking all the features available to us as input features and the house price `medv` as the output feature. We can see the features of the trained model by just using a print statement. Next, you can see the model declaration for a generalized linear regression model, and its result after training on both training and validation datasets:

```
model_glm = GLM(model_id='boston_glm')
model_glm.train(training_frame= train_df,\
        validation_frame=valid_df, \
        y = 'medv', x=features)
print(model_glm)
```

```
glm Model Build progress: |████████████████████████████| 100%
k to expand output; double click to hide output

H2OGeneralizedLinearEstimator :  Generalized Linear Modeling
Model Key:  boston_glm


ModelMetricsRegressionGLM: glm
** Reported on train data. **

MSE: 25.29061565365854
RMSE: 5.028977595263131
MAE: 3.5119806236622573
RMSLE: 0.21879597717063684
R^2: 0.6585836959508422
Mean Residual Deviance: 25.29061565365854
Null degrees of freedom: 199
Residual degrees of freedom: 188
Null deviance: 14815.118876113953
Residual deviance: 5058.123130731708
AIC: 1239.662094110731


ModelMetricsRegressionGLM: glm
** Reported on validation data. **

MSE: 29.45943429400654
RMSE: 5.427654584994014
MAE: 3.9827620428290818
RMSLE: 0.23155132773489584
R^2: 0.6075220878659529
Mean Residual Deviance: 29.45943429400654
Null degrees of freedom: 57
Residual degrees of freedom: 46
Null deviance: 4379.649896571945
Residual deviance: 1708.6471890523794
AIC: 386.81169393537243
```

6. After training, the next step is checking the performance on the test dataset, which can be easily done using the `model_performance()` function. We can also pass it to any of the datasets: the train, validation, test, or some new similar dataset:

```
test_glm = model_glm.model_performance(test_df)
print(test_glm)
```

```
ModelMetricsRegressionGLM: glm
** Reported on test data. **

MSE: 58.79022368779993
RMSE: 7.667478313487423
MAE: 4.535525812229012
RMSLE: 0.2716211906586539
R^2: 0.4911310682143256
Mean Residual Deviance: 58.79022368779993
Null degrees of freedom: 74
Residual degrees of freedom: 63
Null deviance: 8748.76368890764
Residual deviance: 4409.266776584995
AIC: 544.388948275823
```

7. If we want to use gradient boost estimator regression, or random forest regression, we will instantiate the respective class object; the following steps will remain the same. What will vary is the output parameters; in the case of gradient boost estimator and random forest, we will also learn the relative importance of the different input features:

```
#Gradient Boost Estimator
model_gbm = GBM(model_id='boston_gbm')
model_gbm.train(training_frame= train_df, \
        validation_frame=valid_df, \
        y = 'medv', x=features)

test_gbm = model_gbm.model_performance(test_df)

#Random Forest
model_rf = RF(model_id='boston_rf')
model_rf.train(training_frame= train_df,\
        validation_frame=valid_df, \
        y = 'medv', x=features)

test_rf = model_rf.model_performance(test_df)
```

8. The most difficult part of machine and deep learning is choosing the right hyperparameters. In H2O, the task becomes quite easy with the help of its `H2OGridSearch` class. The following code snippet performs the grid search on the hyperparameter depth for the gradient boost estimator defined previously:

```
from h2o.grid.grid_search import H2OGridSearch as Grid
hyper_params = {'max_depth':[2,4,6,8,10,12,14,16]}
grid = Grid(model_gbm, hyper_params, grid_id='depth_grid')
grid.train(training_frame= train_df,\
        validation_frame=valid_df,\
        y = 'medv', x=features)
```

9. The best part of H2O is using AutoML to find the best models automatically. Let's ask it to search for us among the 10 models, with the constraint on time being 100 seconds. AutoML will, with these parameters, build 10 different models, excluding the Stacked Ensembles. It will run, at the most, for 100 seconds before training the final Stacked Ensemble models:

```
from h2o.automl import H2OAutoML as AutoML
aml = AutoML(max_models = 10, max_runtime_secs=100, seed=2)
aml.train(training_frame= train_df, \
        validation_frame=valid_df, \
        y = 'medv', x=features)
```

10. The leaderboard for our regression task is as follows:

In [25]:	print(aml.leaderboard)					
	model_id	mean_residual_deviance	rmse	mse	mae	rmsle
	StackedEnsemble_AllModels_AutoML_20181210_223722	9.82793	3.13495	9.82793	2.13917	0.139589
	StackedEnsemble_BestOfFamily_AutoML_20181210_223722	9.94461	3.15351	9.94461	2.14671	0.138903
	GBM_3_AutoML_20181210_223722	10.2273	3.19802	10.2273	2.24126	0.14437
	GBM_2_AutoML_20181210_223722	10.2627	3.20355	10.2627	2.23899	0.143894
	GBM_1_AutoML_20181210_223722	10.2719	3.20498	10.2719	2.21991	0.147681
	GBM_4_AutoML_20181210_223722	10.287	3.20734	10.287	2.24546	0.144326
	XGBoost_2_AutoML_20181210_223722	10.3645	3.21939	10.3645	2.05124	0.143118
	XGBoost_1_AutoML_20181210_223722	11.068	3.32686	11.068	2.16475	0.14958
	XGBoost_3_AutoML_20181210_223722	11.3421	3.3678	11.3421	2.26389	0.147565
	XRT_1_AutoML_20181210_223722	12.0748	3.47488	12.0748	2.31572	0.141624

Different models in the leaderboard can be accessed using their respective `model_id`. The best model is accessed with the leader parameter. In our case, `aml.leader` represents the best model, the Stacked Ensemble of all the models. We can save the best model using the `h2o.save_model` function in either binary or MOJO format.

Classification in H20

The same models can be used for classification in H2O, with only one change; we will need to change the output features from numeric values to categorical values using the `asfactor()` function. We will perform the classification on the quality of red wine, and use our old red wine database (Chapter 3, *Machine Learning for IoT*). We will need to import the same modules and initiate the H2O server. The full code is available at in the `Chapter08/wine_classification_h2o.ipynb` file:

1. Here is the code to import the necessary modules and initiate the H2O server:

```
import h2o
import time
import seaborn
import itertools
import numpy as np
import pandas as pd
import seaborn as sns
import matplotlib.pyplot as plt
from h2o.estimators.glm import H2OGeneralizedLinearEstimator as GLM
from h2o.estimators.gbm import H2OGradientBoostingEstimator as GBM
from h2o.estimators.random_forest import H2ORandomForestEstimator as RF

%matplotlib inline

h2o.init()
```

2. The next step is to read the data file. We modify the output feature first to account for two classes (good wine and bad wine) and then convert it to a categorical variable using the `asfactor()` function. This is an important step in H2O; since we are using the same class objects for both regression and classification, they require the output label to be numeric in the case of regression, and categorical in the case of classification, as seen in the code block:

```
wine_df = h2o.import_file("../Chapter08/winequality-red.csv",\
        destination_frame="wine_df")
features = wine_df.columns[:-1]
print(features)
wine_df['quality'] = (wine_df['quality'] > 7).ifelse(1,0)
wine_df['quality'] = wine_df['quality'].asfactor()
```

3. Next, split the data into training, validation, and testing datasets. We feed the training and validation datasets to the generalized linear estimator, with one change; we specify the `family=binomial` argument because here, we have only two categorical classes, good wine or bad wine. If you have more than two classes use `family=multinomial`. Remember, specifying the argument is optional; H2O automatically detects the output feature:

```
train_df,valid_df,test_df = wine_df.split_frame(ratios=[0.6, 0.2],\
        seed=133)

model_glm = GLM(model_id='wine_glm', family = 'binomial')
model_glm.train(training_frame= train_df, \
        validation_frame=valid_df,\
        y = 'quality', x=features)
print(model_glm)
```

4. After being trained, you can see the model performance on all the performance metrics: accuracy, precision, recall, F1 measure, and AUC, even the confusion metrics. You can get them for all the three datasets (training, validation, and testing). The following are the metrics obtained for the test dataset from the generalized linear estimator:

```
In [9]:  test_glm = model_glm.model_performance(test_df)
         print(test_glm)


         ModelMetricsBinomialGLM: glm
         ** Reported on test data. **

         MSE: 0.017228193204603934
         RMSE: 0.1312562120610066
         LogLoss: 0.13988271775187358
         Null degrees of freedom: 317
         Residual degrees of freedom: 306
         Null deviance: 53.187557984070224
         Residual deviance: 88.96540849019598
         AIC: 112.96540849019598
         AUC: 0.6038338658146964
         pr_auc: 0.03346490361472496
         Gini: 0.2076677316293929
         Confusion Matrix (Act/Pred) for max f1 @ threshold = 0.17042651179749857:
```

	0	1	Error	Rate
0	308.0	5.0	0.016	(5.0/313.0)
1	4.0	1.0	0.8	(4.0/5.0)
Total	312.0	6.0	0.0283	(9.0/318.0)

```
Maximum Metrics: Maximum metrics at their respective thresholds
```

metric	threshold	value	idx
max f1	0.1704265	0.1818182	5.0
max f2	0.1704265	0.1923077	5.0
max f0point5	0.1704265	0.1724138	5.0
max accuracy	0.4984876	0.9811321	0.0
max precision	0.1704265	0.1666667	5.0
max recall	0.0000002	1.0	253.0
max specificity	0.4984876	0.9968051	0.0
max absolute_mcc	0.1704265	0.1682606	5.0
max min_per_class_accuracy	0.0006228	0.6	109.0
max mean_per_class_accuracy	0.0006228	0.6226837	109.0

```
Gains/Lift Table: Avg response rate:  1.57 %, avg score:  1.20 %
```

5. Without changing anything else in the previous code, we can perform hyper tuning and use H2O's AutoML to get the better model:

```
from h2o.automl import H2OAutoML as AutoML
aml = AutoML(max_models = 10, max_runtime_secs=100, seed=2)
aml.train(training_frame= train_df, \
        validation_frame=valid_df, \
        y = 'quality', x=features)
```

```
In [25]: print(aml.leaderboard)
```

model_id	mean_residual_deviance	rmse	mse	mae	rmsle
StackedEnsemble_AllModels_AutoML_20181210_223722	9.82793	3.13495	9.82793	2.13917	0.139589
StackedEnsemble_BestOfFamily_AutoML_20181210_223722	9.94461	3.15351	9.94461	2.14671	0.138903
GBM_3_AutoML_20181210_223722	10.2273	3.19802	10.2273	2.24126	0.14437
GBM_2_AutoML_20181210_223722	10.2627	3.20355	10.2627	2.23899	0.143894
GBM_1_AutoML_20181210_223722	10.2719	3.20498	10.2719	2.21991	0.147681
GBM_4_AutoML_20181210_223722	10.287	3.20734	10.287	2.24546	0.144326
XGBoost_2_AutoML_20181210_223722	10.3645	3.21939	10.3645	2.05124	0.143118
XGBoost_1_AutoML_20181210_223722	11.068	3.32686	11.068	2.16475	0.14958
XGBoost_3_AutoML_20181210_223722	11.3421	3.3678	11.3421	2.26389	0.147565
XRT_1_AutoML_20181210_223722	12.0748	3.47488	12.0748	2.31572	0.141624

We see that, for wine quality classification, the best model is XGBoost.

Summary

With the ubiquitous status of IoT, the data being generated is growing at an exponential rate. This data, mostly unstructured and available in vast quantities, is often referred to as big data. A large number of frameworks and solutions have been proposed to deal with the large set of data. One of the promising solutions is DAI, distributing the model or data among the cluster of machines. We can use distributed TensorFlow, or TFoS frameworks to perform distributed model training. In recent years, some easy-to-use open source solutions have been proposed. Two of the most popular and successful solutions are Apache Spark's MLlib and H2O.ai's H2O. In this chapter, we showed how to train ML models for both regression and classification in MLlib and H2O. The Apache Spark MLlib supports SparkDL, which provides excellent support for image classification and detection tasks. The chapter used SparkDL to classify flower images using the pre-trained InceptionV3. The H2O.ai's H2O, on the other hand, works well with numeric and tabular data. It provides an interesting and useful AutoML feature, which allows even non-experts to tune and search through a large number of ML/deep learning models, with very little details from the user. The chapter covered an example of how to use AutoML for both regression and classification tasks.

One can take the best advantage of these distributed platforms when working on a cluster of machines. With computing and data shifting to the cloud at affordable rates, it makes sense to shift the task of ML to the cloud. Thus follows the next chapter, where you will learn about different cloud platforms, and how you can use them to analyze the data generated by your IoT devices.

Personal and Home IoT

9

Now that you are fully equipped with **machine learning (ML)** and **deep learning (DL)** knowledge, and have learned how to use it for big data, image tasks, text tasks, and time series data, it is time to explore some real uses of the algorithms and the techniques that you have learned. This chapter and the following two chapters will now concentrate on some specific case studies. This chapter will focus on personal and home **Internet of Things (IoT)** use cases. We will cover the following in this chapter:

- Successful IoT applications
- Wearables and their role in personal IoT
- How to monitor heart using ML
- What makes home smart home
- Devices used in smart home
- The application of Artificial Intelligence in predicting human activity recognition

Personal IoT

The personal IoT is dominated by the use of wearables, technological devices designed to be worn on body, they are used in tandem with an app on a smartphone. The first wearable available was the Pulsar Calculator watch made by Time Computer Inc, USA (at that time known as **Hamilton Watch Company**). It was a standalone device not connected to the internet. Soon, with the growth of the internet, wearables that can connect to the internet became a fad. The wearables market is expected to jump from an estimate of **325 million** in **2016** to over **830 million** by **2020**:

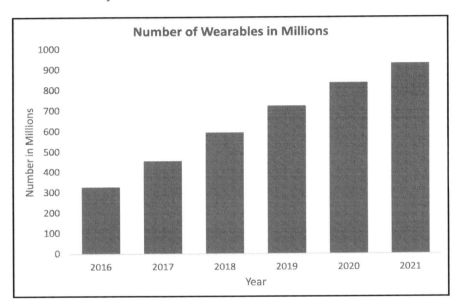

This graph shows the number of wearables worldwide from 2016–2021 (data source: Statista). With so many devices connected online, continuously generating data, AI/ML tools are a natural choice to analyze this data and make informed decisions. In this section, you will learn about some successful personal IoT applications.

SuperShoes by MIT

Holding your mobile in one hand and navigating your way along the road with the help of *Google Maps*, how often have you thought that it is cumbersome? How often have you wished for magic slippers that will take you anywhere you want? SuperShoes by *MIT Media Lab* (`https://www.media.mit.edu/projects/supershoes/overview/`) are almost like those magic slippers; they allow the user to navigate through the sidewalks without any need to check the smartphone screen.

SuperShoes have flexible insoles, embedded with vibrating motors under the toes. They connect wirelessly to an app on the smartphone. The app not only allows the user to interface with the SuperShoes, but it also stores likes/dislikes, hobbies, shops, foods, people, interests, and so on in a cloud account. The vibrating motors generate tickles that communicate with the user. Once the user enters a destination on the app, the shoes start their work. If the left toe tickles then the user is supposed to take a left turn; if the right toe tickles then the user has to take a right turn. When there is no tickle, then the user has to continue straight. If both tickle repeatedly, the user has arrived at their destination.

Besides navigation, it can also recommend places of interest nearby; the user updates their likes and dislikes on the cloud. Based on the likes and dislikes of the user, SuperShoe also gives an indication (both toes tickle once) when the user is near a recommended place of interest. Another interesting feature of SuperShoes is that it can give reminders as well; it can remind you if you have a task on a location nearby.

The hardware required to make this shoe is very simple, it requires the following:

- Three vibrotactile ticklers to tickle the toes
- A capacitive pad to sense the walk
- A microcontroller that takes the commands from the app, and accordingly, controls the ticklers
- A Bluetooth device to connect with the smartphone
- Batteries to power the entire system

The magic is performed by the software coded into the app. You can learn more about the SuperShoes at this website: `http://dhairyadand.com/works/supershoes`.

Continuous glucose monitoring

A major application of AI has been in IoT for healthcare, with one of the most successful commercial applications being continuous monitoring of the body's glucose level. Abbott's FreeStyle CGM, DexCom CGM, and Medtronic CGM are some of the commercially available brands.

Continuous glucose monitoring (CGM) allows people suffering from diabetes to check their body's glucose level in real time. It helps them in monitoring the readings over a period of time, and the data can also be used to prediction of future glucose level, thus helping them to deal with conditions like hypoglycemia.

In CGM, normally a sensor is placed either under the skin of the belly or adhered to the back of your arm. The sensor sends the readings to a connected pager/smartphone app. The app has additional AI-based algorithms that can inform the user of any clinically relevant glucose patterns. The availability of this data not only helps the user to proactively manage their glucose highs and lows, but additionally, it can also provide an insight into the impact that meals, exercise, or illness may have on a person's glucose levels.

The sensors have a lifespan ranging from 7 to 14 days, normally this time is sufficient for a medical practitioner to understand the person's lifestyle, and accordingly, suggest changes.

Hypoglycemia prediction using CGM data

Once a person has CGM data, it can be analyzed using AI/ML to gather more information or to make a prediction about hypoglycemia. In this section, we see how we can use the algorithms we had learned in the previous chapters to make a glucose-predictor system.

We will build our predictor based on the research paper *Glucose Concentration can be Predicted Ahead in Time From Continuous Glucose Monitoring sensor Time-Series* by Sparacino et al. (10.1109/TBME.2006.889774).

In the paper, the CGM time series glucose data is described by a times series model; the paper considered two models, one a simple first order polynomial and second a first order autoregressive model. The model parameters are fitted at each sampling time, t_s, against the past glucose data. Here, we will implement the simple first order polynomial using scikit linear regressor that we learned about in Chapter 3, *Machine Learning for IoT*:

1. We import the modules pandas to read the csv file, NumpPy for data processing, Matplolib for plotting, and scikit-learn for the linear regressor, as follows:

```
import pandas as pd
import numpy as np
import matplotlib.pyplot as plt
from sklearn.linear_model import LinearRegression
%matplotlib inline
```

2. Save the data obtained from your CGM in the data folder and read it. We require two values, the glucose reading and its time. The data that we are using has these available in two CSV files, ys.csv and ts.csv. The first one contains the glucose value and the second one contains the corresponding time, as follows:

```
# Read the data
ys = pd.read_csv('data/ys.csv')
ts = pd.read_csv('data/ts.csv')
```

3. According to the paper, we define two parameters of the predictive model ph, the prediction horizon, and mu the forgetting factor. Please refer to the we mentioned earlier paper for more details on these two parameters:

```
# MODEL FIT AND PREDICTION

# Parameters of the predictive model. ph is Prediction horizon, mu
is Forgetting factor.
ph = 10
mu = 0.98
```

4. We create the arrays to hold our predicted values, shown as follows:

```
n_s = len(ys)

# Arrays to hold predicted values
tp_pred = np.zeros(n_s-1)
yp_pred = np.zeros(n_s-1)
```

5. We now read the CGM data simulating the real-time acquisition and predict the glucose level ph minutes forward. All the past data is used to determine the model parameters, however, each has a different contribution decided by the individual weight assigned to it mu^k (to the sample taken k instants before the actual sampling time):

```
# At every iteration of the for loop a new sample from CGM is
acquired.
for i in range(2, n_s+1):
    ts_tmp = ts[0:i]
    ys_tmp = ys[0:i]
    ns = len(ys_tmp)

    # The mu**k assigns the weight to the previous samples.
    weights = np.ones(ns)*mu
    for k in range(ns):
        weights[k] = weights[k]**k
    weights = np.flip(weights, 0)
    # MODEL
    # Linear Regression.
    lm_tmp = LinearRegression()
    model_tmp = lm_tmp.fit(ts_tmp, ys_tmp, sample_weight=weights)
    # Coefficients of the linear model, y = mx + q
    m_tmp = model_tmp.coef_
    q_tmp = modeltmp.intercept

    # PREDICTION
    tp = ts.iloc[ns-1,0] + ph
    yp = m_tmp*tp + q_tmp

    tp_pred[i-2] = tp
    yp_pred[i-2] = yp
```

6. We can see that the prediction is lagging behind the actual. The normal glucose level lies in the range 70 to 180. Below 70, the patient can suffer from hypoglycemia and above 180 it can lead to hyperglycemia. Let us see the plot of our predicted data:

```
# PLOT
# Hypoglycemia threshold vector.
t_tot = [l for l in range(int(ts.min()), int(tp_pred.max())+1)]
hypoglycemiaTH = 70*np.ones(len(t_tot))
#hyperglycemiaTH = 180*np.ones(len(t_tot))

fig, ax = plt.subplots(figsize=(10,10))
fig.suptitle('Glucose Level Prediction', fontsize=22,
fontweight='bold')
```

```
ax.set_title('mu = %g, ph=%g ' %(mu, ph))
ax.plot(tp_pred, yp_pred, label='Predicted Value')
ax.plot(ts.iloc[:,0], ys.iloc[:,0], label='CGM data')
ax.plot(t_tot, hypoglycemiaTH, label='Hypoglycemia threshold')
#ax.plot(t_tot, hyperglycemiaTH, label='Hyperglycemia threshold')
ax.set_xlabel('time (min)')
ax.set_ylabel('glucose (mg/dl)')
ax.legend()
```

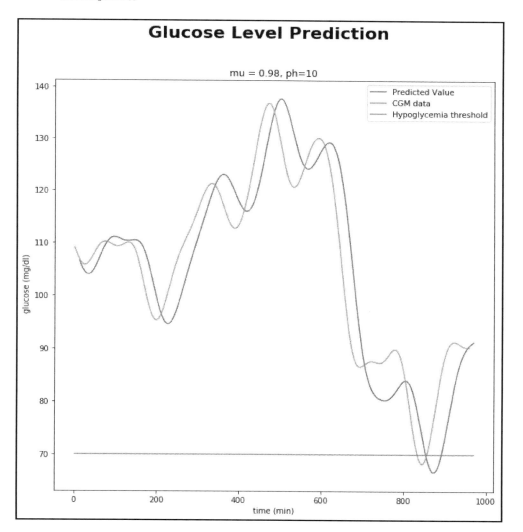

7. The RMSE error will be 27 for the following code:

```
from sklearn.metrics import mean_squared_error as mse
print("RMSE is", mse(ys[1:],yp_pred))
```

The code is located at `Chapter09/Hypoglycemia_Prediction.ipynb` notebook. The glucose-prediction system is available in many commercial products. You can make one too, based on the model that we just made. You can also use an artificial neural network to make a similar prediction with better results (refer to `https://www.ncbi.nlm.nih.gov/pubmed/20082589`).

Heart monitor

Another very useful personal application of AI in IoT is in the detection of heart disease. A large number of wearables exist that can be used to monitor and record heart rate. The data can be used to predict any harmful heart condition. Here, we will employ AI/ML tools to predict cardiac **arrhythmia**, a group of conditions where the heart rate is irregular; it can be either too fast (above 100 beats per minute) or too slow (below 60 beats per minute). The data used is taken from the *UCI Machine learning Repository* dataset: `https://archive.ics.uci.edu/ml/datasets/heart+Disease`. The dataset consists of 76 attributes, not all required for prediction of the presence of disease; the dataset has a goal field associated with each data row. It has five possible values 0–4, the value 0 indicates a healthy heart, any other value means there is a disease. The problem can be broken into a binary classification problems for better accuracy. The code is inspired from the GitHub link of Mohammed Rashad, it is shared under the GNU GPL 3.0 license: `https://github.com/MohammedRashad/Deep-Learning-and-Wearable-IoT-to-Monitor-and-Predict-Cardiac-Arrhytmia`. The complete code can be accessed from GitHub repository under `Chapter09/Heart_Disease_Prediction.ipynb` file:

1. The first step as always is to import the necessary modules. Since we are now classifying the patients as suffering from heart disease or not, we will need a classifier. Here for simplicity, we use the SVC classifier. You can experiment with the MLP classifier, shown as follows:

```
# importing required libraries
import numpy as np
import pandas as pd
import matplotlib.pyplot as plt

from sklearn.svm import SVC
from sklearn import metrics
from sklearn.metrics import confusion_matrix
from sklearn.model_selection import train_test_split
```

2. Next, read the dataset, preprocess the dataset to select the attributes you will be considering. We chose 13 attributes from 76, and then we convert the target from a multi-class value to binary class. Finally, the data is split into the train and test dataset, as follows:

```
# reading csv file and extracting class column to y.
dataset = pd.read_csv("data.csv")
dataset.fillna(dataset.mean(), inplace=True)

dataset_to_array = np.array(dataset)
label = dataset_to_array[:,57] # "Target" classes having 0 and 1
label = label.astype('int')
label[label>0] = 1 # When it is 0 heart is healthy, 1 otherwise

# extracting 13 features
dataset = np.column_stack((
    dataset_to_array[:,4] ,  # pain location
    dataset_to_array[:,6] ,  # relieved after rest
    dataset_to_array[:,9] ,  # pain type
    dataset_to_array[:,11],  # resting blood pressure
    dataset_to_array[:,33],  # maximum heart rate achieve
    dataset_to_array[:,34],  # resting heart rate
    dataset_to_array[:,35],  # peak exercise blood pressure (first
of 2 parts)
    dataset_to_array[:,36],  # peak exercise blood pressure (second
of 2 parts)
    dataset_to_array[:,38],  # resting blood pressure
    dataset_to_array[:,39],  # exercise induced angina (1 = yes; 0 =
no)
    dataset.age, # age
    dataset.sex , # sex
    dataset.hypertension # hyper tension
 ))

print ("The Dataset dimensions are : " , dataset.shape , "\n")

# dividing data into train and test data
X_train, X_test, y_train, y_test = train_test_split(dataset, label,
random_state = 223)
```

3. Now, we define the model to be used. Here we are using a support vector classifier, using the `fit` function to train the dataset:

```
model = SVC(kernel = 'linear').fit(X_train, y_train)
```

4. Let us see its performance on the test dataset:

```
model_predictions = model.predict(X_test)
# model accuracy for X_test
accuracy = metrics.accuracy_score(y_test, model_predictions)
print ("Accuracy of the model is :" ,
    accuracy , "\nApproximately : ",
    round(accuracy*100) , "%\n")
```

5. You can see that it provides an accuracy of 74%, using MLP, we can increase it further. But do remember to normalize all the input features before using the MLP classifier. Following is the confusion matrix of our trained support vector classifier on the test dataset:

```
#creating a confusion matrix
cm = confusion_matrix(y_test, model_predictions)

import pandas as pd
import seaborn as sn
import matplotlib.pyplot as plt
%matplotlib inline
df_cm = pd.DataFrame(cm, index = [i for i in "01"],
columns = [i for i in "01"])
plt.figure(figsize = (10,7))
sn.heatmap(df_cm, annot=True)
```

The following output shows the confusion matrix for the test dataset:

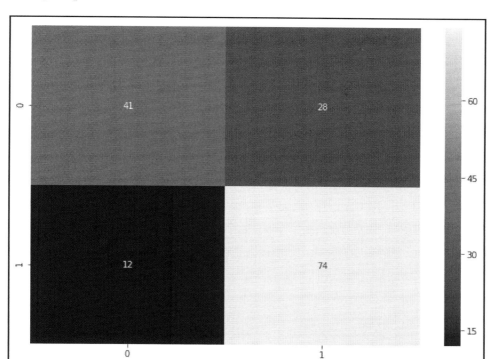

You can train your model on the same dataset and use your trained model to predict heart conditions for your friends, family, or clients.

Digital assistants

Digital assistants are one of the oldest conceived AI applications. Initial attempts at digital assistants never really took off. But with the advent and mass spread of smartphones, today we have a large number of digital assistants providing services such as dialing a phone number, writing a text message, scheduling appointments, or even searching the internet for you. You can ask them for recommendations for nearby restaurants and bars or any other similar thing.

Some of the following are popular digital assistants:

- **Siri**: Developed by Apple, it allows the user to send/make calls, add appointments in the calendar, play music or video, and even send a text. Today, a voice-activated interface is available on almost all Apple products.
- **Cortana**: Created by Microsoft, it helps you to stay on schedule by reminding you to do things based on time, place, or even people. You can ask Cortana to order lunch for you or use any other app it partners with. It comes integrated with Edge and invokes a voice-activated speaker featuring Cortana.
- **Alexa**: Developed by Amazon, this is available with Amazon Echo smart speakers. It can play music, make a to-do list, set alarms for you, play audio books, and provide real-time information on stocks, weather, and more. It is also capable of voice interaction.
- **Google Assistant**: This is a voice-controlled smart assistant. It provides continued conversation, that is you don't have to say *Hey Google* for any follow-up requests, once you start talking, it listens for a response without needing the triggering phrase. It can also recognize the voice profiles for different people and can tailor its response according to the personal likes and dislikes of that person. It is available not only on Android smartphones but also on Google Home.

In 2018, Google went even further, releasing Google Duplex, an assistant that can make calls for you and book your appointments. It talks like a human, and also understands the context when speaking.

IoT and smart homes

A close friend of mine was always worried about his ageing mother, she was left home alone, while he, his wife, and kids were out. As her health started deteriorating, he asked for a piece of advice. The solution was simple; he installed CCTV cameras in all the rooms, interfaced with a mobile app. The cameras were connected to the internet, now, no matter where he is, he can check-in home to ensure the well-being of his mother.

CCTV, smart lightning, smart speakers, and so on connected to the internet help automate a lot of tasks at home, and what you get is a smart home. Most smart home systems at present work through a voice command interface, where you can use a set of commands to control the particular device. For example, in Amazon's Echo Dot, you can ask it to search or play a particular song. You can ask Apple's Siri to use your phone to call a friend, all by simple voice interface. Most of these devices are using AI/ML in some form, but home automation can be further advanced by employing AI/ML. For example, in the case of my friend, an AI system can be trained to identify activity from video, or to detect intrusion in the home. The possibilities are infinite. With the right data and sufficient computing power, you are limited only by your imagination.

In this section, we will see some existing home automation products, and see how we can further use AI to augment the automation.

Human activity recognition

One of the most researched smart home application is **human activity recognition (HAR)**. There are many companies trying to develop apps that keep track of physical activity and its corresponding calorie burn count. Health and fitness no doubt is big business. Besides its application in fitness and health, HAR can also be useful in elder care or rehabilitation centers. There have been many approaches to perform HAR, two of which as the follows:

- Use cameras (or radar or similar devices) to record human activity and classify it using a DL approach
- The individuals use wearable sensors (similar to accelerometers in smartphones) whose data is recorded and used to predict the activity

Both approaches have their pros and cons. We will go through them in further detail in the following sections.

HAR using wearable sensors

A large number of vendors have wearable watches and bracelets with fitness trackers. These watches and bracelets have GPS, accelerometer, gyroscope, heart rate sensor, and/or ambient light sensors. Employing **sensor fusion**, they combine the output of these sensors to make a prediction about the activity. Due to the temporal nature of the data, it is a challenging time series classification task.

Fitbit (`https://www.fitbit.com/smarttrack`), a premier company in the field of fitness trackers, use a technology it calls **SmartTrack**, which recognizes activities with continuous movement or light movement. It uses the intensity and patterns of the movement to classify the activity. It classifies the activity in seven classes, as follows:

- Walking
- Running
- Aerobic workout
- Elliptical
- Outdoor bike
- Sports
- Swimming

Apple Watch (`https://www.apple.com/in/apple-watch-series-4/workout/`) offers tough competition to Fitbit. Working on an iOSoperating system, it comes with fall detection, along with many other health tracking features. By analyzing the wrist trajectory and impact acceleration, it detects if the person is falling and can also initiate an emergency call. The Apple watch, by default, classifies activities into three groups: walking, exercise, and standing. The exercise (workouts) are further classified in another domain, such as indoor run, outdoor run, skiing, snowboarding, yoga, and even hiking.

If you want to try making a similar app using your smartphone sensors, the first thing you will need is data. Following, we present an implementation of HAR using random forest, the code has been adapted from the GitHub link of Nilesh Patil, Data Scientist at the University of Rochester: `https://github.com/nilesh-patil/human-activity-recognition-smartphone-sensors`.

The dataset is from the paper *Davide Anguita, Alessandro Ghio, Luca Oneto, Xavier Parra and Jorge L. Reyes-Ortiz. A Public Domain Dataset for Human Activity Recognition Using Smartphones. 21th European Symposium on Artificial Neural Networks, Computational Intelligence and Machine Learning, ESANN 2013. Bruges, Belgium 24-26 April 2013.*

Available at the UCI ML website: `https://archive.ics.uci.edu/ml/datasets/Human+Activity+Recognition+Using+Smartphones#`.

For each record in the dataset contains:

- Triaxial acceleration from the accelerometer (total acceleration) and the estimated body acceleration
- Triaxial angular velocity from the gyroscope
- A 561-feature vector with time and frequency domain variables
- Its activity label
- An identifier of the subject who carried out the experiment

The data is classified into six categories:

- Laying
- Sitting
- Standing
- Walk
- Walk-down
- Walk-up

1. Here, we use random forest classifier of the scikit-learn to classify the data. The necessary modules needed for the implementation are imported in the first step:

```
import pandas as pd
import numpy as np
import seaborn as sns
import matplotlib.pyplot as plt

from sklearn.ensemble import RandomForestClassifier as rfc
from sklearn.metrics import confusion_matrix
from sklearn.metrics import accuracy_score
%matplotlib inline
```

2. We read the data and divide it into `train` and `test` datasets, as follows:

```
data = pd.read_csv('data/samsung_data.txt',sep='|')
train = data.sample(frac=0.7,
        random_state=42)
test = data[~data.index.isin(train.index)]

X = train[train.columns[:-2]]
Y = train.activity
```

3. The data consists of 561 features however, not all are equally important. We can choose the more important features by making a simple random forest classifier, and choosing only the most important ones. In this implementation, it is done using two steps. Initially, we get the list of important features and arrange them in descending order of importance. Then the number and the features are found by grid hypertuning. The results of hypertuning are shown in the curve. We can see that after about 20 features, there is no significant improvement in **out of bag (OOB)** accuracy using the following code:

```
randomState = 42
ntree = 25

model0 = rfc(n_estimators=ntree,
random_state=randomState,
n_jobs=4,
warm_start=True,
oob_score=True)
model0 = model0.fit(X, Y)

# Arrange the features in ascending order
model_vars0 = pd.DataFrame(
    {'variable':X.columns,
    'importance':model0.feature_importances_})

model_vars0.sort_values(by='importance',
    ascending=False,
    inplace=True)

# Build a feature vector with most important 25 features

n = 25
cols_model = [col for col in model_vars0.variable[:n].values]
```

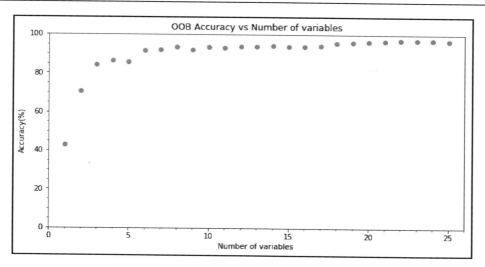

4. We can also see the average importance of the top 25 features in the following diagram:

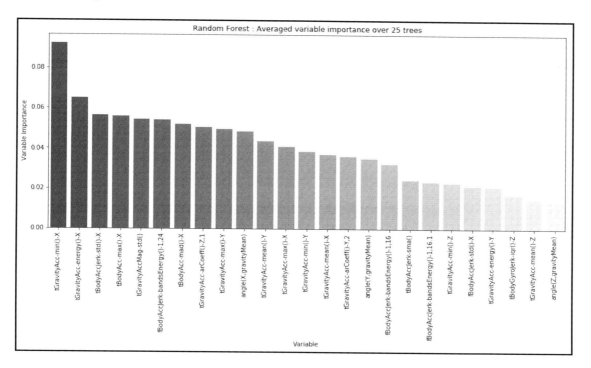

5. In the same manner, we can hypertune the number of tree parameter. Here, we restricted ourselves to four important features:

```
n_used = 4
cols_model = [col for col in model_vars0.variable[:n_used].values]\
    + [model_vars0.variable[6]]
X = train[cols_model]
Y = train.activity

ntree_determination = {}
for ntree in range(5,150,5):
    model = rfc(n_estimators=ntree,
        random_state=randomState,
        n_jobs=4,
        warm_start=False,
        oob_score=True)
model = model.fit(X, Y)
ntree_determination[ntree]=model.oob_score_
```

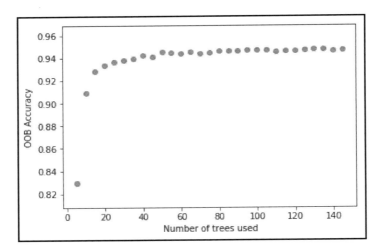

6. Thus, we can see that a random forest with about four important features and 50 trees can give a good OOB accuracy. Hence our final model is as follows:

```
model2 = rfc(n_estimators=50,
    random_state=randomState,
    n_jobs=4,
    warm_start=False,
    oob_score=True)
model2 = model2.fit(X, Y)
```

7. This results in a test data accuracy of 94%. Following you can see the confusion matrix for the test dataset:

```
test_actual = test.activity
test_pred = model2.predict(test[X.columns])
cm = confusion_matrix(test_actual,test_pred)
sns.heatmap(data=cm,
    fmt='.0f',
    annot=True,
    xticklabels=np.unique(test_actual),
    yticklabels=np.unique(test_actual))
```

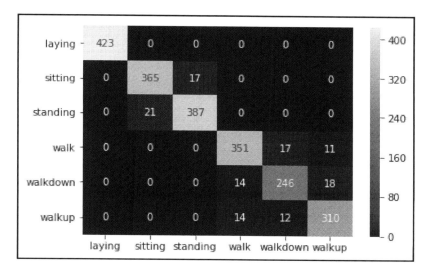

The complete code, along with the data exploration, is available at the GitHub repository, `Chapter09/Human_activity_recognition_using_accelerometer.ipynb`. The advantage of using accelerometer data is that it is gathered from wearable devices, and hence, requires no installation on the premises. Another advantage is that it is textual data, hence, requires fewer computation resources than video data.

HAR from videos

Another way to detect human activity is through videos. In this case, we will have to use a DL model such as CNN to get good results. A good dataset for classified videos is available from Ivan Laptev and Barbara Caputo (`http://www.nada.kth.se/cvap/actions/`). It contains six types of action: walking, jogging, running, boxing, hand waving, and hand clapping, in different scenarios. Each video has been recorded using a camera with 25 fps. The spatial resolution is 160 × 120, and of an average length of four seconds. It has in total 599 videos with about 100 for each of the six categories.

One of the problems with video data is that it is computationally expensive, thus it will be important to reduce the dataset, and a few ways of doing this are as follows:

- Since color has no role in the activity, the images can be converted from three-channel color images to two-dimensional grayscale images.
- The video is of four seconds at 25 frames in one second, most of these frames contain redundant data, so instead of (25 × 4 = 100) frames corresponding to one data row, we can reduce the number of frames to say 5 frames per second resulting in 20 frames. (It would be best if the total number of frames extracted per video is fixed).
- Reduce the spatial resolution of individual frames from 160 × 120.

Next, when it comes to modeling, we should be using three-dimensional convolutional layers. So let us say if have taken only 20 frames per video, and reduced the size of each frame to 128 × 128, then a single sample will be: 20 × 128 × 128 × 1, this corresponds to the volume of 20 × 128 × 128 with a single channel.

Smart lighting

The first home automation application that comes to mind when talking about smart homes is using smart light. Most of the smart lighting systems that exist at present offer an option to control the switching on and off of the lights, as well as their intensity, using an app on your smartphone or via the internet. Some also allow you to change the color/hue. Motion detecting lights, which automatically switch on after detecting any motion, are part of almost all households today:

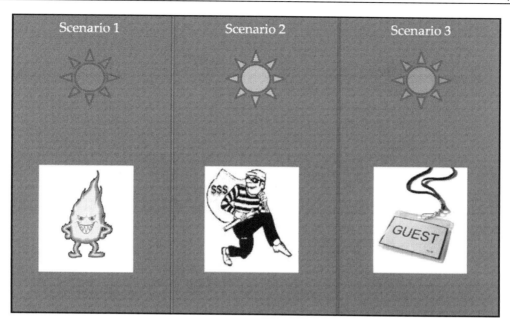

Smart light for people with hearing impairments changes color based on the situation

Using AI, we can make these smart lights even smarter. In case of emergency, they can be programmed to work in collaboration and guide you to the right exit. For people with hearing impairments, the smart lights can be used instead of alarms, for example, a red light when the fire alarm goes off, but an orange light when there's a burglar, and a welcoming green when someone rings the door bell. With the help of services such as **If This Then That (IFTTT)** you can set up smarter and more complex support systems.

The IFTTT provides a free service to control your devices. An action by one device (or service) can trigger one or more other devices. It is very simple to use, you just create an applet at the IFTTT website: `https://ifttt.com`, you select the device (point and click) or service you want to use as a trigger, and link it with your IFTTT account. Next you select (point and click) the service or the device you want should act when the trigger is activated. The site contains thousands of pre-made applets to make your job even easier.

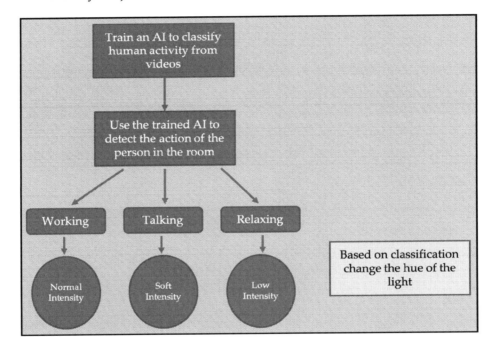

Algorithm for a personalized smart light system

These are just some examples of what you can do with existing smart lights. But if you are adventurous and are ready to interface new sensors with these smart lights, you can build a personal light for yourself, one that changes its hue/intensity based on the mental activity of the person. It gets dim when you feel sleepy, and is full intensity when you are working, but when you are talking and spending time with friends, it simply provides a pleasant hue. Sounds far-fetched? Not really, you can first use an AI algorithm that detects human activity from video (or wearable fitness trackers) and classifies it into three classes: work, leisure, and sleep, and then use its output to control the smart light hue/intensity.

Home surveillance

Home surveillance is a very useful and much-needed application. With single parents and the elderly population on the rise, the need for security and surveillance, not just on the outer premises, but inside homes, is also needed. Many companies are trying to provide in-home surveillance using videos. One of the successful implementations is by a company named DeepSight AILabs (http://deepsightlabs.com), they have developed proprietary software **SuperSecure**; a universally compatible retrofit solution that works with any CCTV system, any camera, any resolution, and turns it into an **AI-powered smart surveillance solution** to detect potential threats with high accuracy, and trigger instant alerts to save lives and protect assets.

When you try your own implementation of home surveillance, the points we discussed in the implementation of HAR using videos will be useful here as well.

Smart homes are still in their infancy, the major reason being that they involve a high cost of ownership and the inflexibility of the interconnected devices. Normally, one particular system is managed completely by one company. If for some reason the company is closed, the consumer is left in the lurch. The solution would be to allow open source home automation hardware and software. An interesting read on the challenges and opportunities in the field of home automation is an article by Microsoft Research, *Home Automation in the Wild: Challenges and Opportunities* (https://www.microsoft.com/en-us/research/publication/home-automation-in-the-wild-challenges-and-opportunities/).

Summary

The focus of this chapter was personal and home AI-powered IoT solutions. The large-scale use of smartphones has brought wearable sensors to every person's reach, resulting in a plethora of personal apps. In this chapter, we explored and implemented some of the successful personal and home AI-powered IoT solutions. We learned about SuperShoes by MIT, shoes that can find their own path to the destination. We learned about CGM systems and implemented code to predict hyperglycemia. This chapter also demonstrated how personalized heart monitors can be implemented.

While smart homes are still in their infancy, the chapter explored some of the most popular and useful smart home solutions. HAR, an application that exists at the boundary of smart homes and personal IoT, was introduced. We wrote some code using scikit-learn to classify the activity from data obtained using accelerometers. The chapter introduced some cool smart lighting applications and talked about home surveillance using videos.

In the next chapter, we will look at some case studies where the data obtained from IoT sensors is used to improve production and efficiency in industries.

10
AI for the Industrial IoT

Companies from a diverse background today are realizing the importance of **Artificial Intelligence (AI)**, and hence, are incorporating it into their ecosystems. This chapter focuses on some of the successful AI-powered **industrial IoT** solutions. By the end of this chapter, you will have covered the following:

- How AI-powered IoT solutions are changing the industry
- Different industries offering AI-enabled analysis for their data to increase production, optimize logistics, and improve the customer experience
- Preventive maintenance
- Implementing a code to perform preventive maintenance based on aircraft engine sensors data
- Electrical load forecasting
- Implementing a TensorFlow code to perform short-term load forecasting

Introduction to AI-powered industrial IoT

The convergence of IoT, robotics, big data, and **machine learning (ML)** is creating enormous opportunities for industrial firms as well as significant challenges.

The availability of low-cost sensors, multiple cloud platforms, and powerful edge infrastructure is making it easier and profitable for industries to adopt AI. This AI-powered industrial IoT is transforming the way companies provide products and services or interact with customers and partners.

One of the promising areas of the AI-powered industrial IoT is **preventive maintenance**. Until now, industrial firms used to be reactive concerning maintenance, in the sense that they will perform maintenance either as a part of a fixed schedule, such as every six months, or only when some equipment stops functioning. For instance, a logistics company may have biannual service checks of every vehicle in its fleet and replace certain parts or entire vehicles on a set schedule. This reactive maintenance often wastes time and can be expensive. Applying AI algorithms to predict anomalies and errors before they happen can save a lot of time.

Another area where the AI-powered industrial IoT can achieve miracles is collaboration among humans and robots. Robots are already part of the industrial IoT ecosystem; working in assembly-lines and warehouses, they perform tasks that are especially repetitive or dangerous for human workers. The semi-autonomous trucks, trains, and loaders that are presently part of the mining industry are typically guided by pre-programmed routines, fixed tracks, and/or remote human operators.

In many industry situations, the latency introduced by cloud computations may not be acceptable, in such situations, the edge of computation infrastructure is needed.

To provide you with an idea of the spread and usage of AI-powered industrial IoT, the following is a list of some of the hot AI-powered startups providing industrial IoT services and solutions:

- **Uptake Technologies Inc**: A Chicago based startup, co-founded in 2014 by Brad Keywell, makes software to monitor and analyze real-time data generated by industrial equipment and uses it to improve the performance and maintenance of the machinery. It is planning to expand its horizon to heavy target industries such as energy, railroads, oil and gas, mining, and wind power (`https://www.uptake.com/`).
- **C3.ai**: A leading provider of big data, IoT, and AI applications, led by Thomas Siebel, has been declared a leader in the IoT platform by Forrester Research 2018 industrial IoT Wave report. Founded in the year 2009, it has successfully provided industries services in the field of energy management, network efficiency, fraud detection, and inventory optimization (`https://c3.ai`).
- **Alluvium**: Founded in 2015 by Drew Conway, the author of *Machine Learning for Hackers*, Alluvium uses ML and AI to help industrial companies achieve operation stability and improve their production. Their flagship product, Primer, helps companies identify the useful insights from the raw and distilled data from the sensors, allowing them to predict operational faults before they happen (`https://alluvium.io`).

- **Arundo Analytics**: Headed by Jakob Ramsøy, founded in the year 2015, Arundo Analytics provides services to connect live data to ML and other analytical models. They have products to scale deployed models, create and manage live data pipelines (`https://www.arundo.com`).

- **Canvass Analytics**: It helps industries make critical business decisions using predictive analytics based on real-time operational data. The Canvass AI Platform distils the millions of data points generated by industrial machines, sensors, and operations systems and identifies patterns and correlations within the data to create new insights. Headed by Humera Malik, Canvass Analytics was founded in 2016 (`https://www.canvass.io`).

That is not the end software technology giants such as Amazon and Google are spending a lot of funds and infrastructure in industrial IoT. Google is using predictive modeling to reduce their data center cost, and PayPal is using ML to find fraudulent transactions.

Some interesting use cases

A large number of companies from diverse backgrounds are realizing the importance and impact of incorporating data analysis and AI into their eco-systems. From increasing their operations, supply chain, and maintenance efficiency to increasing employee productivity, to creating new business models, products, and services, there is not a facet where AI has not been explored. Following, we list some of the interesting use cases of AI-powered IoT in industries:

- **Predictive maintenance**: In predictive maintenance, AI algorithms are used to predict future failures of equipment before the failure occurs. This allows the company to perform maintenance, and hence, reduce the downtime. In the successive section, we will go into more details of how preventive maintenance is helpful for the industries and what are the various ways in which it can be done.

- **Asset tracking**: Also called **asset management**, this is the method to keep track of key physical assets. Keeping track of key assets, a company can optimize logistics, maintain inventory levels, and detect any inefficiencies. Traditionally, asset tracking was limited to adding RFID or barcodes to the assets, and hence, keeping a tab on their location, however, with the AI algorithms at our perusal, it is now possible to do more active asset tracking. For instance, a windmill power station can sense the change in wind speed, its direction, and even the temperature and use these parameters to align the individual windmill in the best direction to maximize power generation.

- **Fleet management and maintenance**: The transport industry had been using AI for fleet management by optimizing routes for about a decade. The availability of many low-cost sensors and the advancement of edge computing devices have now made it possible for transport companies to collect and use the data received from these sensors to not only optimize the logistics by better vehicle to vehicle communication and preventive maintenance, but to accelerate safety. Installing systems such as drowsiness detection, the risky behavior caused due to fatigue or distraction can be detected, and the driver can be asked to take countermeasures.

Predictive maintenance using AI

Heavy machinery and equipment are the backbone of any industry and like all physical objects, they deteriorate, age, and fail. Initially, companies used to perform reactive maintenance, that is, maintenance was done once the equipment failure was reported. This used to cause unplanned downtime. For any industry, an unscheduled, unplanned downtime can cause significant resource crunch and drastically reduce efficiency, production, and hence, profits. To deal with these problems, industries shifted to preventive maintenance.

In preventive maintenance, regular scheduled routine checks are performed at predetermined intervals. Preventive maintenance required keeping a record of equipment and their scheduled maintenance. The third industrial revolution, where computers were introduced into industries, made it easy to maintain and update these records. While preventive maintenance saves the industry from most unplanned downtimes, it still isn't the best alternative, since regular checks can be an unnecessary expenditure. The following diagram outlines an example of the four industrial revolutions:

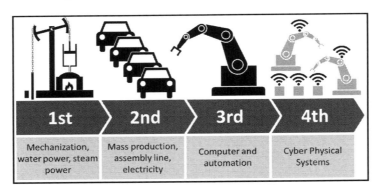

Image shared under Creative Commons Attribution: (https://commons.wikimedia.org/wiki/File:Industry_4.0.png)

The current trend of automation and digitalization has lead to the fourth industrial revolution, also called **Industry 4.0**. This has allowed companies to deploy **machine-to-machine** (**M2M**) and **machine-to-human** (**M2H**) communication, along with AI-powered analytical algorithms, enabling predictive maintenance, that predict the breakdown before it occurs using past data. Predictive maintenance strategies have enormously eased the maintenance and management of the company resources.

The main idea behind predictive maintenance is to predict when equipment breakdown might occur based on condition-monitoring data. The sensors are used to monitor the condition and performance of equipment during their normal operation, depending on the equipment, different types of sensors may be used. Some of the common condition monitoring parameters/sensor values are as follows:

- Vibration sensors mainly used to detect misalignment, imbalance, mechanical looseness, or wear on pumps and motors
- Current/voltage sensors to measure the current and voltage supplied to an electric motor
- Ultrasound analysis to detect leakage in pipe systems or tanks, or mechanical malfunctions of movable parts and faults in electrical equipment
- Infrared thermography to identify temperature fluctuations
- Sensors to detect liquid quality (for example in the case of wine sensors to detect the presence of different elements in the wine)

To implement predictive maintenance, the most important thing is to identify the conditions that need to be monitored. The sensors required to monitor these conditions are then deployed. Finally, the data from the sensors is collected to build a model.

Predictive maintenance using Long Short-Term Memory

For demonstrating predictive maintenance, we'll use the simulated data provided in Azure ML (`https://gallery.azure.ai/Collection/Predictive-Maintenance-Template-3`). The dataset consists of the following three files:

- **Training data**: It contains the aircraft engine run to failure data. The download link for the data is `http://azuremlsamples.azureml.net/templatedata/PM_train.txt`.

- **Testing data**: It contains the aircraft engine operating data without failure events recorded. The data can be loaded from the link: `http://azuremlsamples.azureml.net/templatedata/PM_test.txt`.
- **Ground truth data**: Here, the information about the true remaining cycles for each engine in testing data is available. The link for the ground truth data is `http://azuremlsamples.azureml.net/templatedata/PM_truth.txt`.

According to the data description provided at the data source, the training data (`train_FD001.txt`) consists of multiple multivariate time series with cycle as the time unit, together with 21 sensor readings for each cycle. Each time series can be assumed as being generated from a different engine of the same type. Each engine is assumed to start with different degrees of initial wear and manufacturing variation, and this information is unknown to the user. In this simulated data, the engine is assumed to be operating normally at the start of each time series. It starts to degrade at some point during the series of the operating cycles. This degrades the progresses and grows in magnitude. When a predefined threshold is reached, then the engine is considered unsafe for further operation. In other words, the last cycle in each time series can be considered as the failure point of the corresponding engine. Taking the sample training data as an example, the engine with `id=1` fails at cycle `192`, and engine with `id=2` fails at cycle `287`.

The testing data (`test_FD001.txt`) has the same data schema as the training data. The only difference is that the data does not indicate when the failure occurs (in other words, the last time period does NOT represent the failure point). Taking the sample testing data, the engine with `id=1` runs from cycle `1` through cycle `31`. It is not shown how many more cycles this engine can last before it fails.

The ground truth data (`RUL_FD001.txt`) provides the number of remaining working cycles for the engines in the testing data. Taking the sample ground truth data shown as an example, the engine with `id=1` in the testing data can run another `112` cycles before it fails.

Since this is a time series data, we will use **Long Short-Term Memory (LSTM)** to classify weather the engine will fail in a certain time period or not. The code presented here is based on the implementation provided at the GitHub link of Umberto Griffo: (`https://github.com/umbertogriffo/Predictive-Maintenance-using-LSTM`):

1. The modules needed to implement predictive maintenance are imported in the first step. We also set the seed for random calculations so that the result is reproducible:

```python
import keras
import pandas as pd
import numpy as np
import matplotlib.pyplot as plt
import os

# Setting seed for reproducibility
np.random.seed(1234)
PYTHONHASHSEED = 0

from sklearn import preprocessing
from sklearn.metrics import confusion_matrix, recall_score,
precision_score
from keras.models import Sequential,load_model
from keras.layers import Dense, Dropout, LSTM
```

2. Let's read the data and assign column names, shown in the following code:

```python
# read training data - It is the aircraft engine run-to-failure
data.
train_df = pd.read_csv('PM_train.txt', sep=" ",
        header=None)
train_df.drop(train_df.columns[[26, 27]],
        axis=1,
        inplace=True)
train_df.columns = ['id', 'cycle', 'setting1',
        'setting2', 'setting3', 's1', 's2',
        's3', 's4', 's5', 's6', 's7', 's8',
        's9', 's10', 's11', 's12', 's13',
        's14', 's15', 's16', 's17', 's18',
        's19', 's20', 's21']

train_df = train_df.sort_values(['id','cycle'])

# read test data - It is the aircraft engine operating data without
failure events recorded.
test_df = pd.read_csv('PM_test.txt',
        sep=" ", header=None)
```

```
test_df.drop(test_df.columns[[26, 27]],
        axis=1,
        inplace=True)
test_df.columns = ['id', 'cycle', 'setting1',
        'setting2', 'setting3', 's1', 's2', 's3',
         's4', 's5', 's6', 's7', 's8', 's9',
        's10', 's11', 's12', 's13', 's14',
         's15', 's16', 's17', 's18', 's19',
        's20', 's21']

# read ground truth data - It contains the information of true
remaining cycles for each engine in the testing data.
truth_df = pd.read_csv('PM_truth.txt',
        sep=" ",
        header=None)
truth_df.drop(truth_df.columns[[1]],
        axis=1,
        inplace=True)
```

3. As the first step, we make a prediction whether the engine will fail in the time
   period or not, hence our label will be 1 or 0, that is, this will be a binary
   classification problem. To create the binary label, we preprocess the data and we
   create a new label **remaining useful life** (**RUL**). We also create a binary `label1`
   variable telling if a specific engine is going to fail within w1 cycles or not. And
   finally, the data (non-sensor) is normalized, shown as follows:

```
# Data Labeling - generate column RUL(Remaining Usefull Life or
Time to Failure)
rul = pd.DataFrame(train_df.groupby('id')
        ['cycle'].max()).reset_index()
rul.columns = ['id', 'max']
train_df = train_df.merge(rul,
        on=['id'],
        how='left')
train_df['RUL'] = train_df['max'] -     train_df['cycle']
train_df.drop('max',
        axis=1,
        inplace=True)

# Let us generate label columns for training data
# we will only use "label1" for binary classification,
# The question: is a specific engine going to fail within w1
cycles?
w1 = 30
w0 = 15
train_df['label1'] = np.where(train_df['RUL'] <= w1, 1, 0 )
```

```
# MinMax normalization (from 0 to 1)
train_df['cycle_norm'] = train_df['cycle']
cols_normalize = train_df.columns.difference
        (['id','cycle','RUL','label1'])
min_max_scaler = preprocessing.MinMaxScaler()
norm_train_df = pd.DataFrame(min_max_scaler.
        fit_transform(train_df[cols_normalize]),
        columns=cols_normalize,
        index=train_df.index)
join_df = train_df[train_df.columns.
        difference(cols_normalize)].
        join(norm_train_df)
train_df = join_df.reindex(columns = train_df.columns)

train_df.head()
```

Out[4]:

	id	cycle	setting1	setting2	setting3	s1	s2	s3	s4	s5	...	s15	s1
0	1	1	0.459770	0.166667	0.0	0.0	0.183735	0.406802	0.309757	0.0	...	0.363986	0.
1	1	2	0.609195	0.250000	0.0	0.0	0.283133	0.453019	0.352633	0.0	...	0.411312	0.
2	1	3	0.252874	0.750000	0.0	0.0	0.343373	0.369523	0.370527	0.0	...	0.357445	0.
3	1	4	0.540230	0.500000	0.0	0.0	0.343373	0.256159	0.331195	0.0	...	0.166603	0.
4	1	5	0.390805	0.333333	0.0	0.0	0.349398	0.257467	0.404625	0.0	...	0.402078	0.

5 rows × 29 columns

4. Similar preprocessing is performed on the test dataset, with just one change—the RUL value is obtained from the ground truth data:

```
# MinMax normalization (from 0 to 1)
test_df['cycle_norm'] = test_df['cycle']
norm_test_df = pd.DataFrame(
        min_max_scaler.
        transform(test_df[cols_normalize]),
        columns=cols_normalize,
         index=test_df.index)
test_join_df = test_df[test_df.
        columns.difference(cols_normalize)].
        join(norm_test_df)
test_df = test_join_df.
        reindex(columns = test_df.columns)
test_df = test_df.reset_index(drop=True)
```

```
# We use the ground truth dataset to generate labels for the test
data.
# generate column max for test data
rul = pd.DataFrame(test_df.
        groupby('id')['cycle'].max()).
        reset_index()
rul.columns = ['id', 'max']
truth_df.columns = ['more']
truth_df['id'] = truth_df.index + 1
truth_df['max'] = rul['max'] + truth_df['more']
truth_df.drop('more',
        axis=1,
        inplace=True)

# generate RUL for test data
test_df = test_df.merge(truth_df,
        on=['id'], how='left')
test_df['RUL'] = test_df['max'] - test_df['cycle']
test_df.drop('max',
        axis=1,
        inplace=True)

# generate label columns w0 and w1 for test data
test_df['label1'] = np.where
        (test_df['RUL'] <= w1, 1, 0 )
test_df.head()
```

Out[5]:	id	cycle	setting1	setting2	setting3	s1	s2	s3	s4	s5	...	s15	s1
0	1	1	0.632184	0.750000	0.0	0.0	0.545181	0.310661	0.269413	0.0	...	0.308965	0.
1	1	2	0.344828	0.250000	0.0	0.0	0.150602	0.379551	0.222316	0.0	...	0.213159	0.
2	1	3	0.517241	0.583333	0.0	0.0	0.376506	0.346632	0.322248	0.0	...	0.458638	0.
3	1	4	0.741379	0.500000	0.0	0.0	0.370482	0.285154	0.408001	0.0	...	0.257022	0.
4	1	5	0.580460	0.500000	0.0	0.0	0.391566	0.352082	0.332039	0.0	...	0.300885	0.

5 rows × 29 columns

5. Since we are using LSTM for time-series modeling, we create a function that will generate the sequence to be fed to the LSTM as per the window size. We have chosen the window size of 50. We will also need a function to generate the corresponding label:

```
# function to reshape features into
# (samples, time steps, features)
```

```
def gen_sequence(id_df, seq_length, seq_cols):
    """ Only sequences that meet the window-length
    are considered, no padding is used. This
    means for testing we need to drop those which
    are below the window-length. An alternative
    would be to pad sequences so that
    we can use shorter ones """

    # for one id we put all the rows in a single matrix
    data_matrix = id_df[seq_cols].values
    num_elements = data_matrix.shape[0]
    # Iterate over two lists in parallel.
    # For example id1 have 192 rows and
    # sequence_length is equal to 50
    # so zip iterate over two following list of
    # numbers (0,112),(50,192)
    # 0 50 -> from row 0 to row 50
    # 1 51 -> from row 1 to row 51
    # 2 52 -> from row 2 to row 52
    # ...
    # 111 191 -> from row 111 to 191
    for start, stop in zip(range(0, num_elements-seq_length),
range(seq_length, num_elements)):
        yield data_matrix[start:stop, :]


def gen_labels(id_df, seq_length, label):
    # For one id we put all the labels in a
    # single matrix.
    # For example:
    # [[1]
    # [4]
    # [1]
    # [5]
    # [9]
    # ...
    # [200]]
    data_matrix = id_df[label].values
    num_elements = data_matrix.shape[0]
    # I have to remove the first seq_length labels
    # because for one id the first sequence of
    # seq_length size have as target
    # the last label (the previus ones are
    # discarded).
    # All the next id's sequences will have
    # associated step by step one label as target.
    return data_matrix[seq_length:num_elements, :]
```

6. Let's now generate the training sequence and corresponding label for our data, shown in the following code:

```
# pick a large window size of 50 cycles
sequence_length = 50

# pick the feature columns
sensor_cols = ['s' + str(i) for i in range(1,22)]
sequence_cols = ['setting1', 'setting2',
        'setting3', 'cycle_norm']
sequence_cols.extend(sensor_cols)

# generator for the sequences
seq_gen = (list(gen_sequence
        (train_df[train_df['id']==id],
        sequence_length, sequence_cols))
        for id in train_df['id'].unique())

# generate sequences and convert to numpy array
seq_array = np.concatenate(list(seq_gen)).
        astype(np.float32)
print(seq_array.shape)

# generate labels
label_gen = [gen_labels(train_df[train_df['id']==id],
        sequence_length, ['label1'])
        for id in train_df['id'].unique()]
label_array = np.concatenate(label_gen).
        astype(np.float32)
print(label_array.shape)
```

7. We now build an LSTM model with two LSTM layers and a fully connected layer. The model is trained for binary classification, and therefore, it tries to reduce the binary cross entropy loss. The `Adam` optimizer is used to update the model parameters:

```
nb_features = seq_array.shape[2]
nb_out = label_array.shape[1]

model = Sequential()

model.add(LSTM(
        input_shape=(sequence_length, nb_features),
        units=100,
        return_sequences=True))
model.add(Dropout(0.2))
```

```
model.add(LSTM(
    units=50,
    return_sequences=False))
model.add(Dropout(0.2))

model.add(Dense(units=nb_out,
    activation='sigmoid'))
model.compile(loss='binary_crossentropy',
    optimizer='adam',
    metrics=['accuracy'])

print(model.summary())
```

Layer (type)	Output Shape	Param #
lstm_1 (LSTM)	(None, 50, 100)	50400
dropout_1 (Dropout)	(None, 50, 100)	0
lstm_2 (LSTM)	(None, 50)	30200
dropout_2 (Dropout)	(None, 50)	0
dense_1 (Dense)	(None, 1)	51

Total params: 80,651
Trainable params: 80,651
Non-trainable params: 0

8. We train the model, shown as follows:

```
history = model.fit(seq_array, label_array,
        epochs=100, batch_size=200,
        validation_split=0.05, verbose=2,
         callbacks = [keras.callbacks.
            EarlyStopping(monitor='val_loss',
            min_delta=0, patience=10,
            verbose=0, mode='min'),
        keras.callbacks.
            ModelCheckpoint
            (model_path,monitor='val_loss',
            save_best_only=True,
            mode='min', verbose=0)])
```

9. The trained model gives 98% accuracy on the test dataset and 98.9% accuracy on the validation dataset. The precision value is 0.96, and there is a recall of 1.0 and an F1 score of 0.98. Not bad, right! The following diagram shows these results of the train model:

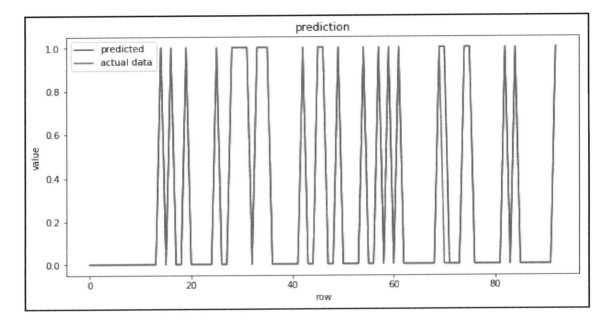

We can use the same data to also predict the RUL of the aircraft engines, that is, predict the engines time to failure. This will be a regression problem now we can use the LSTM model to perform regression as well. The initial steps will be the same as before, but from the fifth step onwards we will have changes. While the input data sequence generated will remain the same as before, the target will no longer be the binary label, instead, we will use RUL as the target for our regression model:

1. We create the target value using the same `gen_labels()` function. We also create a validation set using the `gen_sequence()` function:

```
# generate labels
label_gen = [gen_labels(train_df[train_df['id']==id],
      sequence_length, ['RUL'])
      for id in train_df['id'].unique()]
label_array = np.concatenate(label_gen).astype(np.float32)

# val is a list of 192 - 50 = 142 bi-dimensional array
# (50 rows x 25 columns)
val=list(gen_sequence(train_df[train_df['id']==1],
      sequence_length, sequence_cols))
```

2. Create an LSTM model. We are using r2 as the metrics during training, therefore, we use the Keras custom metric feature and our own metrics function:

```
def r2_keras(y_true, y_pred):
    """Coefficient of Determination
    """
    SS_res = K.sum(K.square( y_true - y_pred ))
    SS_tot = K.sum(K.square( y_true - K.mean(y_true) ) )
    return ( 1 - SS_res/(SS_tot + K.epsilon()) )

# Next, we build a deep network.
# The first layer is an LSTM layer with 100 units followed by
# another LSTM layer with 50 units.
# Dropout is also applied after each LSTM layer to control
# overfitting.
# Final layer is a Dense output layer with single unit and linear
# activation since this is a regression problem.
nb_features = seq_array.shape[2]
nb_out = label_array.shape[1]


model = Sequential()
model.add(LSTM(
      input_shape=(sequence_length, nb_features),
      units=100,
      return_sequences=True))
```

```
model.add(Dropout(0.2))
model.add(LSTM(
    units=50,
    return_sequences=False))
model.add(Dropout(0.2))
model.add(Dense(units=nb_out))
model.add(Activation("linear"))
model.compile(loss='mean_squared_error',
optimizer='rmsprop',metrics=['mae',r2_keras])


print(model.summary())
```

Layer (type)	Output Shape	Param #
lstm_3 (LSTM)	(None, 50, 100)	50400
dropout_3 (Dropout)	(None, 50, 100)	0
lstm_4 (LSTM)	(None, 50)	30200
dropout_4 (Dropout)	(None, 50)	0
dense_2 (Dense)	(None, 1)	51
activation_2 (Activation)	(None, 1)	0

```
Total params: 80,651
Trainable params: 80,651
Non-trainable params: 0
```

3. Train the model on the training dataset, shown as follows:

```
# fit the network
history = model.fit(seq_array, label_array, epochs=100,
    batch_size=200, validation_split=0.05, verbose=2,
    callbacks = [keras.callbacks.EarlyStopping
    (monitor='val_loss', min_delta=0, patience=10,
    verbose=0, mode='min'),
    keras.callbacks.ModelCheckpoint
    (model_path,monitor='val_loss',
    save_best_only=True, mode='min',
    verbose=0)])
```

4. The trained model provides an r2 value of 0.80 on test dataset and 0.72 on the validation dataset. We can improve our results by hypertuning the model parameters. Following, you can see the loss of the model for train and validation datasets during training:

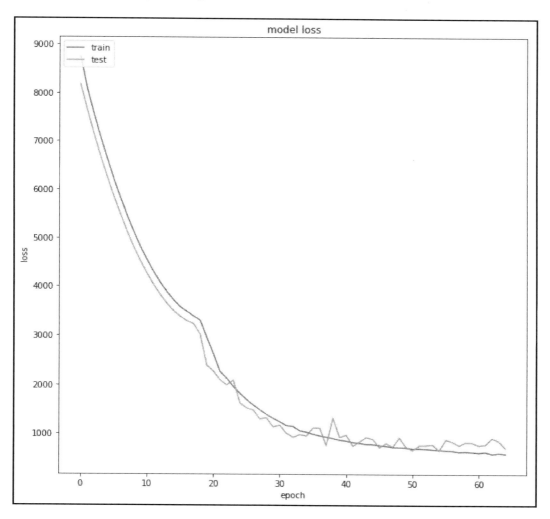

To run this code, please ensure you have Tensorflow 1.4<, and Keras 2.1.2. If you have a higher version of Keras, first uninstall it using `pip uninstall keras` and then reinstall it using `pip install keras==2.1.2`.

The complete code with both the binary classification and regression model are available at the GitHub repository, `Chapter10/Predictive_Maintenance_using_LSTM.ipynb`. We can also create a model to determine if the failure will occur in different time windows, for example, fails in the window $(1, w_0)$ or fails in the window (w_{0+1}, w_1) days, and so on. This will then be a multi-classification problem, and data will need to be preprocessed accordingly. You can read more about this predictive maintenance template from Azure AI Gallery: `https://gallery.azure.ai/Experiment/Predictive-Maintenance-Step-2A-of-3-train-and-evaluate-regression-models-2`.

Predictive maintenance advantages and disadvantages

According to a survey report by GE (`https://www.gemeasurement.com/sites/gemc.dev/files/ge_the_impact_of_digital_on_unplanned_downtime_0.pdf`). The downtime negatively affects the performance of the oil and gas industry. This is true, not only for the oil and gas industry, but all industries. Hence, to reduce downtime, and increase efficiency, it is important that predictive maintenance is adopted. However, the cost of establishing predictive maintenance is quite high, but once a predictive maintenance system has been properly established, it helps to provide several cost-effective benefits, such as the following:

- Minimized time is required for equipment maintenance
- Minimum production time is lost due to maintenance
- And finally, the spare parts cost is also minimized

Successful predictive maintenance can reshape the company as a whole in a positive way.

Electrical load forecasting in industry

Electricity is presently the most important energy vector in both the domestic and industrial sectors. Since, unlike fuels, it is hard and expensive to store electricity, there is a need for a precise coupling between its generation and demand. Electrical energy load forecasting, hence, is very vital. Depending upon the time range (forecasting horizon) electrical load forecasting is classified into the following three categories:

- **Short-term load forecasting**: The forecast is made for one hour to a few weeks
- **Medium-term load forecasting**: The forecast duration spreads from a few weeks to a few months
- **Long-term load forecasting**: Here, the forecasting is done from a few months to years

Depending upon the need and application one may have to plan either one or all of the previous load forecasting categories. In recent years, a lot of research work has been done in the area of **short-term load forecasting (STLF)**. STLF can assist industries by providing an accurate means to predict future load, which can help in precise planning, decrease in operating cost, and thus, increase profit and provide a more reliable electrical supply. STLF predicts the future energy demands based on historical data (acquired through smart meters) and predicted whether conditions.

The load forecasting problem is a regression problem. It can be modeled as a time series problem or as a static model. Modeling load forecasting as a time series data is the most popular choice. With time series modeling, we can use the standard ML time series models like ARIMA, or we can make use of deep learning models such as recurrent neural networks and LSTM.

For a comprehensive review of various strategies and models used in the electrical load forecasting, refer to this paper:
Fallah, S., Deo, R., Shojafar, M., Conti, M., and Shamshirband, S. (2018). *Computational Intelligence Approaches for Energy Load forecasting in Smart Energy Management Grids: State of the Art, Future Challenges, and Research Directions*. Energies, 11(3), 596.

STLF using LSTM

Here, we present the code for performing a short-term load forecasting with the help of LSTM. The data for training and testing is taken from the UCI ML website (`https://archive.ics.uci.edu/ml/datasets/Individual+household+electric+power+consumption#`). The code for STLF has been adapted from GitHub (`https://github.com/demmojo/lstm-electric-load-forecast`):

1. We import the necessary modules and set random seeds, shown as follows:

```
import time
from keras.layers import LSTM
from keras.layers import Activation, Dense, Dropout
from keras.models import Sequential, load_model
from numpy.random import seed

from tensorflow import set_random_seed
set_random_seed(2) # seed random numbers for Tensorflow backend
seed(1234) # seed random numbers for Keras
import numpy as np
import csv
import matplotlib.pyplot as plt

%matplotlib inline
```

2. Define utility functions for loading the data and converting it into a sequence suited for LSTM input:

```
def load_data(dataset_path, sequence_length=60, prediction_steps=5,
ratio_of_data=1.0):
    # 2075259 is the total number of measurements
    # from Dec 2006 to Nov 2010
    max_values = ratio_of_data * 2075259

    # Load data from file
    with open(dataset_path) as file:
        data_file = csv.reader(file, delimiter=";")
        power_consumption = []
        number_of_values = 0
        for line in data_file:
            try:
                power_consumption.append(float(line[2]))
                number_of_values += 1
            except ValueError:
                pass

        # limit data to be considered by
```

```
            # model according to max_values
            if number_of_values >= max_values:
                break

print('Loaded data from csv.')
windowed_data = []
# Format data into rolling window sequences
# for e.g: index=0 => 123, index=1 => 234 etc.
for index in range(len(power_consumption) - sequence_length):
        windowed_data.append(
        power_consumption[
        index: index + sequence_length])

# shape (number of samples, sequence length)
windowed_data = np.array(windowed_data)

# Center data
data_mean = windowed_data.mean()
windowed_data -= data_mean
print('Center data so mean is zero
        (subtract each data point by mean of value: ',
        data_mean, ')')
print('Data : ', windowed_data.shape)

# Split data into training and testing sets
train_set_ratio = 0.9
row = int(round(train_set_ratio * windowed_data.shape[0]))
train = windowed_data[:row, :]

# remove last prediction_steps from train set
x_train = train[:, :-prediction_steps]
# take last prediction_steps from train set
y_train = train[:, -prediction_steps:]
x_test = windowed_data[row:, :-prediction_steps]

# take last prediction_steps from test set
y_test = windowed_data[row:, -prediction_steps:]

x_train = np.reshape(x_train,
        (x_train.shape[0], x_train.shape[1], 1))
x_test = np.reshape(x_test,
        (x_test.shape[0], x_test.shape[1], 1))

return [x_train, y_train, x_test, y_test, data_mean]
```

3. Build the LSTM model, the model we have built contains two LSTM and one fully connected layer:

```
def build_model(prediction_steps):
    model = Sequential()
    layers = [1, 75, 100, prediction_steps]
    model.add(LSTM(layers[1],
        input_shape=(None, layers[0]),
        return_sequences=True)) # add first layer
    model.add(Dropout(0.2)) # add dropout for first layer
    model.add(LSTM(layers[2],
        return_sequences=False)) # add second layer
    model.add(Dropout(0.2)) # add dropout for second layer
    model.add(Dense(layers[3])) # add output layer
    model.add(Activation('linear')) # output layer
    start = time.time()
    model.compile(loss="mse", optimizer="rmsprop")
    print('Compilation Time : ', time.time() - start)
    return model
```

4. Train the model, as shown in the following code:

```
def run_lstm(model, sequence_length, prediction_steps):
    data = None
    global_start_time = time.time()
    epochs = 1
    ratio_of_data = 1 # ratio of data to use from 2+ million data
points
    path_to_dataset = 'data/household_power_consumption.txt'

    if data is None:
        print('Loading data... ')
        x_train, y_train, x_test, y_test, result_mean =
load_data(path_to_dataset, sequence_length,
prediction_steps, ratio_of_data)
    else:
        x_train, y_train, x_test, y_test = data

    print('\nData Loaded. Compiling...\n')
    model.fit(x_train, y_train, batch_size=128, epochs=epochs,
validation_split=0.05)
    predicted = model.predict(x_test)
    # predicted = np.reshape(predicted, (predicted.size,))
    model.save('LSTM_power_consumption_model.h5') # save LSTM model

    plot_predictions(result_mean, prediction_steps, predicted,
y_test, global_start_time)
```

```
    return None

sequence_length = 10 # number of past minutes of data for model to
consider
prediction_steps = 5 # number of future minutes of data for model
to predict
model = build_model(prediction_steps)
run_lstm(model, sequence_length, prediction_steps)
```

5. We can see from the following graph that our model is making good predictions:

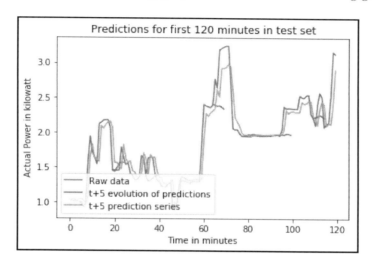

The complete code is available at
GitHub: `Chapter10/Electrical_load_Forecasting.ipynb`.

Summary

In this chapter, we saw that AI-empowered IoT has had a significant impact on industries. From manufacturing, logistics, agriculture, and mining to creating new products and services, AI has touched every facet. We can hopefully assume that the AI-powered industrial IoT will alter and disrupt current business processes and models for the better.

The next chapter will showcase how AI and the IoT can help to shape better cities.

AI for Smart Cities IoT 11

This chapter introduces the reader to smart cities. Case studies will be used to demonstrate how the concepts learned in this book can be applied in developing various smart city components. When reading this chapter, you'll learn about the following:

- What's a smart city
- The essential components of a smart city
- Cities across the globe implementing smart solutions
- The challenges in building smart cities
- Writing a code to detect crime description from San Francisco crime data

Why do we need smart cities?

According to UN data (`https://population.un.org/wup/DataQuery/`), the world population will reach 9.7 billion (9.7×10^9) by the end of 2050. It's presumed that almost 70% of that population will be an urban population with many cities having over 10 million inhabitants. It's a significant number and, as the number grows, not only are we presented with new opportunities, but we also face many unique challenges:

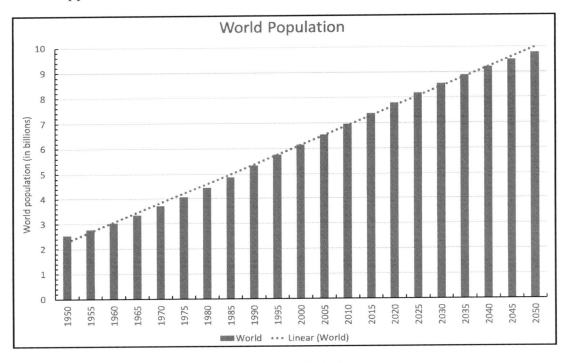

Predicted world population (data from UN)

The most difficult challenge is making resources and energy available to all of the inhabitants and, at the same time, avoiding environment deterioration. At present, cities consume 75% of the world's resources and energy and generate 80% of greenhouse gases; while there's a trend towards green energy sources, we all understand that the earth's resources, such as food and water, are limited. Another critical challenge is administration and management; with the growing population, strategies will be needed to prevent sanitation problems, mitigate traffic congestion, and thwart crime.

Many of these problems can be tamed by the use of AI-enabled IoT. It's possible to use technological advancement to facilitate a new experience for city inhabitants and make their day-to-day living more comfortable and secure. This has given rise to the concept of smart cities.

According to techopedia (https://www.techopedia.com/definition/31494/smart-city), a **smart city** is a city that utilizes information and communication technologies so that it enhances the quality and performance of urban services (such as energy and transportation) so that there's a reduction in resource consumption, wastage, and overall costs. Deakin and AI Waer list four factors that contribute to the definition of a smart city:

- Using a wide range of electronic and digital technologies in the city infrastructure
- Employing **Information and Communication Technology (ICT)** to transform living and working environment
- Embedding ICT in government systems
- Implementing practices and policies that bring people and ICT together to promote innovation and enhance the knowledge that they offer

Hence, a smart city would be a city that not only possesses ICT, but also employs technology in a way that positively impacts the inhabitants.

The paper by Deakin and AI Waer defines a smart city and focuses on the transition required:
Deakin, M., and Al Waer, H. (2011). *From intelligent to smart cities. Intelligent Buildings International, 3(3), 140-152.*

Artificial Intelligence (AI), together with IoT, has the potential to address the key challenges posed by excessive urban population; they can help with traffic management, healthcare, energy crisis, and many other issues. IoT data and AI technology can improve the lives of the citizens and businesses that inhabit a smart city.

Components of a smart city

A smart city has lots of use cases for AI-powered IoT-enabled technology, from maintaining a healthier environment to enhancing public transport and safety. In the following diagram, you can see some the of use cases for a smart city:

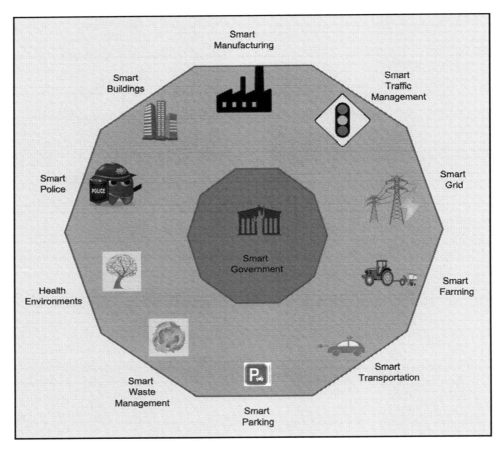

Smart city components

In this section, we'll provide an overview of the most popular use cases—some of them already implemented in smart cities across the world.

Smart traffic management

AI and IoT can implement smart traffic solutions to ensure that inhabitants of a smart city get from one point to another in the city as safely and efficiently as possible.

Los Angeles, one of the most congested cities in the world, has implemented a smart traffic solution to control the flow of traffic. It has installed road-surface sensors and closed-circuit television cameras that send real-time updates about the traffic flow to a central traffic management system. The data feed from the sensors and cameras is analyzed, and it notifies the users of congestion and traffic signal malfunctions. In July 2018, the city further installed **Advanced Transportation Controller** (**ATC**) cabinets at each intersection. Enabled with **vehicle-to-infrastructure** (**V2I**) communications and 5G connectivity, this allows them to communicate with cars that have the traffic light information feature, such as Audi A4 or Q7. You can learn more about the Los Angeles smart transportation system from their website (`https://dpw.lacounty.gov/TNL/ITS/`).

The launch of automated vehicles embedded with sensors can provide both the location and speed of the vehicle; they can directly communicate with the smart traffic lights and prevent congestion. Additionally, using historical data, future traffic could be predicted and used to prevent any possible congestion.

Smart parking

Anyone living in a city must have felt the struggle of finding a parking spot, especially during the holiday time. Smart parking can ease the struggle. With road surface sensors embedded in the ground on parking spots, smart parking solutions can determine whether the parking spots are free or occupied and create a real-time parking map.

The city of Adelaide installed a smart parking system in February 2018, they are also launching a mobile app: Park Adelaide, which will provide the user with accurate and real-time parking information. The app can provide users with the ability to locate, pay for, and even extend the parking session remotely. It'll also give directions to available parking bays, information about parking controls, and alerts when the parking session is about to expire. The smart parking system of the city of Adelaide aims to also improve traffic flow, reduce traffic congestion, and decrease carbon emissions. The details of the smart parking system are available in the city of Adelaide website (`https://www.cityofadelaide.com.au/city-business/why-adelaide/adelaide-smart-city/smart-parking`).

The **San Francisco Municipal Transportation Agency (SAFTA)** implemented (http://sfpark.org), SFpark a smart parking system. They use wireless sensors to detect real-time parking-space occupancy in metered spaces. Launched in the year 2013, SFpark has reduced weekday greenhouse gas emissions by 25%, the traffic volume has gone down, and drivers' search time has reduced by 50%. Another benefit reported by SAFTA is that, by making it easier for people to pay for their parking, the loss due to broken parking meters has reduced, and hence there's an increase in the parking-related revenue by about $1.9 million.

In London, the city of Westminster (https://iotuk.org.uk/smart-parking/#1463069773359-c0d6f90f-4dca) also established a smart parking system in the year 2014 in association with Machina Research (https://machinaresearch.com/login/?next=/forecasts/usecase/). Earlier, drivers had to wait an average of 12 minutes, resulting in congestion and pollution, but since the installation of the smart parking system, there's no need to wait; drivers can find an available parking spot using the mobile. This hasn't only reduced congestion and pollution, but has also increased revenue generation.

Smart waste management

Waste collection and its proper management and disposal is an essential city service. The increase in the urban population necessitates that better smart methods for waste management should be adopted. A smart city should holistically address its waste management. Adopting AI for smart recycling and waste management can provide a sustainable waste management system. In the year 2011, ZenRobotics (https://zenrobotics.com/), a Finnish company, demonstrated how using computer vision and artificial intelligence (a robot) can be trained to sort and pick recycle materials from moving conveyor belts. Since then, we have come a long way; many companies provide smart waste management solutions and cities and buildings are adopting them. There's a growing awareness among leaders and community builders of the potential benefits of the deployment of smart city infrastructure.

Barcelona's waste management system (http://ajuntament.barcelona.cat/ecologiaurbana/en/services/the-city-works/maintenance-of-public-areas/waste-management-and-cleaning-services/household-waste-collection) is a good case study. They had sensors and devices fitted on waste bins, which can send alert notifications to the authorities that then dispatch the waste collection trucks as soon as they are about to be filled. They maintain separate bins for paper, plastic, glass, and waste food items in every locality. The Barcelona authorities have set up a network of containers connected with underground vacuum pipes, which can suck up the trash and leave it in the processing unit; this eliminates the need for trash trucks to collect the garbage.

Another good case study is Denmark, waste management (`https://www.smartbin.com/tdc-denmark-cisco-showcase-the-future-of-smart-city-waste-collection/`), provided by SmartBin. Collaborating with TDC, Denmark's largest telecom service and Cisco, SmartBin has installed sensors to a range of the containers and these sensors are integrated with the City Digital Platform. Additionally, lamp posts, and traffic lights also have been installed with the sensors that send data to the control console at the town hall. The real-time data obtained from these sensors help the cleaner services to plan their route for garbage collection more efficiently; they only need to go where there's a need for emptying.

Ten solar-powered Bigbelly bins equipped with Wi-Fi units are installed in Sharjah, United Arab Emirates; they plan to deploy several hundreds of these smart bins in the near future to achieve sustainability goals.

Smart policing

Crime is unfortunately omnipresent. Every city has a police force trying to catch criminals and reduce the crime rate. Smart cities also require policing: smart policing, where law enforcement agencies employ evidence-based data-driven strategies that are effective, efficient, and economical. The concept of smart policing emerged somewhere in 2009, driven mainly due to limited budget constraints. The fundamental idea driving the smart policing concept was given by Herman Goldstein (University of Wisconsin, 1979). He argued that police shouldn't view criminal incidents as isolated events but, instead, as overt systems of problems that have a history and a future.

In the US, the **Bureau of Justice Assistance (BJA)** has funded many **Smart Policing Initiatives (SPI)** and according to its findings, these initiatives have resulted in significantly reducing the violent crimes. The SPI focuses on police-research partnership, where the research partner provides ongoing data collection and analysis, monitors the data, participates in solution development, and assesses its impact. These initiatives have helped police identify the following:

- Hot-spots of crime
- Prolific offenders

Singapore has also initiated its smart nation initiative. A network of cameras and sensors have been installed on almost every corner of the city. They use the feed obtained from them to identify where people are smoking in prohibited zones, or are loitering from a high-rise housing. The cameras enable the authorities to monitor crowd density, cleanliness of public places, and even track the exact movement of all registered vehicles. The camera feed is fed into an online platform called **Virtual Singapore**, which provides information about how the city is working on a real-time basis.

Smart lighting

Street lights are necessary, but they consume a lot of energy. Smart lighting systems can help make street light energy efficient. Besides this, the lamp posts can also be fitted with additional sensors, or serve as Wi-Fi network hotspots.

One such invention that can help install smart lighting in any city is CitySense (`https://www.tvilight.com/citysense/`), an award-winning streetlight motion sensor; it has integrated wireless lighting control. Designed for harsh external environments, CitySense offers on-demand adaptive lighting. The lamps can adjust their brightness based on the presence of pedestrians, cyclists or cars. It employs a real-time mesh network to trigger neighboring lights, and creates a safe circle of light around a human occupant. It has intelligent filters, which can filter out the interference caused by small animals or moving trees. The system can automatically detect any lamp failures and trigger a maintenance call. The Van Gogh Village in the Netherlands has employed CitySense for their smart street lighting systems.

It's also worth mentioning Barcelona's lighting master plan initiative; it has reported a significant reduction in streetlight power consumption. Around 2014, most of the city's lampposts were fitted with LED lights and IoT powered sensors were installed in them. The sensors automatically turn the lights dim when streets are empty and this has helped in lowering energy consumption. Additionally, these lampposts also serve as Wi-Fi network hotspots and are fitted with sensors to monitor air quality.

Smart governance

The main purpose of smart cities is to make a comfortable and convenient life for its inhabitants. Therefore, a smart city infrastructure is not complete without smart governance. Smart governance means the intelligent use of information and communication technology to improve decision making through better collaboration among different stakeholders, including government, and citizens. Smart governance can be seen as a basis to smart, open, and participatory government. This requires reshaping the role of governments, citizens, and other social actors, as well as exploring the new technologies to frame a new governance model, including new relationships, new processes, and new government structures. Smart governance would be able to use data, evidence, and other resources to improve decision making and would be able to deliver the results that meet the needs of the citizens. This will enhance the decision-making process and increase the quality of public services.

Adapting IoT for smart cities and the necessary steps

Building a smart city is not a one-day business, neither is it the work of one person or organization. It requires the collaboration of many strategic partners, leaders, and even citizens. The dynamics of such a collaboration is beyond the scope of this book, but, since the book is for AI enthusiasts and engineers, let's explore what the AI community can do, what are the areas that provide us with a career or entrepreneurship opportunity. Any IoT platform will necessarily require the following:

- A network of smart things (sensors, cameras, actuators, and so on) for gathering data
- Field (cloud) gateways that can gather the data from low power IoT devices, store it, and forward it securely to the cloud
- Streaming data processor for aggregating numerous data streams and distributing them to a data lake and control applications
- A data lake for storing all the raw data, even the ones that seem of no value yet
- A data warehouse that can clean and structure the collected data
- Tools for analyzing and visualizing the data collected by sensors

- AI algorithms and techniques for automating city services based on long-term data analysis and finding ways to improve the performance of control applications
- Control applications for sending commands to the IoT actuators
- User applications for connecting smart things and citizens

Besides this, there will be issues regarding security and privacy, and the service provider will have to ensure that these smart services do not pose any threat to citizens' wellbeing. The services themselves should be easy to use and employ so that citizens can adopt them.

As you can see, this offers a range of job opportunities, specifically for AI engineers. The IoT-generated data needs to be processed, and to benefit from it truly, we will need to go beyond monitoring and basic analysis. The AI tools will be required to identify patterns and hidden correlations in the sensor data. Analysis of historical sensor data using ML/AI tools can help in identifying trends and create predictive models based on them. These models can then be used by control applications that send commands to IoT devices' actuators.

The process of building a smart city will be an iterative process, with more processing and analysis added at each iteration. Consider the case of a smart traffic light, let's see how we can iteratively improve it.

Compared to a traditional traffic light, our smart traffic light adapts its signal timings, depending upon the traffic. We can use the historical traffic data to train a model to reveal traffic patterns and adjust signal timings to maximize the average vehicle speed, and thus, avoid congestions. Such isolated smart traffic lights are good, but not sufficient. Supposing an area has congestion, then it'll be great if the drivers on the road are informed to avoid that route. To do this now, we can add an additional processing system; it identifies the congestion using the traffic light sensor data, and using the GPS from the vehicle or driver's smartphone, informs the drivers near the region of congestion to avoid that route.

As the next step, the traffic lights can be added with more sensors, like sensors that can monitor the air quality, and then train the model to ensure the alerts to be generated before a critical air quality is reached.

Cities with open data

In the last decade, many cities around the world have established open data portals. These open data portals not only help citizens to stay informed, but are boon for AI coders, since data drive AI. Let's look at a number of the interesting data portals and the data they provide.

This article on Forbes lists the 90 US cities with open data: `https://www.forbes.com/sites/metabrown/2018/04/29/city-gov ernments-making-public-data-easier-to-get-90-municipal-open-data-portals/#4542e6f95a0d`.

Atlanta city Metropolitan Atlanta Rapid Transit Authority data

The **Metropolitan Atlanta Rapid Transit Authority (MARTA)** releases real-time public transport data with an aim to provide the developers with an opportunity to develop custom web and mobile applications. The MARTA platform provides the developers with resources to access the data and use it to develop an application (`https://www.itsmarta.com/app-developer-resources.aspx`).

General Transit Feed Specification (GTFS) format is used to provide the data. GTFS is a standard format for public transportation schedules and geographic information. It's composed of a series of text files, each file models a particular aspect of transit information: stops, routes, trips, and similar scheduled data.

MARTA also provides data through RESTful APIs. To access the API, you will need to install MARTA-Python the Python library for accessing MARTA real-time API. The Python library can be installed using `pip`:

```
pip install tox
```

Before using the API, you will need to register and sign up for the API key (`https://www.itsmarta.com/developer-reg-rtt.aspx`). The API key would be stored in the `MARTA_API_KEY` environment variable. To set the `MARTA_API_KEY` you can use the following:

On Windows, use the following:

```
set MARTA_API_KEY=<your_api_key_here>
```

On Linux/MAC, use the following:

```
export MARTA_API_KEY=<your_api_key_here>
```

It provides two primary wrapper functions `get_buses()` and `get_trains()`, and both functions take keyword arguments to filter the result:

```python
from marta.api import get_buses, get_trains

# To obtain list of all buses
all_buses = get_buses()

# To obtain a list of buses by route
buses_route = get_buses(route=1)

# To obtain list of all trains
trains = get_trains()

# To obtain list of trains specified by line
trains_red = get_trains(line='red')

# To obtain list of trains by station
trains_station = get_trains(station='Midtown Station')

# To obtain list of trains by destination
trains_doraville = get_trains(station='Doraville')

# To obtain list of trains by line, station, and destination
trains_all = get_trains(line='blue',
            station='Five Points Station',
            destination='Indian Creek')
```

The `get_buses()` and `get_trains()` functions return `Bus` and `Train` dictionary objects, respectively.

Chicago Array of Things data

Launched in the year 2016, **Array of Things (AoT)** project consists of installing a network of sensor-boxes mounted on light posts. The sensors collect a host of real-time data on environmental surroundings and urban activity. The data generated is available for developers and enthusiasts via bulk download and also through APIs.

The sensors are deployed across several geographic areas, each deployment region is named **projects**, with the largest deployment in Chicago, under the project named Chicago.

The physical devices that are deployed are called **nodes**, each node is identified by its unique serial number VSN. These nodes are connected together to comprise a network. The nodes contain **sensors**, these sensors observe various facets of the environment, like temperature, humidity, light intensity, and particulate matter. The information recorded by sensors is called **observations**.

The observations have redundancy and are available in their raw form through the API. There exist one-to many relationships between nodes and observations, sensors, and observations. There are also many-to-many relationships between projects, nodes and sensors. The complete data and details of the AoT project can be accessed from the Chicago city open data portal: `https://data.cityofchicago.org/`.

Detecting crime using San Francisco crime data

The San Francisco city also has an open data portal (`https://datasf.org/opendata/`) providing data from different departments online. In this section, we take the dataset providing about 12 years (from January 2003 to May 2015) of crime reports from across all of San Francisco's neighborhoods and train a model to predict the category of crime that occurred. There are 39 discreet crime categories, thus it's a multi-class classification problem.

We will use make use of Apache's PySpark and use its easy to use text processing features for this dataset. So the first step will be to create a Spark session:

1. The first step is to import the necessary modules and create a Spark session:

```
from pyspark.ml.classification import LogisticRegression as LR
from pyspark.ml.feature import RegexTokenizer as RT
from pyspark.ml.feature import StopWordsRemover as SWR
from pyspark.ml.feature import CountVectorizer
from pyspark.ml.feature import OneHotEncoder, StringIndexer,
VectorAssembler
from pyspark.ml import Pipeline
from pyspark.sql.functions import col
from pyspark.sql import SparkSession

spark = SparkSession.builder \
        .appName("Crime Category Prediction") \
        .config("spark.executor.memory", "70g") \
        .config("spark.driver.memory", "50g") \
        .config("spark.memory.offHeap.enabled",True) \
        .config("spark.memory.offHeap.size","16g") \
        .getOrCreate()
```

2. We load the dataset available in a csv file:

```
data = spark.read.format("csv"). \
        options(header="true", inferschema="true"). \
        load("sf_crime_dataset.csv")

data.columns
```

```
Out[3]: ['Dates',
         'Category',
         'Descript',
         'DayOfWeek',
         'PdDistrict',
         'Resolution',
         'Address',
         'X',
         'Y']
```

3. The data contains nine columns: [Dates, Category, Descript, DayOfWeek, PdDistrict, Resolution, Address, X, Y], we will need only Category and Descript fields for training and testing dataset:

```
drop_data = ['Dates', 'DayOfWeek', 'PdDistrict', 'Resolution',
'Address', 'X', 'Y']
data = data.select([column for column in data.columns if column not
in drop_data])

data.show(5)
```

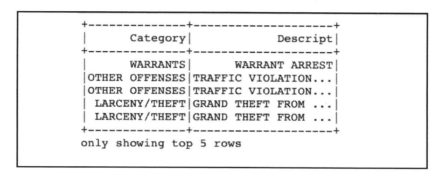

4. Now the dataset we have has textual data, so we will need to perform text processing. The three important text processing steps are: tokenizing the data, remove the stop words and vectorize the words into vectors. We will use RegexTokenizer which will uses regex to tokenize the sentence into a list of words, since punctuation or special characters do not add anything to the meaning, we retain only the words containing alphanumeric content. There are some words like the, which will be very commonly present in the text, but not add any meaning to context. We can remove these words (also called **stop words**) using the inbuilt StopWordsRemover class. We use standard stop words ["http","https","amp","rt","t","c","the"]. And finally using the CountVectorizer, we convert the words to numeric vector (features). It's these numeric features that will be used as input to train the model. The output for our data is the Category column, but it's also textual with 36 distinct categories, and so, we need to convert it to one hot encoded vector; the PySpark's StringIndexer can be easily used for it. We add all these transformations into our data Pipeline:

```
# regular expression tokenizer
re_Tokenizer = RT(inputCol="Descript",
        outputCol="words", pattern="\\W")
```

```
# stop words
stop_words = ["http","https","amp","rt","t","c","the"]
stop_words_remover = SWR(inputCol="words",
            outputCol="filtered").setStopWords(stop_words)

# bag of words count
count_vectors = CountVectorizer(inputCol="filtered",
        outputCol="features", vocabSize=10000, minDF=5)

#One hot encoding the label
label_string_Idx = StringIndexer(inputCol = "Category",
            outputCol = "label")

# Create the pipeline
pipeline = Pipeline(stages=[re_Tokenizer, stop_words_remover,
            count_vectors, label_string_Idx])

# Fit the pipeline to data.
pipeline_fit = pipeline.fit(data)
dataset = pipeline_fit.transform(data)

dataset.show(5)
```

```
+--------------+--------------------+--------------------+--------------------+--------------------+-----+
|      Category|            Descript|               words|            filtered|            features|label|
+--------------+--------------------+--------------------+--------------------+--------------------+-----+
|      WARRANTS|      WARRANT ARREST|   [warrant, arrest]|   [warrant, arrest]|(809,[17,32],[1.0...|  7.0|
|OTHER OFFENSES|TRAFFIC VIOLATION...|[traffic, violati...|[traffic, violati...|(809,[11,17,35],[...|  1.0|
|OTHER OFFENSES|TRAFFIC VIOLATION...|[traffic, violati...|[traffic, violati...|(809,[11,17,35],[...|  1.0|
| LARCENY/THEFT|GRAND THEFT FROM ...|[grand, theft, fr...|[grand, theft, fr...|(809,[0,2,3,4,6],...|  0.0|
| LARCENY/THEFT|GRAND THEFT FROM ...|[grand, theft, fr...|[grand, theft, fr...|(809,[0,2,3,4,6],...|  0.0|
+--------------+--------------------+--------------------+--------------------+--------------------+-----+
only showing top 5 rows
```

5. Now, the data is ready, we split it into training and test dataset:

```
# Split the data randomly into training and test data sets.
(trainingData, testData) = dataset.randomSplit([0.7, 0.3], seed =
100)
print("Training Dataset Size: " + str(trainingData.count()))
print("Test Dataset Size: " + str(testData.count()))
```

6. Let's fit a simple logistic regression model for it. On the test dataset, it provides a 97% accuracy. Yahoo!:

```
# Build the model
logistic_regrssor = LR(maxIter=20,
                regParam=0.3, elasticNetParam=0)
# Train model with Training Data
model = logistic_regrssor.fit(trainingData)

# Make predictions on Test Data
predictions = model.transform(testData)

# evaluate the model on test data set
evaluator =
MulticlassClassificationEvaluator(predictionCol="prediction")
evaluator.evaluate(predictions)
```

The complete code is available in the GitHub repository `Chapter11/SF_crime_category_detection.ipynb` Jupyter Notebook.

Challenges and benefits

AI is changing the way cities operate, deliver, and maintain public amenities, from lighting and transportation to connectivity and health services. However, the adoption can be obstructed by the selection of technology that doesn't efficiently work together or integrate with other city services. Hence, it's important to think for retrofitted solutions.

Another important thing to take care of is collaboration. For cities to truly benefit from the potential that smart cities offer, a change in mindset is required. The authorities should plan longer and across multiple departments. Everyone—technologists, local governments, businesses, environmentalists, and the general public—must work together to enable cities to transform into a smart city, successfully.

Though budget can be a big issue, the results of the successful implementation of smart city components across different cities of the world show that, by proper implementation, smart cities are more economical. Smart city transition not only creates jobs, but can help save the environment, reduce energy expenditure, and generate more revenue. The city of Barcelona is a prime example of this; through the implementation of IoT systems, it created an estimated 47,000 jobs, saved €42.5 million on water, and generated an extra €36.5 million a year through smart parking. We can easily see that cities can benefit tremendously from the technological advances that utilize AI-powered IoT solutions.

Summary

AI-powered IoT solutions can help connect cities and manage multiple infrastructure, and public services. This chapter covered diverse use cases of smart cities, from smart lighting and road traffic to connected public transport, and waste management. From the successful case studies, we also learned that smart cities can lead to reduced costs for energy, optimized use of natural resources, safer cities, and a healthier environment. This chapter listed some of the open city data portals and the information available there. We use the tools learned in this book to categorize the data from the San Francisco crime reports done in a period of 12 years. And finally, this chapter discussed some challenges and benefits in the building of smart cities.

Combining It All Together

12

Now that we have understood and implemented different **Artificial Intelligence (AI)/machine learning (ML)** algorithms, it is time to combine it all together, understand which type of data is best suited for each, and, at the same time, understand the basic preprocessing required for each type of data. By the end of this chapter, you will know the following:

- The different types of data that can be fed to your model
- How to process time series data
- Preprocessing of textual data
- Different transforms that can be done on image data
- How to handle video files
- How to handle speech data
- Cloud computing options

Processing different types of data

Data is available in all shapes, sizes, and forms: tweets, daily stock prices, per minute heartbeat signals, photos from cameras, video obtained from CCTV, audio recordings, and so on. Each of them contain information and when properly processed and used with the right model, we can analyze the data and, obtain advanced information about the underlying patterns. In this section, we will cover the basic preprocessing required for each type of data before it can be fed to a model and the models that can be used for it.

Time series modeling

Time underlies many interesting human behaviors, and hence, it is important that AI-powered IoT systems know how to deal with time-dependent data. Time can be represented either explicitly, for example, capturing data at regular intervals where the time-stamp is also part of data, or implicitly, for example, in speech or written text. The methods that allow us to capture inherent patterns in time-dependent data is called **time series modeling**.

The data that is captured at regular intervals is a time series data, for example, stock price data is a time series data. Let's take a look at Apple stock price data; this data can be downloaded from the NASDAQ site (https://www.nasdaq.com/symbol/aapl/historical). Alternatively, you can use the pandas_datareader module to directly download the data by specifying the data source. To install pandas_datareader in your working environment, use the following:

```
pip install pandas_datareader
```

1. The following code downloads the Apple Inc stock price from Yahoo Finance from 1st January 2010 to 31st December 2015:

    ```
    import datetime
    from pandas_datareader import DataReader
    %matplotlib inline


    Apple = DataReader("AAPL", "yahoo",
            start=datetime.datetime(2010, 1, 1),
            end=datetime.datetime(2015,12,31))
    Apple.head()
    ```

2. The downloaded DataFrame provides High, Low, Open, Close, Volume, and Adj Close values for each working day:

Out[2]:						
	High	**Low**	**Open**	**Close**	**Volume**	**Adj Close**
Date						
2009-12-31	30.478571	30.080000	30.447144	30.104286	88102700.0	20.159719
2010-01-04	30.642857	30.340000	30.490000	30.572857	123432400.0	20.473503
2010-01-05	30.798571	30.464285	30.657143	30.625713	150476200.0	20.508902
2010-01-06	30.747143	30.107143	30.625713	30.138571	138040000.0	20.182680
2010-01-07	30.285715	29.864286	30.250000	30.082857	119282800.0	20.145369

3. Let's now plot it, shown as follows:

```
close = Apple['Adj Close']
plt.figure(figsize= (10,10))
close.plot()
plt.ylabel("Apple stocj close price")
plt.show()
```

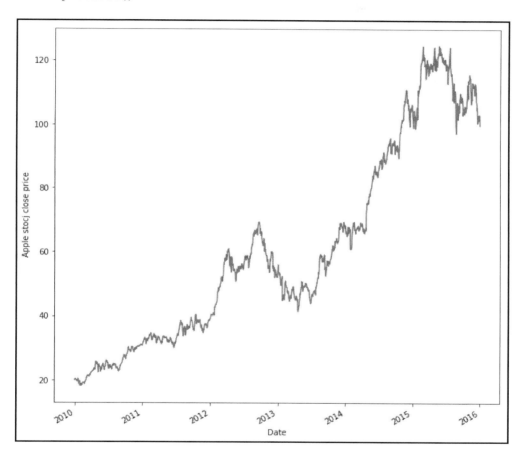

To be able to model time series data, we need to identify a few things: trend, seasonality, and stationarity.

4. **Trend** means to find whether, on average, the measurements tend to decrease (or increase) over time. The most common way to find a trend is by plotting a moving average, shown as follows:

```
moving_average = close.rolling(window=20).mean()

plt.figure(figsize= (10,10))
close.plot(label='Adj Close')
moving_average.plot(label='Moving Average Window 20')
plt.legend(loc='best')
plt.show()
```

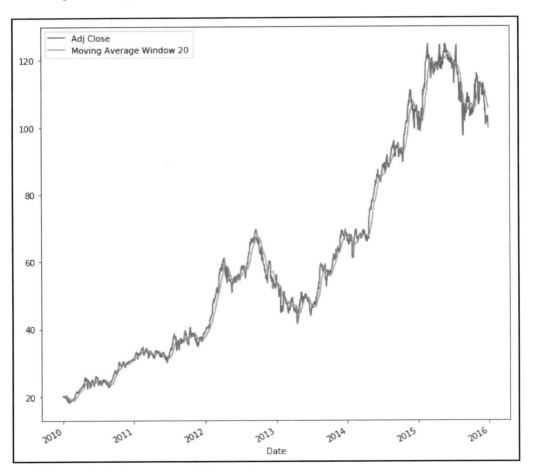

5. We can see, with a window of 20, the upward and downward trend. For time series modeling, we should detrend the data. Detrending can be done by subtracting the trend (moving average) from the original signal. Another popular way is using the first order difference method, where you take the difference between successive data points:

```
fod = close.diff()
plt.figure(figsize= (10,10))
fod.plot(label='First order difference')
fod.rolling(window=40).mean().\
        plot(label='Rolling Average')
plt.legend(loc='best')
plt.show()
```

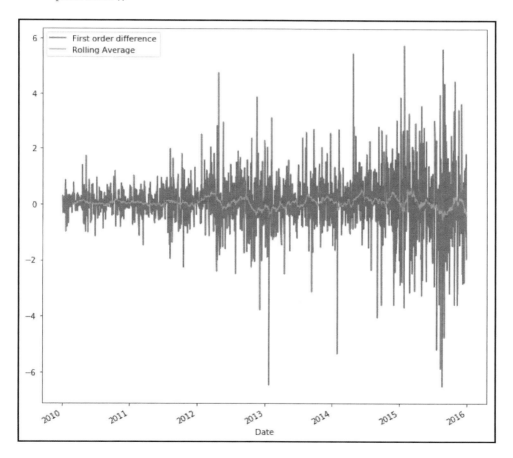

6. **Seasonality** is the presence of a regularly repeating pattern of highs and lows related to time (for example, sine series). The easiest way is to find autocorrelation in the data. Once you find the seasonality, you can remove it by differencing the data by a time lag corresponding to the season length:

```
# Autocorrelation
plt.figure(figsize= (10,10))
fod.plot(label='First order difference')
fod.rolling(window=40).mean().\
        plot(label='Rolling Average')
fod.rolling(window=40).corr(fod.shift(5)).\
        plot(label='Auto correlation')
plt.legend(loc='best')
plt.show()
```

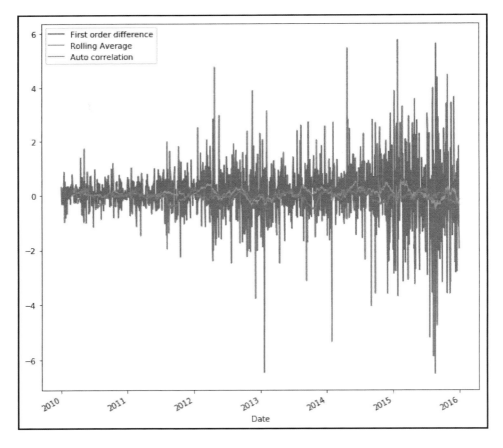

7. The last thing is to ensure whether the series is **stationary**, that is, the mean of the series is no longer a function of time. Stationarity of data is essential for time series modeling. We achieve stationarity by removing any trends or seasonality present within the data. Once the data is stationary, we can use regression models to model it.

Traditionally, time series data was modeled using auto-regressive and moving average based models like ARMA and ARIMA. To learn more about time series modeling, the interested reader can refer to these books:

- Pandit, S. M., and Wu, S. M. (1983). *Time Series and System Analysis with Applications*(Vol. 3). New York: Wiley.
- Brockwell, P. J., Davis, R. A., and Calder, M. V. (2002). *Introduction to Time Series and Forecasting*(Vol. 2). New York: Springer.

The stationarity is an important property for any time series data, whether you are using traditional time series modeling or deep learning models. This is so because, if a series has stationarity (even if it is weak stationarity), then it means the data has same distribution across time, and hence, can be estimated in time. If you are planning to use deep learning models such as RNN or LSTM, then after confirming stationarity of the time series, additionally, you need to normalize the data and use a sliding window transform to convert the series in to input-output pairs on which regression can be done. This can be very easily done using the scikit-learn library and NumPy:

1. Let's normalize the `close` DataFrame. Normalization ensures that data lies between 0 and 1. Observe that the following plot is the same as the plot of the `close` DataFrame in the preceding *step 3* , however, the *y*-axis scale is now different:

```
# Normalization
from sklearn.preprocessing import MinMaxScaler
def normalize(data):
    x = data.values.reshape(-1,1)
    pre_process = MinMaxScaler()
    x_normalized = pre_process.fit_transform(x)
    return x_normalized

x_norm = normalize(close)

plt.figure(figsize= (10,10))
pd.DataFrame(x_norm, index = close.index).plot(label="Normalized
Stock prices")
```

```
plt.legend(loc='best')
plt.show()
```

2. We define a `window_transform()` function, which will convert the data series into a sequence of input-output pairs. For example, you want to construct an RNN that takes the previous five values as output and predicts the sixth value. Then, you choose `window_size = 5`:

```
# Create window from the normalized data
def window_transform(series, window_size):
    X = []
    y = []

    # Generate a sequence input/output pairs from series
    # x= <s1,s2,s3,s4,s5,... s_n> y = s_n+1 and so on
    for i in range(len(series) - window_size):
        X.append(series[i:i+window_size])
        y.append(series[i+window_size])

    # reshape each
    X = np.asarray(X)
    X.shape = (np.shape(X)[0:2])
    y = np.asarray(y)
    y.shape = (len(y),1)

    return X,y

window_size = 7
X,y = window_transform(x_norm,window_size = window_size)
```

Please refer to the GitHub
repository, `Chapter-12/time_series_data_preprocessing.ipynb`, for the complete
code of this section.

Preprocessing textual data

Language plays a very important role in our daily life. For us, reading a written text is very
natural, but what about computers? Can they read it? Can we make our deep learning
models generate new text based on the old pattern? For example, if I say, "Yesterday, I had
____ at Starbucks," most of us will be able to guess that the blank space is coffee, but can
our deep learning models do it? The answer is yes; we can train our deep learning models
to guess the next word (or character). However, deep learning models run on computers,
and computers understand only binary, only 0s and 1s. Hence, we need a way to process
out textual data so that it can be converted in to a form that is easy for the computer to
handle. Moreover, while cat or CAT or Cat have different ASCII representation, they mean
the same; it is easy for us to see, but for models to take them as the same, we need to
preprocess the textual data. This section will list the necessary preprocessing steps for the
textual data, and you will learn how to do it in Python:

1. For this section, we will consider a small text from my favorite science fiction
   novel, *Foundation*, by Isaac Asimov. The text is in the `foundation.txt` file. The
   first step is, we read in the text:

   ```
   f = open('foundation.txt')
   text = f.read()
   print(text)
   ```

2. The next step in text processing is cleaning the data. We retain only that part of
   the text that is relevant. In most cases, punctuation does not add any additional
   meaning to the text, so we can safely remove it:

   ```
   # clean data
   import re
   # remove Punctuation
   text = re.sub(r"[^a-zA-Z0-9]", " ", text)
   print(text)
   ```

3. After cleaning the data, we need to normalize the text. In text processing, normalizing the text means converting all text in to the same case, lowercase or uppercase. Conventionally, lowercase is preferred, so we convert the text in to lowercase:

```
# Normalize text
# Convert to lowercase
text = text.lower()
print(text)
```

4. Once the text is normalized, the next step is tokenizing the text. We can tokenize a text in word tokens or sentence tokens. To do this, you can use either the split function or use the powerful NLTK module. If you do not have NLTK installed in your system, you can do it using `pip install nltk`. In the following, we use NLTK's word tokenizer to do the task:

```
import os
import nltk
nltk.download('punkt')
from nltk.tokenize import word_tokenize

# Split text into words using NLTK
words_nltk = word_tokenize(text)
print(words_nltk)
```

5. Depending on the type of text you have and the work you are doing, you will need to remove stop words. Stop words are words that are present in most text samples, and hence, do not add any information to the context or meaning of the text. For example, the, a, and an. You can declare your own stop words or use the stop words provided by NLTK. Here, we remove `stopwords` of the `english` language from our text:

```
from nltk.corpus import stopwords
nltk.download('stopwords')
#Remove stop words
words = [w for w in words \
        if w not in stopwords.words("english")]
```

6. Another thing that you can perform on the textual data is stemming and lemmatization. These are used to convert the words into canonical form:

```
from nltk.stem.porter import PorterStemmer

# Reduce words to their stems
stemmed = [PorterStemmer().stem(w) for w in words]
print(stemmed)

from nltk.stem.wordnet import WordNetLemmatizer

# Reduce words to their root form
lemmed = [WordNetLemmatizer().lemmatize(w) for w in words]
print(lemmed)
```

You can access the notebook with this code at GitHub:
`Chapter12/text_processing.ipynb`.

Data augmentation for images

Python has OpenCV, which provides very good support for images. OpenCV can be downloaded from both Conda channels and PyPi for installation. Once the image is read using the OpenCV `imread()` function, the image is represented as an array. In case the image is coloured, the channels are stored in BGR order. Each element of the array represents the intensity of the corresponding pixel value (the values lie in the range 0 to 255).

Let's say you have trained a model to recognize a ball: you present it with a tennis ball, and it recognizes it as a ball. The next image of the ball that we present is taken after zooming: will our model still recognize it? A model is just as good as the dataset it has been trained on, and so, if the model while training had seen rescaled images, it will be easy for it to identify the zoomed ball as a ball. One way to ensure that such images are available in your dataset is to implicitly include such variable images, however, since images are represented as an array, we can perform mathematical transformations to rescale, flip, rotate, and even change intensities. The process of performing these transformations on existing training images to generate new images is called **data augmentation**. Another advantage of using data augmentation is that you are able to increase the size of your training dataset (when used with data generators, we can get infinite images).

Most deep learning libraries have standard APIs to perform data augmentation. In Keras (`https://keras.io/preprocessing/image/`), there is `ImageDataGenerator`, and in TensorFlow-TfLearn, we have `ImageAugmentation`. TensorFlow also has Ops to perform image conversions and transformations (`https://www.tensorflow.org/api_guides/python/image`). Here we will see how we can use OpenCV's powerful library for data augmentation and create our own data generator:

1. We import the necessary modules: OpenCV to read and process images, numpy for matrix manipulations, Matplotlib to visualize images, `shuffle` from scikit-learn for randomly shuffling the data, and Glob to find files within directories:

```
import cv2 # for image reading and processsing
import numpy as np
from glob import glob
import matplotlib.pyplot as plt
from sklearn.utils import shuffle
%matplotlib inline
```

2. We read the necessary files. For this example, we downloaded some images of the previous President of the United States, Barack Obama, from Google image search:

```
img_files = np.array(glob("Obama/*"))
```

3. We create a function that can randomly introduce any of the following distortions in the image: random rotation in the range 0–50 degrees, randomly change the intensity, randomly shift the image horizontally and vertically by up to 50 pixels, or randomly flip the image:

```
def distort_image(img, rot = 50, shift_px = 40):
    """
    Function to introduce random distortion: brightness, flip,
    rotation, and shift
    """
    rows, cols,_ = img.shape
    choice = np.random.randint(5)
    #print(choice)
    if choice == 0: # Randomly rotate 0-50 degreee
        rot *= np.random.random()
        M = cv2.getRotationMatrix2D((cols/2,rows/2), rot, 1)
        dst = cv2.warpAffine(img,M,(cols,rows))
    elif choice == 1: # Randomly change the intensity
        hsv = cv2.cvtColor(img, cv2.COLOR_RGB2HSV)
        ratio = 1.0 + 0.4 * (np.random.rand() - 0.5)
        hsv[:, :, 2] = hsv[:, :, 2] * ratio
        dst = cv2.cvtColor(hsv, cv2.COLOR_HSV2RGB)
```

```
elif choice == 2: # Randomly shift the image in horizontal and
vertical direction
    x_shift,y_shift = np.random.randint(-shift_px,shift_px,2)
    M = np.float32([[1,0,x_shift],[0,1,y_shift]])
    dst = cv2.warpAffine(img,M,(cols,rows))
elif choice == 3: # Randomly flip the image
    dst = np.fliplr(img)
else:
    dst = img

return dst
```

4. In the following image, you can see the result of the preceding function on randomly chosen images from our dataset:

5. And finally, you can create a data generator using Python `yield` to generate as many images as you want:

```
# data generator
def data_generator(samples, batch_size=32, validation_flag =
False):
    """
    Function to generate data after, it reads the image files,
    performs random distortions and finally
    returns a batch of training or validation data
    """
    num_samples = len(samples)
    while True: # Loop forever so the generator never terminates
 shuffle(samples)
        for offset in range(0, num_samples, batch_size):
            batch_samples = samples[offset:offset+batch_size]
            images = []

            for batch_sample in batch_samples:
                if validation_flag: # The validation data consists
only of center image and without distortions
                    image = cv2.imread(batch_sample)
                    images.append(image)
                    continue
                else: # In training dataset we introduce
distortions to augment it and improve performance
                    image = cv2.imread(batch_sample)
                    # Randomly augment the training dataset to
reduce overfitting
                    image = distort_image(image)
                    images.append(image)

        # Convert the data into numpy arrays
        X_train = np.array(images)

        yield X_train

train_generator = data_generator(img_files,  batch_size=32)
```

The `Chapter12/data_augmentation.ipynb` file contains the code for this section.

Handling videos files

Videos are nothing but a collection of still images (frames), therefore, if we can extract images from the videos, we can apply our trusted CNN networks on the same. The only necessary thing to do is convert the video in to a list of frames:

1. The first thing we import are the requisite modules. We will need OpenCV to read the video and convert it in to frames. We will also need the `math` module for basic mathematical operations and Matplotlib for visualizing the frames:

```
import cv2 # for capturing videos
import math # for mathematical operations
import matplotlib.pyplot as plt # for plotting the images
%matplotlib inline
```

2. We read the video file using the OpenCV function and get its frame rate by using the property identifier, 5 (https://docs.opencv.org/2.4/modules/highgui/doc/reading_and_writing_images_and_video.html#videocapture-get):

```
videoFile = "video.avi" # Video file with complete path
cap = cv2.VideoCapture(videoFile) # capturing the video from the
given path
frameRate = cap.get(5) #frame rate
```

3. We loop through all of the frames of the video one by one using the `read()` function. Although we read only one frame at a time, we save only the first frame in each second. This way, we can cover the whole video, and yet reduce the data size:

```
count = 0
while(cap.isOpened()):
    frameId = cap.get(1) #current frame number
    ret, frame = cap.read()
    if (ret != True):
        break
    if (frameId % math.floor(frameRate) == 0):
        filename ="frame%d.jpg" % count
        count += 1
        cv2.imwrite(filename, frame)

cap.release()
print ("Finished!")
```

4. Let's visualize the fifth frame that we saved:

```
img = plt.imread('frame5.jpg') # reading image using its name
plt.imshow(img)
```

The video file for this code was taken from the site maintained by Ivan Laptev and Barbara Caputo (http://www.nada.kth.se/cvap/actions/). The code is available at GitHub: Chapter12/Video_to_frames.ipynb.

One of the best papers that uses CNN for classifying videos is *Large-scale Video Classification with Convolutional Neural Networks* by Andrej Karpathy et al.. You can access here: https://www.cv-foundation.org/openaccess/content_cvpr_2014/html/Karpathy_Large-scale_Video_Classification_2014_CVPR_paper.html.

Audio files as input data

Another interesting data type is audio files. Models that convert speech in to text or classify audio sounds take as input audio files. If you want to work with audio files, then you will need the `librosa` module. There are many ways to treat an audio file; we can convert it into a time series and use a recurrent network. Another way that has given good results is to use them as one-dimensional or two-dimensional patterns, and train a CNN to classify them. Some good papers that adopt this approach are as follows:

- Hershey, S., Chaudhuri, S., Ellis, D. P., Gemmeke, J. F., Jansen, A., Moore, R. C., and Slaney, M. (2017, March). *CNN architectures for large-scale audio classification.* In Acoustics, Speech, and Signal Processing (ICASSP), 2017 IEEE International Conference on (pp. 131-135). IEEE.

- Palaz, D., Magimai-Doss, M., and Collobert, R. (2015). *Analysis of CNN-based speech recognition system using raw speech as input.* In Sixteenth Annual Conference of the International Speech Communication Association.

- Zhang, H., McLoughlin, I., and Song, Y. (2015, April). *Robust sound event recognition using convolutional neural networks.* In Acoustics, Speech, and Signal Processing (ICASSP), 2015 IEEE International Conference on (pp. 559-563). IEEE.

- Costa, Y. M., Oliveira, L. S., and Silla Jr, C. N. (2017). *An evaluation of convolutional neural networks for music classification using spectrograms.* Applied soft computing, 52, 28–38.

We will use the `librosa` module to read an audio file and convert it in to a one-dimensional sound pattern and two-dimensional spectrogram. You can install `librosa` in your Anaconda environment using the following:

```
pip install librosa
```

1. Here, we will import `numpy`, `matplotlib`, and `librosa`. We will take the example audio file from the `librosa` datasets:

```
import librosa
import numpy as np
import matplotlib.pyplot as plt
%matplotlib inline
# Get the file path to the included audio example
filename = librosa.util.example_audio_file()
```

2. The `librosa` load function returns the audio data as time series represented as a one-dimensional NumPy floating-point array. We can use them as time series or even as a one-dimensional pattern for a CNN:

```
input_length=16000*4
def audio_norm(data):
    # Function to Normalize
    max_data = np.max(data)
    min_data = np.min(data)
    data = (data-min_data)/(max_data-min_data)
    return data


def load_audio_file(file_path,
            input_length=input_length):
    # Function to load an audio file and
    # return a 1D numpy array
    data, sr = librosa.load(file_path, sr=None)

    max_offset = abs(len(data)-input_length)
    offset = np.random.randint(max_offset)
    if len(data)>input_length:
        data = data[offset:(input_length+offset)]
    else:
        data = np.pad(data, (offset,
            input_size - len(data) - offset),
            "constant")

    data = audio_norm(data)
    return data
```

3. In the following, you can see the one-dimensional audio wave pattern after normalization:

```
data_base = load_audio_file(filename)
fig = plt.figure(figsize=(14, 8))
plt.title('Raw wave ')
plt.ylabel('Amplitude')
plt.plot(np.linspace(0, 1, input_length), data_base)
plt.show()
```

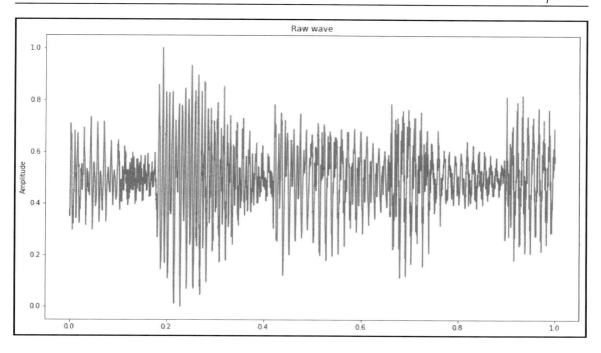

4. librosa also has a melspectrogram function that we can use to form a mel
spectrogram, which can be used as a two-dimensional image for a CNN:

```
def preprocess_audio_mel_T(audio, sample_rate=16000,
        window_size=20, #log_specgram
        step_size=10, eps=1e-10):

    mel_spec = librosa.feature.melspectrogram(y=audio,
            sr=sample_rate, n_mels= 256)
    mel_db = (librosa.power_to_db(mel_spec,
        ref=np.max) + 40)/40
    return mel_db.T


def load_audio_file2(file_path,
            input_length=input_length):
    #Function to load the audio file
    data, sr = librosa.load(file_path, sr=None)

    max_offset = abs(len(data)-input_length)
    offset = np.random.randint(max_offset)
    if len(data)>input_length:
        data = data[offset:(input_length+offset)]
    else:
```

```
        data = np.pad(data, (offset,
            input_size - len(data) - offset),
            "constant")

    data = preprocess_audio_mel_T(data, sr)
    return data
```

5. Here is a mel spectrogram of the same audio signal:

```
data_base = load_audio_file2(filename)
print(data_base.shape)
fig = plt.figure(figsize=(14, 8))
plt.imshow(data_base)
```

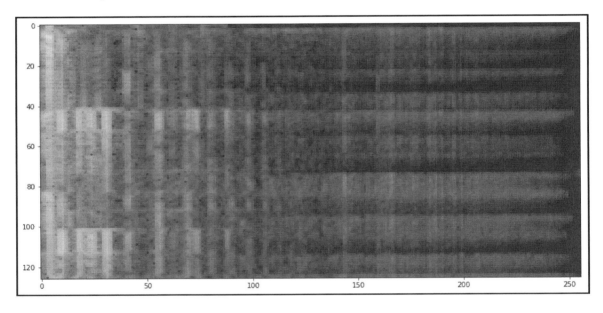

You can find the code file for the example in the GitHub repository under the Chapter12/audio_processing.ipynb file.

Computing in the cloud

Applying AI algorithms to IoT-generated data requires computing resources. With the availability of a large number of cloud platforms offering service at competitive prices, cloud computing offers a cost-effective solution. Out of the many cloud platforms available today, we will talk about three main cloud platform providers that occupy the majority of the market share: **Amazon Web Service (AWS)**, **Google Cloud Platform (GCP)**, and Microsoft Azure.

AWS

Amazon offers almost every feature under the cloud, from a cloud database, to cloud computing resources, to even cloud analytics. It even provides space to build a secure data lake. Its IoT core allows users to connect devices to the cloud. It provides a single dashboard that can be used to control the services you sign for. It charges per hour for its services. It has been offering these services for almost 15 years. Amazon continuously upgrades the service providing a better user experience. You can learn more about AWS from its site: `https://aws.amazon.com/`.

It allows new users to make use of many of its services for free for one whole year.

Google Cloud Platform

Google Cloud Platform (`https://cloud.google.com/`) also offers a myriad of services. It offers cloud computing, data analytics, data storage, and even cloud AI products that provide users with pre-trained models and service to generate their own tailored models. The platform allows you to pay per minute. It offers enterprise-level secure services. The Google Cloud console is the one place stop to access and control all of your GCP services. GCP offers $300 credit for the first year, which allows you to access all of its services for free.

Microsoft Azure

Microsoft Azure offers a wide variety of cloud services too. The best part of Microsoft Cloud services (`https://azure.microsoft.com/en-in/`) is its ease of use; you can integrate it easily with available Microsoft tools. It claims to be five times less expensive compared to AWS. Like AWS and GCP, Azure also offers a one-year free trial worth $200 credits.

You can use these cloud services to develop, test, and deploy your applications.

Summary

This chapter focused on providing the reader with tools to handle different types of data and how to prepare them for the deep learning models. We started with time series data. This chapter next detailed how textual data needs to be preprocessed. This chapter showed how to perform data augmentation, an important technique for image classification and object detection. We next moved on to handling video; we show how to form image frames from a video. Next, this chapter covered audio files; we formed a time series and mel spectrogram from an audio file. Finally, we moved on to cloud platforms and discussed the features and services provided by three major cloud service providers.

Other Books You May Enjoy

If you enjoyed this book, you may be interested in these other books by Packt:

Artificial Intelligence with Python
Prateek Joshi

ISBN: 9781786464392

- Realize different classification and regression techniques
- Understand the concept of clustering and how to use it to automatically segment data
- See how to build an intelligent recommender system
- Understand logic programming and how to use it
- Build automatic speech recognition systems
- Understand the basics of heuristic search and genetic programming
- Develop games using Artificial Intelligence
- Learn how reinforcement learning works
- Discover how to build intelligent applications centered on images, text, and time series data
- See how to use deep learning algorithms and build applications based on it

Artificial Intelligence By Example

Denis Rothman

ISBN: 9781788990547

- Use adaptive thinking to solve real-life AI case studies
- Rise beyond being a modern-day factory code worker
- Acquire advanced AI, machine learning, and deep learning designing skills
- Learn about cognitive NLP chatbots, quantum computing, and IoT and blockchain technology
- Understand future AI solutions and adapt quickly to them
- Develop out-of-the-box thinking to face any challenge the market presents

Leave a review - let other readers know what you think

Please share your thoughts on this book with others by leaving a review on the site that you bought it from. If you purchased the book from Amazon, please leave us an honest review on this book's Amazon page. This is vital so that other potential readers can see and use your unbiased opinion to make purchasing decisions, we can understand what our customers think about our products, and our authors can see your feedback on the title that they have worked with Packt to create. It will only take a few minutes of your time, but is valuable to other potential customers, our authors, and Packt. Thank you!

Index

Printed in Great
Britain
by Amazon